LIBERAL ROOTS OF FAR RIGHT ACTIVISM

This book explores the anti-Islamic turn and expansion of the far right in Western Europe, North America, and beyond from 2001 onwards.

Driven by terror attacks and other moral shocks, the anti-Islamic cause has undergone four waves of transnational expansion in the period since 2001. The leaders and intellectuals involved have varied backgrounds, many coming from the left, uniting historically opposed sets of values under their banner of a civilizational struggle against Islam. The findings presented in this book indicate that anti-Islamic initiatives in Western Europe and the United States form a transnational movement and subculture characterized by a fragile balance between liberal and authoritarian values. The author draws on a broad array of data sources and methods, including network analysis and sentiment analysis, to analyze the impact of the anti-Islamic expansion and turn at a macro level, and the theoretical implications for our understanding of the current far right flowing from this. Offering an overview of anti-Islamic activism, the book explores the background of their leaders and ideologues, provides an in-depth look at their ideology, online organizational networks, and the views expressed by their online members as well as which emotions and messages continue to drive their mobilization.

The book will be of interest to scholars in the social movement field, as well as political scientists, sociologists, and general readers interested in issues such as populism, extremism, and understanding the ways in which the contemporary far right challenges liberal democracies.

Lars Erik Berntzen is a Postdoctoral Research Fellow at the Department of Comparative Politics, University of Bergen, Norway. Berntzen currently studies affective, identity-based polarization in Western Europe using a combination of panel-based survey experiments and social media experiments. He studied sociology at the University of Bergen, before taking his PhD at the European University Institute in Florence, Italy.

Routledge Studies in Extremism and Democracy

Series Editors: Roger Eatwell, *University of Bath*, and Matthew Goodwin, *University of Kent.*
Founding Series Editors: Roger Eatwell, *University of Bath* and Cas Mudde, *University of Antwerp-UFSIA.*

This new series encompasses academic studies within the broad fields of 'extremism' and 'democracy'. These topics have traditionally been considered largely in isolation by academics. A key focus of the series, therefore, is the (inter-)*relation* between extremism and democracy. Works will seek to answer questions such as to what extent 'extremist' groups pose a major threat to democratic parties, or how democracy can respond to extremism without undermining its own democratic credentials.

The books encompass two strands:

Routledge Studies in Extremism and Democracy includes books with an introductory and broad focus which are aimed at students and teachers. These books will be available in hardback and paperback.

The People and the Nation
Populism and Ethno-Territorial Politics in Europe
Edited by Reinhard Heinisch, Emanuele Massetti and Oscar Mazzoleni

The Anti-Islamic Movement
Far Right and Liberal?
Lars Berntzen

Routledge Research in Extremism and Democracy offers a forum for innovative new research intended for a more specialist readership. These books will be in hardback only.

Liberal Roots of Far Right Activism
The Anti-Islamic Movement in the 21st Century
Lars Erik Berntzen

For more information about this series, please visit: www.routledge.com/politics/series/ED

LIBERAL ROOTS OF FAR RIGHT ACTIVISM

The Anti-Islamic Movement in the 21st Century

Lars Erik Berntzen

Routledge
Taylor & Francis Group
LONDON AND NEW YORK

First published 2020
by Routledge
2 Park Square, Milton Park, Abingdon, Oxon OX14 4RN

and by Routledge
52 Vanderbilt Avenue, New York, NY 10017

Routledge is an imprint of the Taylor & Francis Group, an informa business

© 2020 Lars Erik Berntzen

British Library Cataloguing-in-Publication Data
A catalogue record for this book is available from the British Library

Library of Congress Cataloging-in-Publication Data
A catalog record for this book has been requested

ISBN: 978-0-367-22465-3 (hbk)
ISBN: 978-0-367-22466-0 (pbk)
ISBN: 978-0-429-27501-2 (ebk)

Typeset in Bembo
by Apex CoVantage, LLC

CONTENTS

FIGURES

TABLES

PICTURES

PREFACE

Writing this book has been a long journey. I want to give you a little preamble before you delve into it, so that you can understand the premises for it.

I start by winding the clock back to the very beginning of my academic career, and then some. My journey into academia began August 2006 at the Department of Sociology, University of Bergen. Bergen is my hometown, and the region of Norway where my ancestors come from as far back as anybody has traced them. I am among the first persons in my family who have completed a higher education. My mother was a hairdresser, while my father began as a carpenter before he gradually advanced to a higher management position in a construction company. The generations before them have been farmers, fishermen, factory workers, and housewives. Today, many of my relatives work in the oil industry or related fields. This journey of upward mobility through the generations is not unique to my family or me, but has been one core characteristic of Norwegian society during the last century.

Perhaps not surprisingly, when I began studying sociology, most of the classes I took were on the welfare state, class differences, and questions of poverty and inequality. Already instilled with a sense of pride in Norwegian social democracy, my understanding of the welfare state as the single greatest achievement of our society was solidified during these years.

Then I came across Sigurd Skirbekk's *Nasjonalstaten: Velferdsstatens grunnlag* (*The Nation-state: Foundation of the Welfare State*). Skirbekk claimed that the support necessary to maintain this costly welfare state was being eroded. Not only that, it was being eroded by the increased ethnic and cultural diversity which immigration brings with it. The premise was that the Norwegian majority population would withdraw their support for economic redistribution as society became more diverse. Was he right?

My own sociological background and its emphasis on the explanatory power of economic issues and class differences over notions of ethnic and cultural differences made me resistant to the idea. I nonetheless decided to delve into the matter. Based on a limited amount of survey data between the 1980s and 2008, my tentative answer was that the normative foundations for the Norwegian welfare state had until that point in time not been substantially undermined through immigration. However, this work had made me increasingly aware of the organized and popular opposition against immigration. Particularly Muslim immigration.

Inspired by the social anthropologist Marianne Gullestad and her book *Det norske sett med nye øyne* (*Norwegianess Seen with New Eyes*), I decided to study this opposition from the point of view of the majority rather than looking at the Muslim minority and how it impacted them. The result was the first study of anti-Islamic and anti-Muslim mobilization in Norway, finished in May 2011. The anti-Islamic movement in Norway, I argued, was a peaceful one. But its view of Islam and Muslims as an existential and totalitarian threat contained the seeds of anti-democratic and violent solutions.

No more than two months later, Norway was struck by two large-scale terror attacks on the fateful summer day of 22 July. Of the 77 people killed, most were youths. Another 46 had been severely injured. It was by far the most devastating attack in Norwegian peacetime, and the consequences of which reverberate through our society to this day.

To most people's surprise, the perpetrator turned out to be Anders Behring Breivik – a white Norwegian man from Oslo. Just before committing these attacks, Breivik had uploaded a 1,518-page manifesto titled *2083: A European Declaration of Independence*. I immediately downloaded the manifesto, and together with Sveinung Sandberg (Department of Criminology and Sociology of Law, University of Oslo Professor), I analyzed the extent to which his views overlapped with the broader Norwegian anti-Islamic movement. The overlap was considerable. Considering this, we argued that the violent solutions he championed – and committed – were just as plausible an outcome as peaceful ones for those who believed that the West was in danger of going under. This would indicate that the potential for radicalization among anti-Islamic activists was considerable.

After that, I began delving into the support Breivik received among these activist groups and online forums. It quickly became apparent that Breivik and his choice of violence in fact had little or no support among anti-Islamic activists. What meagre support there was came from a fringe collection of individuals who got together online – mass murderer and school shooting fans, some ideologically motivated people and a collection of people who seemed drawn into this small community through the allure of romance and brotherhood. The anti-Islamic scene remained largely peaceful, and Breivik represented a clear outlier.

At that point in time, two distinct pathways lay before me. First, either continue down the track of studying the important but marginal phenomenon of actual extreme right political violence. Second, continue studying the broader and largely peaceful anti-Islamic mobilization. Both remained heavily underexplored. Furthermore, both dimensions are needed to explain the intertwined issues of the dynamics and mechanisms that lead to right-wing violence and those that lead to an absence of violence. Of the two, I chose to focus on the anti-Islamic mobilization.

Studying the broader anti-Islamic mobilization also means that my work is precisely that – broad. A project can be both ambitious in its scope and informative in its outcome, but the obvious risk is that it ends up saying too little about too much. Whether I managed to walk that tightrope is up to you, the reader, to decide. It certainly would have been broader still without the excellent input and guidance I got along the way.

ACKNOWLEDGEMENTS

This book is based on doctoral work undertaken at the European University Institute (2013–2017). A special debt of gratitude is owed to my thesis supervisor, Professor Donatella della Porta, and to the other faculty and fellow PhD candidates at the European University Institute's Department of Social and Political Sciences. A debt of gratitude is also owed to the Department of Comparative Politics at the University of Bergen for taking me in on a research exchange (2015) and the Center for Research on Extremism, Department of Political Science at the University of Oslo for housing me and subsequently providing the necessary support for this book to come into fruition (2016–2019). I am also particularly grateful to colleagues who have provided input and advice, namely: Stefano Bartolini, Hanspeter Kriesi, Manès Weisskircher, Swen Hutter, Elisabeth Ivarsflaten, Mikael Johannesson, Jan Oskar Engene, Lise Lund Bjånesøy, Carl Norlund, Sveinung Sandberg, Tore Bjørgo, Anders Jupskås, Jacob Ravndal, Pietro Castelli, Caterina Froio, Joel Busher, Graham Macklin, and Hugo Lewi Hammer. Finally, I wish to thank my family: my father, Svein Erik Berntzen; my partner, Linn Sandberg; and finally, Linn's parents, Laine Gnista and Per Sandberg.

ACRONYMS

Acronym	Original name	English name
4F		Four Freedoms Community
AFA		Anti-Fascist Action
AfD	Alternative für Deutschland	Alternative for Germany
AIG	al-Jama'ah al-Islamiyah al-Musallaha	Algerian Islamic Group
BFP		British Freedom Party
BNP		British National Party
BPE	Bürgerbewegung Pax Europa	Citizens' Movement Pax Europa
BPI	Blok proti islámu	Bloc Against Islam
CDU	Christlich Demokratische Union Deutschlands	Christian Democratic Union
CVF		Center for Vigilant Freedom
DDE	Direkte Demokratie für Europa	Direct Democracy for Europe
DDF	Den Danske Forening	Danish Association
DDL		Danish Defence League
DF	Dansk Folkeparti	Danish Peoples' Party
DFG	Die Freiheit – Bürgerrechtspartei für mehr Freiheit und Demokratie	German Freedom Party
FDV	Freiheitlich	Liberal Direct Democratic People's Party
	Direktdemokratische Volkspartei	
FMI	Folkevebegelsen mot innvandring	People's movement against immigration
FN	Front National	Front National
FPÖ	Freiheitliche Partei Österreichs	Freedom Party of Austria
FrP	Fremskrittspartiet	Progress Party
GoV		Gates of Vienna
HRS		Human Rights Service
IFPS		International Free Press Society

Acronym	Original name	English name
ISIS		Islamic State in Iraq and Syria
Jobbik	Jobbik Magyarországért Mozgalom	Hungarian Jobbik, the Movement for a Better Hungary
LGB		Liberty Great Britain
LGF		Little Green Footballs
LN	Lega Nord	Northern League
LPF	Lijst Pim Fortuyn	Pim Fortuyn List
NdIE	Nie dla Ilamizacji Europy	No to the Islamization of Europe
NDL		Norwegian Defence League
ONR	Oboz Narodowo-Radykalny	Radical Nationalist Camp
PEGIDA	Patriotische Europäer gegen die Islamisierung des Abendlandes	Patriotic Europeans against the Islamization of the West
PI		Politically Incorrect
PP	Partido Popular	Peoples Party
PKK	Partiya Karkerên Kurdistanê	Kurdistan Workers Party
PVV	Partij voor de Vrijheid	Party for Freedom
SD	Sverigedemokraterna	Sweden Democrats
SIAD	Stop Islamiseringen af Danmark	Stop Islamization of Denmark
SIAN	Stopp Islamiseringen av Norge	Stop Islamization of Norway
SIOA		Stop Islamization of America
SIOE		Stop Islamization of Europe
SIOED	Stop Islamization og Europe Deutschland	Stop Islamization of Europe Germany
SION		Stop Islamization of Nations
SIOTW		Stop Islamization of the World
SVP	Schweizerische Volkspartei	Swiss People's Party
TFS	Trykkefrihedsselskabet	Free Press Society
UKIP		United Kingdom Independence Party
VB	Vlaams Belang	Flemish Interest
ViS	Verdier i Sentrum	Core Values

1

FAR RIGHT AND LIBERAL?

Introduction

Europe is currently undergoing large-scale demographic and cultural change. An otherwise ageing and secularizing corner of the world has received an influx of younger, non-Western and often religious migrants. This influx has been increasingly and consistently contested by a resurgent far right from the 1980s onwards (Klandermans & Mayer, 2006, p. 3). For decades, as the conflict revolved around race, ethnicity and nationality – Africans and Arabs, Turks, Moroccans, and Pakistanis – some on the far-right upheld Islam as a positive, conservative force.

That has changed. In tandem with a long list of spectacular acts of political violence committed in the name of Islam and controversies such as the Muhammed cartoon crisis[1], Muslims and Islam have now become the predominant enemy for the far right in Europe and beyond.

This book is about that anti-Islamic turn and expansion of the far right. It is about a growing movement and subculture that is transnational in scope ranging from the United States, Western Europe, and, increasingly, Central and Eastern Europe. It has old ideological roots, but the movement began to coalesce online in the wake of the terror attacks on the United States by Al-Qaeda on 11 September 2001 (9/11). Since then, the anti-Islamic struggle has given rise to several distinct waves of activism under the names of Stop Islamization, Defense League, Patriotic Europeans against the Islamization of the West (*Patriotische Europäer gegen die Islamisierung des Abendlandes*, PEGIDA) and others. Anti-Islamic and anti-Muslim groups flourish online. In party politics, new initiatives such as the Dutch Pim Fortuyn List (*Lijst Pim Fortuyn*, LPF) and later Geert Wilders' Freedom Party (*Partij voor de Vrijheid*, PVV) made opposition to Islam their main issue.

The parties that mobilize on anti-Muslim and anti-Islamic ideas and arguments are now the most studied of all the party families (Mudde, 2016). In contrast, we know less about the broader movement and subculture.[2] An important reason for precisely why far-right parties are the subject of so much research, and why the anti-Islamic movement(s) and subculture merit closer scrutiny, is the idea that these initiatives either want to destroy democratic society itself or will in some way lead to its corrosion.

Franz Timmermans, the first Vice President of the European Commission, stated in an official speech that "The rise of islamophobia is one of the biggest challenges in Europe. It is a challenge to our vital values, to the core of who we are" (2015). Given this notion of a threat to "our" values, it is striking that the anti-Islamic far right in Western Europe and North America argue that they are defending democracy and freedom of speech (Betz & Meret, 2009, p. 313), while often proclaiming their support for Jews, gender equality, and lesbian, gay, bisexual, and transsexual (LGBT) rights (e.g. Dauber, 2017, p. 52).[3] If we turn the clock back two decades, we find a surge in neo-Nazi violence (Koopmans, 1996) and outspoken hostility towards Jews, homosexuals, and modern gender norms was commonplace.

Hearing far-right politicians and activists talk in such different terms today may appear paradoxical, given the legacy of opposition towards both progressive and liberal ideals, movements, and parties. Is the far right, which has been so closely tied to antagonism towards these very groups, now one of their defenders?

Viewed through the lens of history, it is their apparent self-portrayal as defenders of progressive and liberal ideals – and *not* their opposition to Islam and Muslims – that is most distinctive. In academic circles, this is often portrayed as being only skin deep, a thin veneer masking their true positions – and that the far right hides a radical "back stage" behind its moderate "front stage" (Fleck & Müller, 1998, p. 438) which is racist, anti-Semitic, homophobic, against women's rights, and hostile to democracy.

It is defined as a transparently strategic vocabulary (Scrinzi, 2017) used to circumvent and defend against allegations of racism. This is deemed a necessity on their part, since openly racist remarks have been stigmatized and pathologized (Lentin & Titley, 2011, p. 20) ever since the total defeat of the Axis powers in World War II (Jackson & Feldman, 2014, p. 7). The claims by Marine Le Pen of the French Front National (FN) to defend women's rights are, for instance, understood as "instrumental" and "pseudo-feminist" (Larzillière & Sal, 2011). In much the same way, Mayer, Ajanovic, and Sauer (2014) state that the far right exploits gender and LGBT arguments strategically in order to denigrate Muslim men. Others have conceptualized this as *homonationalism* (Puar, 2013; Zanghellini, 2012),[4] and *femonationalism* (Farris, 2012, 2017).[5]

Critical positions and scepticism are not without merit. For instance, studies of the British National Party (BNP) that go beyond the "front stage" by examining speeches and memos not intended for the public reveal that they toned down their anti-Semitism and anti-democratic positions as a ploy to win over new recruits and circumvent opposition from mainstream society (Jackson & Feldman, 2014, p. 10). These findings are in line with the broad consensus in the literature. Yet, we risk misconstruing the anti-Islamic turn and expansion if we limit ourselves to a theoretically based rejection or if we rely exclusively on single-case evidence from organizations with a clear fascist legacy. As a starting point for mapping the anti-Islamic movement and to investigate this apparent paradox and its ramifications on a broader scale, I pose the two following research questions:

RQ1 What characterizes the anti-Islamic movements' structure and composition?
RQ2 How, and to what extent, does the anti-Islamic movement incorporate progressive and liberal values?

In order to investigate the movements' configuration and degree of entanglement with progressive and liberal ideals, this book provides a study of four specific dimensions: 1) the background of leaders; 2) their official ideology; 3) organizational networks; and 4) the mobilization of sympathizers. The extent to which liberal and progressive positions and arguments permeate the anti-Islamic movement has far-reaching consequences for our basic understanding of what the anti-Islamic movement *is*. In addition to saying something about their entanglement with progressive and liberal ideals, these dimensions give us insight about the anti-Islamic turn on the far right.

First, tracing the waves of activism and the biographies of the leaders, representatives, and ideologues provides us with insight into their motivation for joining the anti-Islamic cause and whether they have their roots in the old far right or not. Second, studying their official ideology (front stage) gives an indication of whether their positions are consistent or fragmented across countries and organizations. Third, network analysis tells us whether these initiatives form a cohesive whole or consist of disjointed communities. Taken together, the historical and biographical overview, alongside the analyses of ideology and networks, go to the core of the matter. Is this really a movement, or is it just a question of different groups driven by national, regional, and local legacies and peculiarities? And do they represent a continuation of the old far right or not? By studying their mobilization, we uncover whether they have managed to recruit moderates or extremists, and to what extent they are aligned with the official ideological platform espoused by the leaders. It also provides insight into the drivers of their continued online mobilization and ability to spread their message, and why certain messages get more traction than others.

The four steps

The broader anti-Islamic turn consists of two parallel developments: first, an anti-Islamic reorientation of pre-existing radical right parties; second, an anti-Islamic expansion of the far right with new political initiatives. While the expansion includes some electorally successful parties, such as Pim Fortuyn's LPF and Geert Wilders' PVV, both in the Netherlands, it largely consists of alternative news sites and blogs, think-tanks, street protest groups such as the English Defence League (EDL) and PEGIDA, and minor political parties. Empirically speaking, the universe of cases dealt with in this book is limited to the anti-Islamic expansion. The findings and theoretical claims, however, have some bearing on the broader anti-Islamic turn.

The book starts by tracing the growth of anti-Islamic activism between 2001 and 2017, focussing on initiatives and central figures from six "stronghold" countries: Britain, the United States, the Netherlands, Germany, Norway, and Denmark. This is followed by a frame analysis of official statements by 11 key initiatives known for their anti-Muslim and anti-Islamic rhetoric in Germany, Norway, and Britain. All three countries are epicentres of anti-Islamic activism. Norway was the first country to have an explicitly anti-Islamic activist organization in Stop Islamization of Norway (SIAN) in 2000. Britain was the location where the online communities first gathered for a street march in 2005, and which witnessed the rise of the EDL in 2009. Finally, Germany gave birth to the latest version of anti-Islamic activism with PEGIDA in 2014, which has since spread across Europe (Berntzen & Weisskircher, 2016). I then trace the online anti-Islamic network starting with these 11 anti-Islamic initiatives' from Norway, Britain and Germany and 16 of their offshoots across the world in March 2015 and March 2016; that is, before and after the "refugee crisis". When examining members of these networks, the case selection consists of the anti-Islamic groups found in the network analysis that were active during the summer of 2016 – totalling 300 groups across Europe, North America, and Australia (Figure 1.1).

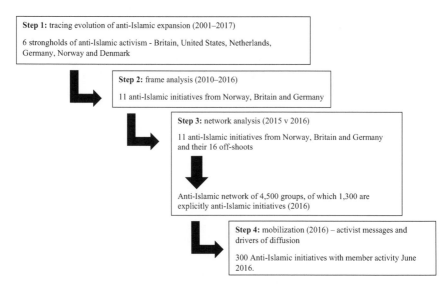

Step 1: tracing evolution of anti-Islamic expansion (2001–2017)

6 strongholds of anti-Islamic activism - Britain, United States, Netherlands, Germany, Norway and Denmark

Step 2: frame analysis (2010–2016)

11 anti-Islamic initiatives from Norway, Britain and Germany

Step 3: network analysis (2015 v 2016)

11 anti-Islamic initiatives from Norway, Britain and Germany and their 16 off-shoots

Anti-Islamic network of 4,500 groups, of which 1,300 are explicitly anti-Islamic initiatives (2016)

Step 4: mobilization (2016) – activist messages and drivers of diffusion

300 Anti-Islamic initiatives with member activity June 2016.

FIGURE 1.1 The four steps taken to explore the anti-Islamic movement and expansion

Findings and the argument(s)

As the old, highly authoritarian and ethnocentric far right lost its vitality, a new phenomenon arose to take its place: anti-Islam. It is a new addition to the far-right family, but no child of the old far right. The anti-Islamic cause was borne by a curious mix of people with leftist and conservative backgrounds, all of whom professed their attachment to many liberal ideals. Their leaders and intellectuals – many of them journalists and historians – came to see their own political camps as ignorant of the dangers posed by Islam. In their eyes, Islam was not a regular religion but a totalitarian ideology equivalent to communism and fascism. Propelled by their belief in a civilizational struggle between the West and Islam, these activists managed to establish a transnational anti-Islamic movement consisting of activist groups, think-tanks, and alternative media outlets, as well as some political parties. The movement itself has undergone four waves of expansion in response to acts of terror and other moral shocks, starting with 9/11. Most of their claims and positions about what they represent resonate with broad majorities in Western Europe: free speech, preservation of the Christian heritage, democracy, gender equality, LGBT rights and the protection of Jews. Their outspoken hostility to Islam and Muslims further resonates with substantial minorities.

Their civilizational worldview, which combines previously divergent political projects, is broadly consistent across organizations and countries. They continuously include both traditional and modern perspectives on a broad range of issues. On the one hand, hostility towards the Muslim minority and defence of traditions sits well with the older far right. On the other hand, their inclusion of modern gender norms and key liberal positions are clearly at odds with the traditional far right with its rigid views on gender roles and hostility toward democracy. For instance, when it comes to the supposed threat posed by Islam and Muslims to women's rights, they vacillate between "protector frames" with a male point of view (our women), and "equality frames" with a female point of view. I define this ideological duality as strategic frame ambiguity.

The anti-Islamic network mirrors this ideological duality. Anti-Islamic groups reach out to animal rights, LGBT, and women's rights groups, as well as Christian conservatives and Jewish and pro-Israeli initiatives. Some, but not all, of these reciprocate. Furthermore, both main components of the ideology – 1) Islam as an existential threat enabled by "the elites" either through a willed conspiracy or due to their sheer ignorance; 2) which undermines Western traditions and Christianity, democracy, gender equality, and minority rights – resonate with the online activists and followers. In terms of the two overarching research questions, the findings in this book can be summarized in one structural and one ideology-centric argument:

First, the initiatives that make up the anti-Islamic expansion of the far right comprise a transnational movement and subculture with a consistent worldview and prominent ideologues.

Second, the anti-Islamic movement and subculture is characterized by a semi-liberal equilibrium.

It is to the second argument I now turn. The transnational anti-Islamic movement exists in a state of balance between modern and liberal values on the one hand, and traditional and authoritarian values on the other. Both components are part of their civilizational, anti-Islamic identity. I have chosen to describe this state of balance as semi-liberal. Therefore, it is also semi-authoritarian. Using the label of liberal instead of authoritarian is justified by the fact that their leftist-to-conservative-liberal stances largely predate clearly authoritarian ones. When looking at the far right in its totality, the anti-Islamic movement represents a profound unmooring from ethnically based nationalism and pervasive authoritarianism, as well as homophobia and anti-Semitism. This sets them apart from the older far right, which is firmly rooted in precisely these values.

Although the old far right with its all-pervasive authoritarianism and ethnocentrism certainly exists in a diminished state today, most pre-existing radical right parties in Western Europe have undergone an ideological transformation that makes them ideologically similar to the anti-Islamic movement that arose after 9/11. Herbert Kitschelt (2012) described this transformation as a partial decoupling between authoritarianism and the radical right through an adoption of liberal positions on many issues. The starting point was an authoritarian one.

For the anti-Islamic movement that emerged after 9/11, the precise opposite holds. As the anti-Islamic movements' roots and original set of ideas come from outside the far right, it represents a partial *coupling* between liberalism and authoritarianism from a liberal starting point.[6] In other words, the anti-Islamic expansion is in fact liberalism that has drifted to the far right. What is the cause of this drift? My material clearly points to the pivotal role of their conception of Islam and Muslims as the ultimate embodiment of authoritarianism, narrow-mindedness, patriarchy and misogyny as the root cause. Ostensibly starting from a position of tolerance, they have concluded, "in order to maintain a tolerant society, the society must be intolerant of intolerance" (Popper, 1945, p. 226).[7] That is, Islam as the ultimate manifestation of intolerance must be met with intolerance itself to preserve a tolerant Western civilization. This demonstrates that it matters who the enemy is.[8]

If the anti-Islamic movements' roots and many of their central ideas are not far right, why call them far right? Labelling them as part of the far-right family hinges on two aspects of their ideology. The first and main aspect is nativism. Just as nativism is the bedrock of older far right ideologies, so it is with anti-Islam. Nevertheless, their qualitative conception of nativism is fundamentally different. The nativism espoused by the anti-Islamic movement is primarily founded on citizenship and adherence to "Western values", not ethnicity or race. It is therefore a more inclusive form of nativism. It is not an awakening of white ethnic identity as white, but a coming together around a civic identity that builds on progressive and conservative varieties of liberalism.[9] Emphasizing broad categories such as nativism therefore masks fundamental differences between the anti-Islamic project and the old far right. There is no strong continuity between the old far right and the anti-Islamic movement in this regard, but rather an abstract similarity. It is, organizationally speaking, a "new" phenomenon with new actors who hold many substantially different beliefs compared to the old far right.

The second criterion is precisely their turn toward intolerance and authoritarian solutions to combat Islam in order to defend and maintain an otherwise tolerant Western civilization. Therefore, while their civic nativism clearly sets the anti-Islamic movement apart from the old far right, their intermittent call for authoritarian solutions makes the difference less clear cut.

The ideological evolution of Hege Storhaug, a prominent female anti-Islamic activist and spokesperson for the Norwegian organization Human Rights Service (HRS) serves to illustrate the gradual coupling of progressive stances with conservative, and eventually some authoritarian stances under an anti-Islamic banner. Storhaug came from a left-wing background, seeing herself as a feminist champion of women's causes. Her main antagonists were Christian conservatives and others opposed to gender equality, abortion rights, and so forth. During the 1990s, she began focussing on the plight of Muslim women living in Norway who had been victims of female gender mutilation and forced marriage. In the years following 9/11, and especially after the Muhammed cartoon crisis, Storhaug became increasingly dogmatic in her focus and hostility toward Islam, seeing it as a threat to Western civilization and in particular, women's rights. In my interview with her, she said she came to the gradual realization that Christianity had largely been a force for good and was something altogether different from Islam. In the aftermath of the refugee crisis, she became outspoken in her praise of Hungarian Prime Minister Viktor Orbán and the Polish Law and Justice Party's authoritarian policies and rejection of Islam and Muslim immigrants. Neither Orbán nor the Polish Law and Justice Party are great defenders of gender equality, LGBT rights, or free speech. By 2017, Storhaug had taken to arguing that mosques should be banned and the Quran rewritten. Geert Wilders and other key players in the anti-Islamic movement came to such conclusions far earlier, whereas some still adhere to a softer approach.

As the case of Storhaug's ideological journey hints at, the current semi-liberal equilibrium characterizing the anti-Islamic far right is fragile. The first source of fragility lies in their view of Islam as an immediate and existential threat to Western civilization. This creates a space for more authoritarian, extreme, and explicitly anti-democratic solutions to gain ground. The second source of fragility stems from their activist base. Anti-Islamic activist groups contain a vocal minority of extreme activists who espouse long-standing hostilities and notions about race, homosexuals, Jews, and democracy. These extremists stand poised to exploit the movements' ideological discrepancies if the opportunity arises. The continued inability to stem the growth of either Muslim minorities or incidents of terror attacks committed by Islamist extremists represents just such an opportunity. Finally, the recent eastward expansion now means that their transnational network includes radical and extreme right groups of the old ideological order. Since the Eastern European groups are closely aligned with the extremist minority within the anti-Islamic movement in Western Europe and North America, this expansion has made the anti-Islamic far right more susceptible to profound internal identity struggles. For these reasons, the pendulum may swing in a decisively authoritarian direction and the semi-liberal equilibrium overturned.

Motivation and limitations

This is an exploratory study whose aim is to better grasp the anti-Islamic expansion at a macro level, and the theoretical implications for our understanding of the current far right flowing from this. As far as I am aware, it is the first study of this nature, and therefore fills a large gap. It helps rectify the fragmented and lopsided knowledge base which pre-existing single case studies of extra-parliamentary initiatives alongside the voluminous body of work on radical right parties provides. I have already described the merits of this approach and the findings that it has produced.

However, as an exploratory study of the anti-Islamic expansion in the aftermath of 9/11, my study also has several clear limitations. First, studying the anti-Islamic expansion entails focussing on the "successful" cases, their networks, and mobilization. My work offers limited insight into "failed" cases, the question of timing or why the old far right remains dominant in many countries. What it does provide, however, are good grounds for investigating these questions in future studies. As a first step, the clues my findings do provide to these questions are leveraged to sketch out some tentative answers in the conclusion.

Second, emphasizing the macro level comes with some clear costs. In particular, my work provides little insight into the variations between organizations and countries when it comes to what their online members and followers write and respond to. Rather, this data is treated in aggregate to discern the major patterns. This means that potentially significant distinctions between anti-Islamic and far-right activism in various countries are glossed over. Further in-depth analyses such as those conducted by Caterina Froio (2018) of the French far right would be the logical next step in fleshing out and nuancing findings and arguments provided in this book.

Furthermore, while this book covers a sizeable share of the anti-Islamic far right, the material does not span the entire width and breadth of anti-Islamic initiatives. In other words, this is a limited galaxy of cases, and the findings represent a partial – but significant – trend. While the incorporation of liberal and progressive claims is an overarching pattern found among the anti-Islamic initiatives scrutinized in this book, this is by no means generalizable to *every individual* anti-Islamic activist group, party, website, or think-tank in Western Europe or North America.

Moreover, my findings concerning the entanglement between anti-Islamic activism and liberal values is not readily generalizable beyond the North American and North-West European core region where the anti-Islamic movement originated. In fact, it is probable that the macro-level patterns I identified are reversed outside of these areas. Instead of having a majority of activists embrace liberal values, with only a minority pushing clear-cut racism, ethno-nationalism, and explicitly anti-democratic ideas, it seems plausible that a majority of those who engage in anti-Islamic activism in regions such as Eastern Europe profess racist and anti-democratic ideas. My own material hints at this. In other words, the attachment between liberalism and mobilization against Islam and Muslims is historically and geographically contingent.

To a certain extent, this study challenges the party-movement distinction by introducing the conceptual categories of ideological reorientation versus expansion. These categories are independent of organizational form. Empirically speaking, however, the focus is on the extra-parliamentary actors. Therefore, I cannot tell the extent which radical right parties have undergone an anti-Islamic, ideological reorientation which includes supplanting ethnic nativism with civic nativism, except by drawing on secondary literature. My findings resonate with some recent studies on these pre-established radical right parties, but the degree to which my findings carry over is nonetheless unclear.

Relatedly, my work does not substantially go into the exchange of ideas between parliamentary and extra-parliamentary actors. Nor does it say anything about the extent to which the new anti-Islamic initiatives have influenced the ideological reorientation of older radical right parties. Although outside the scope of this study, such interactions remain a promising avenue of research.

Finally, the network analysis only captures one online dimension of their interactions with other groups. It does not refer to "deeper" ties, such as economic transactions, membership overlap, or mutual participation in collective action on the streets.

In the following sections, I look at the state of the art and list key contributions on the issues of ideology and framing, networks, and the mobilizational aspects of recruitment and message diffusion.

Anti-Islam, the far right and liberal values

Concepts, ideology and framing

Anti-Muslim prejudices are widespread across Europe (Wike & Grim, 2010; Savelkoul, Scheepers, Veld, & Hagendoorn, 2012), but these prejudices are not directly affected by the actual number of Muslims in any given country (Lucassen & Lubbers, 2012, p. 567). This puts the onus on the anti-Islamic initiatives and their role in diffusing anti-Islamic and anti-Muslim ideas, as well as mobilizing activists and citizens to this cause. Examples of anti-Islamic rhetoric include portraying Europe as in danger of being "overrun" by Muslims and an "Islamization" manifested through the introduction of halal products, Sharia law, Muslim ghettoes, and honour killings, all of which constitutes a totalitarian threat. Some initiatives openly talk of "Eurabia", an alleged conspiracy between amorphous European political elites and Arab rulers whereby the European elites agree to transform the continent into a part of the Islamic world through Muslim colonization in return for access to oil (Bangstad, 2013, p. 3). In the literature, anti-Islamic and anti-Muslim opposition is mainly understood as stemming from the radical and extreme right (e.g. Strabac & Listhaug, 2008; Grabow & Hartleb, 2014). Anti-Islamic initiatives with no organizational links to older extreme or radical right organizations and milieus and that adopt this rhetoric are also labelled as radical right, extreme right, neo-fascist, or simply Islamophobic (e.g. Zúquete, 2008; Jackson & Feldman, 2011; Archer, 2013; Lee, 2015). In short, these initiatives have consistently been defined as belonging to the far right. However, their almost exclusive focus on Islam and Muslims has led some researchers to distinguish between them and the broader far right (e.g. Meleagrou-Hitchens & Brun, 2013; Goodwin, 2013).

Ideology – that is, worldview – is what distinguishes the far right from other political phenomena, not their organizational form or actions. The emphasis on ideology makes the way we define and conceptualize their ideologies vitally important. In this field, we find a profusion of concepts and definitions – all of which have implications and guide our analysis in specific directions. For instance, as far back as 1996, Cas Mudde identified over 26 different definitions of the term "extreme right". As Caiani, Della Porta, and Wagemann state, we have to "acknowledge that the term extreme (or radical) right has multiple facets" (2012, p. 4). Many of these terms are used as slurs in politics and everyday interactions, and this can muddy the field of analysis. Before we move on, some clarification is therefore required. See Chapter 2 for an in-depth discussion.

As there is no clear-cut consensus on the different terms, I draw on some of the most widely cited definitions to compile a taxonomy of far-right ideologies. The term "far right" is not used to define an ideology in itself, but is a highly abstracted conceptual container which includes extreme and radical right ideologies. "Nativism" is broadly considered to be the common denominator for far-right ideologies, whereby the nation-state should only consist of members of the native group. Non-natives are therefore a threat by default (Mudde, 2007, p. 17).[10] If an ideology does not have nativism at its core, it is incorrect to define it as far right. The distinguishing characteristics of radical right versus extreme right ideology lies in their approach to the political system and the solutions they profess. Whereas the extreme right is anti-democratic and willing to use non-state violence to achieve their goals, the radical right is for working within the confines of the democratic system, but is critical of the establishment (e.g. Bornschier, 2010). Within this framework, fascism is one permutation of extreme right ideology, whereas the ethno-pluralism of the *nouvelle droite* and others is a permutation of radical right ideology.

Key to many studies that use these terms is that while they deal with anti-Muslim and anti-Islamic antagonism from parties and activist groups, they generally raise the level of abstraction and define them as, for instance, hostile to immigrants and minorities – thereby stressing the continuity between current and older iterations of the far right. Emphasis on continuity through theoretical abstraction has been a factor in the scant attention afforded to these initiatives' claims of defending liberal and progressive values.

The studies that specifically scrutinize opposition to and mobilization against Islam and Muslims alternate between three concepts: anti-Islam, anti-Muslim, and Islamophobia. The three have been used intermittently, but it is Islamophobia that has received the most attention and which has been most developed (Doyle &

Ahmad, 2013). Although the term "Islamophobia" has a long history (Bangstad, 2016), it resurfaced in Britain in the 1990s, when Muslim rights groups attempted to put the discrimination of Muslims on the political agenda. In 1997, a left-wing think-tank, a Commission of the Runneymede Trust, issued a report on British Muslims and Islamophobia (CBMI) (1997) entitled "Islamophobia: a challenge for us all". The Commission defined Islamophobia as "an unfounded hostility towards Islam, and therefore fear or dislike of all or most Muslims" (ibid., p. 4). The use of the term became widespread, and entered into academic discourse, especially in the Anglo-Saxon sphere. Islamophobia as a concept was – and to a large extent still is – used "because there [was] a new reality that need[ed] naming" – but also as a tool so that in identifying it could be "acted against" (Sayyid & Vakil, 2008, p. 40). Animosity towards Islam, Muslim culture, and immigration takes different shapes, some more moderate and some more extreme – at times seemingly inseparable from secular criticism, at times one of vitriolic racism. Research that relies on the term Islamophobia, however, is often linked with the tradition of fascism studies, describing Muslims as "the new Jews", and paying less attention to the issue of liberal and progressive values. Siding with Sedgwick (2013, p. 209) and Busher (2015, p. 29), I set aside the concept of "Islamophobia" as a confusing term which conflates different phenomena and unneccesarily places the emphasis on irrationality.[11]

Based on an ethnographic logic, Joel Busher (2015) uses the term "anti-Muslim" for two reasons. It reflects the activists own self-portrayal (p. 20) while also keeping present the fact that there are actual people on the receiving end of their activism.[12]

In this book, I use the term "anti-Islamic" in combination with the term "the far right". I specifically rely on the term anti-Islam based on an analysis of the various actors' views of Islam as a political, totalitarian force. Their claims indicate that they are negative not only towards Islamism, but towards Islam in general. On an ideological level, their opposition to Muslim immigration and culture flows from their view of Islam as a totalitarian and destructive force. On a personal level, it may be just the opposite for many people. This book, however, is concerned with the meso and macro levels of organizational actors and ideology, not with the underlying prejudices driving individuals at the micro level. At the meso and macro levels, "anti-Islam" is therefore a more precise label than "anti-Muslim". In line with this reasoning, I define anti-Islam in terms of *framing Islam as a homogenous, totalitarian ideology which threatens Western civilization*; whereas the term "Islamophobia" contains an inherent emphasis on (emotional) reaction, conceptualizing anti-Islam in terms of framing moves the focus to the agency of far-right initiatives.

Ambiguity, the anti-Islamic master frame and GAL/TAN

In essence, this entire book speaks to the ideologically oriented debate about the far right. In the previous section, I sketched out two of my contributions which draw on existing work: first, by providing a taxonomical conceptualization of far-right ideologies, and second, by offering a definition of anti-Islam in terms of framing.

Beyond this, two larger contributions are worth highlighting. The first comes from a ground-up approach in which I compare the collective action frames of anti-Islamic across organizations and countries, followed by an in-depth analysis of how these initiatives frame issues such as women's rights. When exploring the issue of women's rights, I identify two sets of frames that are used intermittently by all the anti-Islamic initiatives examined: protector frames with a male point of view, and equality frames with a female point of view. I characterize the simultaneous use of both as *strategic frame ambiguity*.

Second, in order to contextualize the anti-Islamic turn in relation to other versions of the far right, I expand on Jens Rydgren's conceptualization of far-right ideological evolution since World War II (2005a, 2007). In line with the broader literature, Rydgren argues that the original extreme right ideology – or master frame – became unviable in the political climate after World War II and the defeat of the Nazis and fascists (2005a, p. 413). The situation for the far right only changed after a period of ideological reorientation and moderation – that is, with the invention of a second master frame by the new right (*nouvelle droite*) and the French Front National (FN), which stressed anti-establishment populism and xenophobic ethno-nationalism. The (partial) embrace of democracy embodied by this new master frame signalled a major shift – the establishment of radical right ideology. Furthermore, their xenophobic ethno-nationalism was packaged in the notion of "separate but equal cultures", meaning that the superiority and inferiority of ethnicities and cultures was no longer part of the equation (2005a, p. 427). This is in stark contrast to the supposedly biological, racial hierarchies of the older extreme right. For the sake of clarity, the first master frame is hereafter defined as "fascist", whereas the second is defined as "ethno-pluralist".

The distinction between the two master frames – and as a consequence, between extreme and radical right ideology – rests on two dimensions: their view of the political system, and their conceptualization of "the other". I argue that the anti-Islamic collective action framing (Chapter 5) is sufficiently distinct from both these master frames to be categorized as a third master frame for the far right, but not as a distinct ideology. Instead, in its predominant form, it is a new permutation of radical right ideology. First, unlike the ethno-pluralist radical right, anti-Islam reintroduces notions of superiority and inferiority, but this time they speak in terms of civilizations – Western, Judeo-Christian versus Islamic – and not race. Second, and more importantly, distinguishing anti-Islam as a third master frame rests on introducing a third dimension; their conception of themselves, particularly when it comes to family and gender relations. The fascist and ethno-pluralist master frames more or less overlap on this dimension, as both build on "traditional" family and gender values. In contrast, the anti-Islamic, civilizational master frame incorporates LGBT rights and women's rights, in addition to the historically vilified Jewish minority.

On an abstract level, the anti-Islamic master frame resembles the fascist master frame in its strong emphasis on hierarchies of worth, while the anti-Islamic master frame overlaps directly with the ethno-pluralist master frame in its partial acceptance of democracy. The anti-Islamic master frame basically breaks with both, and incorporates liberal and progressive perspectives on gender and minority rights. This means that the anti-Islamic master frame transcends the libertarian-traditional divide at the core of the so-called Green–Alternative–Libertarian (GAL) versus Traditional–Authoritarian–Nationalist (TAN) cultural cleavage, which some have argued is the most salient struggle in Western politics (Kriesi et al., 2008; van der Brug & Van Spanje, 2009; Bakker et al., 2015). This is important, as the radical right are seen as championing the TAN side in a struggle against the libertarian left (Bornschier, 2010, p. 5).

Far-right networks, movements, and transnationalization

Ideology and framing are interconnected with networks, but the causal relationship is difficult to untangle. Social networks function as channels for the construction of meaning, and operate as both resources and constraints (Caiani et al., 2012, p. 30). The network-oriented perspective helps us to get a grasp on the interplay between competition and cooperation among plural and complex actors (ibid., p. 210). The presence of networks between the initiatives is also one of the necessary factors to establish whether or not we are talking about a movement. A social movement can be defined as "a network of informal interactions between a plurality of individuals, groups and/or organizations, engaged in political or cultural conflict, on the basis of a shared collective identity" (Diani, 1992, p. 165). Social movement research has long stressed the importance of online communication platforms as resources for the mobilization of transnational movements, as information can be disseminated virtually instantaneously (Petit, 2004), overcoming problems of leadership and decision-making (Castells, 2000), and creating transnational solidarity (Chase-Dunn & Boswell, 2002). It has been argued that online networks are important for groups that are marginalized in their own domestic politics (della Porta & Tarrow, 2005, pp. 1–21). Caiani and Wagemann (2009) claim that online networks have been particularly important for the extreme right, due to the constraints they face when taking to the streets or trying to mobilize in other offline arenas. Speaking of the radical right parties, however, Cas Mudde argues that the notion of transnational far right alliances and networks are inflated (2016).

Narrowing things down to extra-parliamentary anti-Islamic initiatives, there is a small but growing body of research that goes beyond the study of particular organizations to look at the network constellations between anti-Islamic and other far-right groups *within* specific countries, primarily the United States (e.g. Bail, 2012, 2014). In one of the first empirical studies of anti-Islamic initiatives in the United States, such as ACT! For America and Stop Islamization of America, Ali et al. (2011, p. 2) claim that "this core group of deeply intertwined [anti-Islamic, sic] individuals and organizations manufacture and exaggerate threats of "creeping Sharia", Islamic domination of the West, and purported obligatory calls to violence against all non-Muslims by the Quran. Detailed network analyses and the plagiarism detection programme (Bail, 2012, 2014) show that the network of anti-Islamic organizations in the United States has grown in influence and become agenda-setting, sometimes dominating the news cycle due to emotionally charged language.[13] While focussing on Norway, Berntzen and Sandberg (2014) claim that these communities form a transnational social movement "sharing an anti-Islamic identity and rhetoric, and have overlapping and close ties" (ibid., p. 761). The transnational character of the anti-Islamic movement, with organizational and ideological roots across Europe and the United States has been further outlined by several scholars. Meleagrou-Hitchens and Brun label it as an "identifiable pan-European far-right movement" (2013, p. 1), and Goodwin describes it as "an amorphous network of think-tanks, bloggers and activists" (2013, p. 1), whereas Denes characterizes it as a "loose global fraternity" (2012, p. 295). Small empirical inroads have been made by Yang and Self (2015) and Lee (2015). Yang and Self conducted a network analysis starting from the anti-Islamic blog, Atlas Shrugs, finding that it primarily had connections to other US right-wing sites. Beginning with five anti-Islamic websites, and tracing their hyperlinks, Lee made a partial mapping of what he defines as the "Counter-Jihadist Nebula", uncovering an online network of 46 websites (2015, p. 256). Furthermore, it has been claimed that "the 'counter-jihad' network seems to have dissolved, as many right-wing populists have branded themselves primarily anti-EU" (Fleischer, 2014, p. 69). Apart from these studies, has been known about the full scope and configuration of the anti-Islamic movement and subculture.

Growing, ideologically diverse, and transnational network

The network analyses (Chapter 6) fill a large gap and can be divided into three categories; size and persistence, ideology, and transnationalization. First, my analysis shows that the anti-Islamic movement and subculture is large and growing. In 2015, the network consisted of just over 3,000 groups. A third of these were explicitly anti-Islamic. By 2016 the network had expanded to over 4,000, with anti-Islamic groups accounting for a somewhat larger share. Although growing and structurally cohesive at the macro level, the movement and subculture which the online network analysis captures also indicates that there is a large degree of fluidity. One-third of the groups present in the network in 2015 were no longer present in 2016, whereas over 2,000 new groups joined. There are also major internal shifts, with close to one-third of the groups present in 2015 migrating from one community to another by 2016. This fluidity may be a function of the media platform itself. Setting up a new group on Facebook does not demand resources, although being noticed and accepted by pre-existing anti-Islamic groups does require some effort. Fluidity aside, the movement and subculture has persisted for over two decades, and can no longer be described as "embryonic" (see e.g. Goodwin, 2013; Busher, 2015).

Second, we see that "birds of a feather flock together". The overview of the various clusters within the network in both 2015 and 2016 gives an immediate picture that closely mirrors what my own and other qualitative studies have uncovered about anti-Islamic initiatives' rhetoric and worldview (e.g. Zúquete, 2008;

Goodwin, 2013; Berntzen & Sandberg, 2014). They have strong ties to Israeli and pro-Israeli groups, which consist of everything from Christians for Israel to the official website of the Israeli Defence Forces. By 2016, the anti-Islamic movement and the pro-Israeli community had become further integrated, with a large chunk of the former Stop Islamization community being absorbed by the pro-Israeli community. This means that the anti-Islamic far right is clearly different from the traditional anti-Semitic extreme right on this dimension. The growing presence of women's rights, animal rights, and LGBT groups within the network also highlight its distinctive quality when compared to the ethno-pluralist far right, which emphasizes traditional gender and family values. Their presence underlines the fundamental shift that the focus on Muslims and Islam means for the far right, particularly in Western Europe and North America. If progressive actors and ideas continue to exert influence, the anti-Islamic movement – and the far right as a whole – seems to be set on a course for continued moderation.

In combination with the comparative frame analysis, the network analyses also contribute to the understanding of the ongoing transnationalization of the far right. As this book shows, the ties between Western European anti-Islamic initiatives and Eastern European radical and extreme right initiatives increased in the wake of the 2015 "refugee crisis". Major far-right parties such as the Hungarian Jobbik, the Movement for a Better Hungary (*Jobbik Magyarországért Mozgalom*), have also adopted anti-Islam positions (Thorleifsson, 2017), moving away from their characteristic focus on anti-ziganism (Roma), anti-Semitism (Jews) and biological racism (Wodak, 2015). Simultaneously, in Western Europe, the "refugee crisis" seems to have led to a resurgent focus on asylum seekers and refugees and a comparative decline in emphasis on Muslims and Islam (see e.g. Haanshuus & Jupskås, 2017). In other words, the refugee crisis has facilitated an increased transnationalization and Europeanization of the far right, and has also led to some degree of breakdown between the (ideal type) ethno-pluralist and anti-Islamic master frame. These two co-occurring processes in the wake of the "refugee crisis" reveal not only the increasing impact of anti-Islam, but also that old and new far right ideologies can to a certain extent be interchangeable without causing major internal ruptures within these initiatives – be it parties or activist groups. In other words, both the eastward expansion and mixture indicate that these two master frames are sufficiently similar to co-exist without causing organizational breakdown, in much same way that extreme right ideas intermittently surface among the members of old populist radical right organizations.

Organizationally speaking, the movement's attempts to reach out to groups championing women's rights, LGBT groups, and animal rights, as well as Christian conservatives and pro-Israeli initiatives, are primarily best understood as ongoing efforts to build a negative coalition. This term comes from the studies of social revolution, which suggest that multiclass coalitions were critical to revolutionary success (Goldstone, 1994, 2011; Goodwin, 2001). For instance, Dix (1984) attributed the degree of success enjoyed by revolutionary movements in Latin America to their ability to construct a negative coalition which brought together different classes united by a common rejection of the ruling regime. More specifically, a negative coalition is "a coalition displaying highly diverse preferences on most major politically salient issues but united primarily by their common rejection of a particular outcome" (Beissinger, 2013, p. 3).

Mobilization

Mobilization – and more specifically, recruitment – is a pivotal aspect in all spheres of politics. David Art argues that it is precisely who the radical right recruit that is crucial when it comes to determining whether or not a given radical right party succeeds or fails (2011, p. 33). What characterizes those recruited by far-right initiatives? In his analysis, which builds on interviews and ethnographic fieldwork, Art distinguishes between three kinds of activists on the basis of their views and motivations: moderates, extremists and opportunists (ibid., pp. 31–33). Extremists reject democracy and espouse racist and anti-Semitic ideas, but moderates embrace democracy and distance themselves from explicitly racist views. Art identifies opportunists as those without a radical right legacy or ideological motivation. Narrowing this down to the anti-Islamic far right, work by Goodwin, Cutts, and Janta-Lipinski (2016) on who sympathized and joined the EDL showed that supporters hold more classic racial prejudice than the population as a whole (ibid., p. 4). Extrapolating from this, we would therefore expect that anti-Islamic initiatives should draw a large amount of what Art defines as extremists.

Why do people join? The social movement literature presents three variables for recruitment: ideological compatibility, or frame alignment (Snow, Rochford, Worden, & Benford, 1986), personal networks (McAdam, 1988; Goodwin & Jasper, 2014), and external shocks (Gould, 2009). First, an underlying assumption is that participation in a movement or group is dependent on the congruence between the goals and ideology of the organization and the individual activist and members (Snow et al., 1986, p. 464). However, with some exceptions (e.g. Beissinger, 2013; Ketelaars, Walgrave, & Wouters, 2014), this has not been tested. In contrast, personal networks and external shocks have now been empirically identified as important in a number of studies. In his ethnographic study of the EDL, Joel Busher (2015) also identified personal networks (ibid., pp. 42–43) and external shocks (in this case, personal trauma) as two of the main factors driving activist recruitment. Only a minority were deeply involved in EDL ideology before joining (the ideologically compatible). Nonetheless, one of the reasons for their importance is because of the meaning they transmit. In other words, they were channels which facilitated ideological compatibility. According to Busher, the same holds for external shocks (critical events). When these aligned with the EDL position, they made the person susceptible to the rest of their views.

As already mentioned, the literature on the far right also indicates that strategic thinking and planning plays a role for far-right initiatives and those people who adopt anti-Islamic and civilizational claims. They are thought to do this to fend off allegations of racism and the potential normative and political sanctions that it entails. They are therefore opportunists, but of a different variety than those cited in Art's research.

Different entry pathways, bound by belonging

Building on these perspectives, I suggest two different, causal pathways for adopting the anti-Islamic, civilizational master frame, and thereby potentially joining the transnational movement (Chapter 8). There is one pathway for people with a far right, nativist outlook, and another for those with a liberal and progressive outlook. The first pathway is strategic, escaping normative sanctions against xenophobic nativism. I call this the strategic calculation (SC) pathway. The second pathway is when jihadist terror attacks and other critical events trigger a fear-based response (moral shock), whereby they come to adopt the civilizational claims about Islam being a totalitarian, existential threat. I call this the emotional response (ER) pathway.

Regardless of their entry pathway, the views activists *express* is probably far more important than the views they *hold* for the trajectory of a single initiative and the broader movement. In this sense, the degree of ideological compatibility and frame alignment becomes the important factor once a person has joined. This book sheds light on what is expressed by those who have become (online) activists (Chapter 7). Orienting myself towards Art (2011), I therefore make a bipartite distinction between moderate and extreme activists in studying the views expressed by those who have become activists. As with previous studies on alignment, my findings indicate a strong congruence on the diagnostic framing of Islam and Muslims as the penultimate threat to Western civilization. Furthermore, a majority seem to embrace the expansive in-group which includes women, LGBT, Jews, and others deemed to be threatened by Islam. Nonetheless, expressions of racist, misogynistic, anti-Semitic, and anti-democratic ideas are also present. This points to a subset of extreme activists who are not (strategically) motivated to disguise their views.

This book also connects with the growing literature on the role of emotions in understanding continued mobilization and message diffusion. It studies which emotions drive online mobilization within anti-Islamic groups active on Facebook and their diffusion on the same platform. According to Klandermans, van der Toorn and van Stekelenburg (2008), the mobilizing role of emotions had previously been neglected in social movement literature. This also holds for those who employ framing theory (e.g. Benford, 1997), even though frames are tailored to elicit emotional responses and, for instance, hot cognition has been recognized as pivotal for mobilizing potential members (Zajonc, 1980; Gamson, 1992). I find that joy and trust are strongly associated with mobilization. The more joy or trust-related words a post contains, the more comments it gets. Increases in joy- and trust-associated words also correlate with an increase in the number of times a post is shared by members and followers, either with friends, on their own Facebook wall, or in other groups they participate in. The pattern is not as clear for anger-associated words, and fear seems to have no effect at all. In contrast, fact-heavy statements seem to drive down responses and shares beyond the specific group. When looking at the content of these posts, mobilizing messages focus on the in-group and the building of a common identity. The core theme is "belonging".

Chapter outline

The book is divided into eight chapters. After this introductory chapter, Chapter 2 provides an overview of the main research traditions and concepts, and how they inform our analysis of anti-Islamic mobilization. The chapter has three main sections. After providing a brief overview of the research field, the first section draws on key literature to construct a taxonomical ladder of far-right ideology. In it, the far right is used as an umbrella term for the extreme and radical right, respectively, whereas fascism is understood as one permutation of the extreme right and ethno-pluralism is understood as one permutation of the radical right. The second section deals with the concepts of Islamophobia, anti-Islam, and anti-Muslim, and how far-right antagonism towards Islam and the inclusion of liberal and progressive positions have been understood. The third section presents the dominant perspectives and claims about far right and anti-Islamic networks and mobilization.

Chapter 3 provides an overview of the methodological tools and data used. It includes qualitative content analysis of statements made by leaders and representatives of anti-Islamic initiatives in Norway, Britain, and Germany, tools used to harvest data from Facebook, network analysis, and the dictionary-based, automated sentiment analysis for large amounts of text.

Chapter 4 provides a chronological overview of the anti-Islamic expansion which emanates from the United States, Britain, the Netherlands, Germany, Norway, and Denmark, as well as a comparative analysis of the background of 30 figureheads (leaders, ideologues, and representatives) from these countries. First, it argues that the anti-Islamic movement has undergone four waves of expansion, precipitated by large-scale critical events and smaller moral shocks. Second, the comparative analysis shows that many of the figureheads have both a left-wing and a right-wing background, with only a few having any previous affiliation with the far right. Just as extreme right legacies can help continue old extreme right ideas, legacies from outside the far right may have contributed to the inclusion of progressive and liberal ideals among the anti-Islamic initiatives.

Chapter 5 consists of three main sections. The first is an analysis of the collective action framing of the leaders and representatives of anti-Islamic initiatives in Norway, Britain, and Germany. Similarities and differences in their diagnostic, prognostic, and motivational framework are identified. The main finding is that their positions are broadly aligned across country cases and organizational forms – parties, activist groups, or online groups. The understanding of Islam as an existential threat is unison, and so is the rejection of the "establishment". Furthermore, they are aligned in their understanding of what and who is threatened (democracy, the Christian cultural heritage, gender equality, and LGBT rights), as well as in their inclusion of pro-democratic solutions. In the second section, I delve down to look at how they frame women's rights. I identify two sets of frames that are used intermittently by all the anti-Islamic initiatives in question: protector frames that operate with a possessive, male point of view; and equality frames operating with a female point of view. I characterize the simultaneous use of both as strategic frame ambiguity. In the third section, I synthesize and discuss these findings in the light of Rydgren's work on the evolution of far-right master frames and the literature on the cultural cleavage between initiatives which represent the Green–Alternative–Libertarian (GAL) versus the Traditional–Authoritarian–Nationalist (TAN) dimensions. Extending Rydgren's argument, I claim that anti-Islam is best understood as a third, distinct master frame. The anti-Islamic, civilizational master frame transcends the fundamental GAL/TAN divide by incorporating the libertarian dimension. Finally, I employ grid/group analysis first developed by Mary Douglas (1982) to further elaborate on the distinctions between the three versions of the far right. Arising from this, I argue that the anti-Islamic far right is characterized by a form of liberal sectarianism. This resonates with Herbert Kitschelt's (2012) argument that some radical right parties have partially decoupled from authoritarianism in their embrace of some liberal positions. For the anti-Islamic movement, however, the process is reverse. Their ideological journey is one where they have embraced some authoritarian positions from an ostensibly liberal starting point. In both cases, the end result is the same: the anti-Islamic far right straddle the gap between liberal and authoritarian values at the core of the GAL/TAN cleavage.

Chapter 6 takes the anti-Islamic organizations in Norway, Britain, and Germany, and offshoots around the world present on Facebook, as a starting point for a network analysis that ends up uncovering a transnational constellation of approximately 3,600 and 4,600 groups in March 2015 and March 2016, respectively. Beyond uncovering the fundamentally transnational nature of the anti-Islamic movement and subculture, the major finding is that extreme right groups were virtually non-existent in the network in 2015, whereas anti-Islamic initiatives do reach out to groups that label themselves as favoring women's rights, LGBT rights, and animal rights, as well as Jewish and pro-Israeli groups. This is in line with the framing activity of the organizations, as identified in Chapter 5. However, by 2016, the share of extreme right initiatives had risen with the introduction of more groups from Eastern Europe. In general, the broad ideological span between the initiatives which anti-Islamic groups attempt to create ties with can be defined as attempts at building *negative coalitions* – united primarily by what they are against.

Chapter 7 looks at the arguments and sentiments expressed by the members and followers of 300 anti-Islamic groups on Facebook, using a selection based on the preceding network analysis. In other words: who have they mobilized? When compared to the framing activity of the organizations in Chapter 5, we can identify a strong alignment on the prognostic framing (what and who is the problem), less so on the solutions. Furthermore, the inclusion of the "progressive" in-group (LGBT, women and people of different religious and from different ethnic backgrounds with the exception of Muslims) is dominant. Nonetheless, the traditional extreme right views of black people, Jews and LGBT and arguments in favour of violent solutions are also present. A second aim is to identify the emotions and messages which drive internal online mobilization in the form of comments and messages disseminated beyond the specific groups in the form of shares. Here I used a dictionary-based sentiment analysis, which ranks emotions connected to specific words. Using multilevel regression analysis, the major findings are that positive emotions of joy and trust, often connected to messages that affirm the in-group identity, drive mobilization. Anger plays a secondary role.

Chapter 8 provides syntheses of the findings and develops the core arguments relating to the two overarching research questions. I argue that the various initiatives that make up the anti-Islamic expansion of the far right comprise a cohesive transnational movement embedded in a larger subculture. This movement and subculture has a consistent worldview and prominent ideologues. Today, the anti-Islamic movement and subculture is no longer an embryonic phenomenon. The anti-Islamic civilizational master frame, or worldview, draws on both liberal and traditional, authoritarian values. This civilizational master frame (partly) structures their organizational online networks and dominates among their online members. I therefore argue that the anti-Islamic movement and subculture is characterized by a semi-liberal equilibrium. This demonstrates that it matters who the enemy is, but not just in the way that earlier research indicates. I suggest two mutually exclusive pathways into adopting the worldviews espoused in the anti-Islamic movement and subculture. In the first, opposition to Islam precedes an inclusion of some progressive and liberal positions, driven by a strategic attempt to escape social and political sanctions. In the other pathway, progressive and liberal positions precedes an understanding of Islam as a totalitarian ideology and an existential threat, driven by an emotional response to jihadi terror attacks and other critical events. The equilibrium is threatened by the eastward expansion of the network; the sizeable minority position, which includes racist and anti-democratic positions. and the inherent tension in their worldview, which portrays Islam as an apocalyptic threat, but which should be met by adhering to democratic procedures. The semi-liberal and peaceful equilibrium is therefore fragile.

Notes

1 The Muhammad cartoon crisis denotes the backlash by Muslims in Western Europe and Muslim majority countries after the Danish newspaper *Jyllands-Posten* published 12 editorial cartoons on 30 September 2005, most of which depicted Muhammad.
2 Art (2011) and Busher (2015) are two prominent and notable exceptions.
   The existing studies of "non-parties" are predominantly case studies of single activist groups. They show that anti-Islamic initiatives like the English Defence League (EDL) (e.g. Allen, 2011; Jackson & Feldman, 2011; Kassimeris & Jackson, 2015; Busher, 2015) and PEGIDA (Daphi et al., 2015; Dostal, 2015; Berntzen & Weisskircher, 2016) are fixtures of the broader political landscape.
   Several authors point out that far right initiatives outside of party politics and the networks they form deserves more attention (e.g. Mudde, 2007, p. 5; Rydgren, 2007, p. 257; Macklin, 2013, p. 177).

3 For instance, following the attack on the gay club in Orlando, where an IS sympathizer killed 50 people, the far-right news site Breitbart commentator Milo Yiannopoulos wrote that "America has to make a choice. Does it want gay rights, women's emancipation, and tolerance for people of all nonviolent faiths – or does it want Islam?" (12 June 2016). Available at: www.breitbart.com/milo/2016/06/12/left-chose-islam-gays-now-100-people-killed-maimed-orlando/?utm_source=facebook&utm_medium=social (accessed 8 November 2016).

4 The concept of homonationalism refers to the use of gay rights for racist and islamophobic ends (Zanghellini, 2012, p. 357).

5 Scepticism of what far-right initiatives say and write precedes the explicit focus on Islam and claims of defending liberal values and the rights of women and minorities. Mudde argues that one explanation for this assumption of is that most authors define them as "the other" (2000, p. 21). The academic othering of those they study mimics the anti-Islamic narrative about Muslims engaging in *taqiyya*; that is, deception and lying about their true goals and beliefs. For as Arne Næss says, "An important ingredient in descriptions of outgroups is the hypothesis that the outgroup says one thing, but means another" (1980, p. 136).

6 The pre-existing radical right in Western Europe and the transnational anti-Islamic movement that emerged after 9/11 had opposite ideological starting points, but the outcome is broadly similar: an anti-Islamic, civilizational identity that draws on many liberal values. Since 2001, then, we have witnessed a convergence between radical right actors using liberal rhetoric to justify their intolerance and authoritarianism, and liberal actors moved in an authoritarian direction by the desire to preserve tolerance against a perceived intolerant force.

7 Karl Popper described this as the paradox of tolerance.

8 Speaking of the then exceptional case of the Dutch List Pim Fortuyn, Tjitske Akkerman defined this as a liberalism turned inward, driven by fear (2005, p. 346).

9 In his book "Whiteshift" (2018), Eric Kaufmann argues that we are witnessing a politicization of the white majority's ethnic identity. In contrast, my study points to a politicization of civic identity vis-a-vis Muslims and Islam, and not whiteness. The ethnic makeup of the majority becomes an incidental and secondary factor in this picture.

10 This is in contrast to Art's relative definition of the far right as "an umbrella term for any political party, voluntary association, or extra-parliamentary movement that differentiates itself from the mainstream right" (2011, p. 10). In Art's definition, the far right is a relative phenomenon precisely because it is dependent on what ideas the mainstream right chooses to adopt.

11 See Chapter 2 for a more in-depth discussion and comparison of these terms.

12 Personal correspondence with Joel Busher.

13 Bail uses the label "anti-Muslim".

Bibliography

Akkerman, T. (2005). Anti-immigration parties and the defence of liberal values: The exceptional case of the list Pim Fortuyn. *Journal of Political Ideologies, 10*(3), 337–354.

Ali, W., Clifton, E., Duss, M., Fang, L., Keyes, S., & Shakir, F. (2011). Fear, Inc. In *The roots of the Islamophobia network in America*. Washington, DC: Center for American Progress.

Allen, C. (2011). Opposing Islamification or promoting Islamophobia? Understanding the English Defence League. *Patterns of Prejudice, 45*(4), 279–294.

Archer, T. (2013). Breivik's mindset: The Counterjihad and the new transatlantic anti-Muslim right. *Extreme Right Wing Political Violence and Terrorism*, 169–185.

Art, D. (2011). *Inside the radical right: The development of anti-immigrant parties in Western Europe.* Cambridge: Cambridge University Press.

Bail, C. A. (2012). The fringe effect: Civil society organizations and the evolution of media discourse about Islam since the September 11th attacks. *American Sociological Review*, 77(6), 855–879.

Bail, C. A. (2014). *Terrified: How anti-Muslim Fringe organizations became mainstream*. Princeton, NJ: Princeton University Press.

Bakker, R., De Vries, C., Edwards, E., Hooghe, L., Jolly, S., Marks, G., & Vachudova, M. A. (2015). Measuring party positions in Europe: The Chapel Hill expert survey trend file, 1999–2010. *Party Politics*, 21(1), 143–152.

Bangstad, S. (2013). Eurabia comes to Norway. *Islam and Christian – Muslim Relations*, 24(3), 369–391.

Bangstad, S. (2016). Islamophobia: What's in a name? *Journal of Muslims in Europe*, 5(2), 145–169.

Beissinger, M. R. (2013). The semblance of democratic revolution: Coalitions in Ukraine's orange revolution. *American Political Science Review*, 107(3), 574–592.

Benford, R. D. (1997). An insider's critique of the social movement framing perspective. *Sociological Inquiry*, 67(4), 409–430.

Berntzen, L. E., & Sandberg, S. (2014). The collective nature of lone wolf terrorism: Anders Behring Breivik and the anti-Islamic social movement. *Terrorism and Political Violence*, 26(5), 759–779.

Berntzen, L. E., & Weisskircher, M. (2016). Anti-Islamic PEGIDA beyond Germany: Explaining differences in mobilisation. *Journal of Intercultural Studies*, 37(6), 556–573.

Betz, H-G., & Meret, S. (2009). Revisiting Lepanto: The political mobilization against Islam in contemporary Western Europe. *Patterns of Prejudice*, 43(3–4), 313–334.

Bornschier, S. (2010). The new cultural divide and the two-dimensional political space in Western Europe. *West European Politics*, 33(3), 419–444.

Busher, J. (2015). *The making of anti-Muslim protest: Grassroots activism in the English Defence League*. London: Routledge.

Caiani, M., Della Porta, D., & Wagemann, C. (2012). *Mobilizing on the extreme right: Germany, Italy, and the United States*. Oxford: Oxford University Press.

Caiani, M., & Wagemann, C. (2009). Online networks of the Italian and German extreme right: An explorative study with social network analysis. *Information, Communication & Society*, 12(1), 66–109.

Castells, M. (2000). Toward a sociology of the network society. *Contemporary Sociology*, 29(5), 693–699.

Chase-Dunn, C., & Boswell, T. (2002). *Transnational social movements and democratic socialist parties in the semiperiphery*. The Institute for Research on World-Systems. Riverside, CA: University of California, unpublished manuscript.

Daphi, P., Kocyba, P., Neuber, M., Roose, J., Rucht, D., Scholl, F., & Zajak, S. (2015). *Protestforschung am Limit. Eine soziologische Annäherung an PEGIDA*. Retrieved from www.wzb.eu/sites/default/fi les/u6/pegida-report_berlin_2015.pdf

Dauber, A. S. (2017). The increasing visibility of right-wing extremist women in contemporary Europe: Is Great Britain an exception? In *Gender and far right politics in Europe* (pp. 49–64). Springer International Publishing. DOI: 10.1007/978-3-319-43533-6

Della Porta, D., & Tarrow, S. G. (Eds.). (2005). *Transnational protest and global activism*. Lanham, MD: Rowman & Littlefield.

Denes, N. (2012). "Welcome to the Counterjihad": Uncivil networks and the narration of European public spheres. *Journal of Civil Society*, 8(3), 289–306.

Diani, M. (1992). The concept of social movement. *The Sociological Review*, 40(1), 1–25.

Dix, R. H. (1984). Why revolutions succeed & fail. *Polity*, 16(3), 423–446.

Douglas, M. (1982). Introduction to grid/group analysis. *Essays in the Sociology of Perception*, 1–8.

Dostal, J. M. (2015). The PEGIDA movement and German political culture: Is right-wing populism here to stay? *The Political Quarterly, 86*(4), 523–531.

Doyle, N. J., & Ahmad, I. (2013). Islamophobia, European modernity and contemporary illiberalism. *Politics, Religion & Ideology, 14*(2), 167–172.

Farris, S. R. (2012). Femonationalism and the "regular" army of labor called migrant women. *History of the Present, 2*(2), 184–199.

Farris, S. R. (2017). *In the name of women s rights: The rise of femonationalism.* Durham: Durham University Press.

Fleck, C., & Müller, A. (1998). Front-stage and back-stage: The problem of measuring post-Nazi antisemitism in Austria. In B. Hagtvet (Ed.), *Modern Europe after fascism, 1943–1980s* (Vol. 2, pp. 436–454). Boulder: Social Science Monographs.

Fleischer, R. (2014). Two fascisms in contemporary Europe? Understanding the ideological split of the radical right. In M. Deland, M. Minkenberg, & C. Mays (Eds.), *In the tracks of Breivik: Far right networks in Northern and Eastern Europe* (pp. 53–70, 54). Vienna and Münster: LIT.

Froio, C. (2018). Race, religion or culture? Framing Islam between racism and neo-racism in the online network of the French far-right. *Perspectives on Politics, 16*(3), 696–709.

Gamson, W. (1992). *Talking politics.* New York: Cambridge University Press.

Goldstone, J. A. (1994). Is revolution individually rational? Groups and individuals in revolutionary collective action. *Rationality and Society, 6*(1), 139–166.

Goldstone, J. A. (2011). Social origins of the French revolution revisited. In D. Van Kley (Ed.), *From deficit to deluge: The origins of the French revolution* (p. 67). Stanford, CA: Stanford University Press.

Goodwin, M. J. (2001). Is the age of revolution over? *Revolution: International Dimensions,* 272–283.

Goodwin, M. J. (2013). *The roots of extremism: The English Defence League and the Counter-Jihad challenge.* London: Chatham House.

Goodwin, M. J., Cutts, D., & Janta-Lipinski, L. (2016). Economic losers, protestors, islamophobes or xenophobes? Predicting public support for a counter-Jihad movement. *Political Studies, 64*(1), 4–26.

Goodwin, M. J., & Jasper, J. M. (Eds.). (2014). *The social movements reader: Cases and concepts.* Oxford: John Wiley & Sons.

Gould, D. B. (2009). *Moving politics: Emotion and ACT UP's fight against AIDS.* Chicago, IL: University of Chicago Press.

Grabow, K., & Hartleb, F. (2014). Europe – no, thanks. In *Study on the right-wing and national populist parties in Europe.* Sankt-Augustin and Berlin: Konrad-Adenauer-Stiftung and Centre for European Studies.

Haanshuus, B. P., & Jupskås, A. R. (2017). Høyreklikk! En analyse av ytre høyre på sosiale medier i Norge. *Tidsskrift for samfunnsforskning, 58*(2), 145–165.

Jackson, P., & Feldman, M. (2011). *The EDL: Britain's "new far right" social movement* (NECTAR, the Northampton Electronic Collection of Theses and Research). The University of Northampton, Northampton.

Jackson, P., & Feldman, M. (2014). *Doublespeak: The framing of the far-right since 1945.* Stuttgart: Ibidem-Verlag.

Kassimeris, G., & Jackson, L. (2015). The ideology and discourse of the English Defence League: "Not racist, not violent, just no longer silent". *The British Journal of Politics and International Relations, 17*(1), 171–188.

Kaufmann, E. (2018). *Whiteshift: Populism, immigration and the future of white majorities.* London, UK: Penguin.

Ketelaars, P., Walgrave, S., & Wouters, R. (2014). Degrees of frame alignment: Comparing organisers' and participants' frames in 29 demonstrations in three countries. *International Sociology, 29*(6), 504–524.

Kitschelt, H. (2012). Social class and the radical right: Conceptualizing political preference formation and partisan choice. In J. Rydgren (Ed.), *Class politics and the radical right* (pp. 224–251). London: Routledge.

Klandermans, B., & Mayer, N. (2006). *Through the magnifying glass: The world of extreme right activists*. London: Routledge.

Klandermans, B., Van der Toorn, J., & Van Stekelenburg, J. (2008). Embeddedness and Identity: How immigrants turn grievances into action. *American Sociological Review, 73*(6), 992–1012.

Koopmans, R. (1996). Explaining the rise of racist and extreme right violence in Western Europe: Grievances or opportunities? *European Journal of Political Research, 30*(2), 185–216.

Kriesi, H., Grande, E., Lachat, R., Dolezal, M., Bornschier, S., & Frey, T. (2008). *West European politics in the age of globalization* (pp. 154–182). Cambridge: Cambridge University Press.

Larzillière, C., & Sal, L. (2011). *Comprendre l'instrumentalisation du féminisme à des fins racistes pour résister*. Retrieved from www.contretemps.eu/interventions/comprendre-instrumentalisation-f%C3%A9minisme-fins-racistes-r%C3%A9sister

Lee, B. (2015). A day in the "swamp": Understanding discourse in the online counter-Jihad nebula. *Democracy and Security, 11*(3), 248–274.

Lentin, A., & Titley, G. (2011). *The crises of multiculturalism: Racism in a neoliberal age*. London: Zed Books.

Lucassen, G., & Lubbers, M. (2012). Who fears what? Explaining far-right-wing preference in Europe by distinguishing perceived cultural and economic ethnic threats. *Comparative Political Studies, 45*(5), 547–574.

Macklin, G. (2013). Transnational networking on the far right: The case of Britain and Germany. *West European Politics, 36*(1), 176–198.

Mayer, S., Ajanovic, E., & Sauer, B. (2014). Intersections and inconsistencies: Framing gender in right wing populist discourses in Austria. *NORA-Nordic Journal of Feminist and Gender Research, 22*(4), 250–266.

McAdam, D. (1988). Micromobilization contexts and recruitment to activism. *International Social Movement Research, 1*(1), 125–154.

Meleagrou-Hitchens, A., & Brun, H. (2013). *A neo-nationalist network: The English Defence League and Europe's counter-Jihad movement*. London: International Centre for the Study of Radicalisation and Political Violence.

Mudde, C. (2000). *The ideology of the extreme right*. Manchester: Manchester University Press.

Mudde, C. (2007). *The populist radical right in Europe*. Cambridge: Cambridge University Press.

Mudde, C. (2016). *The study of populist radical right parties: Towards a fourth wave*. C-REX Working Paper Series, 1. www.nytimes.com/2017/01/26/opinion/the-radical-rights-united-front.html

Næss, A. (1980). Ideology and rationality. In M. Cranston & P. Mair (Eds.), *Ideology and politics – Ideologie et Politique* (pp. 133–142). Alphen aan den Rijn: Sijthoff.

Petit, C. (2004, August). *Social movement networks in Internet discourse*. Annual meetings of the American Sociological Association, San Francisco, Vol. 17.

Popper, K. (1945). *The open society and its enemies*. London: Routledge.

Puar, J. (2013). Rethinking homonationalism. *International Journal of Middle East Studies, 45*(2), 336–339.

Runnymede Trust, L. U. K. (1997). *Islamophobia: A challenge for us all*. London: Runnymede Trust.

Rydgren, J. (2005a). Is extreme right-wing populism contagious? Explaining the emergence of a new party family. *European Journal of Political Research, 44*(3), 413–437.

Rydgren, J. (2005b). *Movements of exclusion: Radical right-wing populism in the Western world*. New York: Nova Publishers.

Rydgren, J. (2007). The sociology of the radical right. *Annual Review of Sociology*, *33*, 241–262.

Savelkoul, M., Scheepers, P., van der Veld, W., & Hagendoorn, L. (2012). Comparing levels of anti-Muslim attitudes across Western countries. *Quality & Quantity*, *46*(5), 1617–1624.

Sayyid, S., & Vakil, A. (2008). *Thinking Thru' Islamophobia*, Symposium, University of Leeds.

Scrinzi, F. (2017). A "new" national front? Gender, religion, secularism and the French populist radical right. In M. Köttig, R. Bitzan, & A. Petö (Eds.), *Gender and far right politics in Europe* (pp. 127–140). Springer International Publishing. DOI:10.1007/978-3-319-43533-6

Snow, D. A., Rochford Jr, E. B., Worden, S. K., & Benford, R. D. (1986). Frame alignment processes, micromobilization, and movement participation. *American Sociological Review*, 464–481.

Strabac, Z., & Listhaug, O. (2008). Anti-Muslim prejudice in Europe: A multilevel analysis of survey data from 30 countries. *Social Science Research*, *37*(1), 268–286.

Thorleifsson, C. (2017). Disposable strangers: Far-right securitisation of forced migration in Hungary. *Social Anthropology*, *25*(3), 318–334.

Timmermans, F. (2015). *Opening remarks of First Vice-President Frans Timmermans at the first annual colloquium on fundamental rights*. Retrieved from https://europa.eu/rapid/press-release_SPEECH-15-5754_en.htm

van der Brug, W., & Van Spanje, J. (2009). Immigration, Europe and the "new" cultural dimension. *European Journal of Political Research*, *48*(3), 309–334.

Wike, R., & Grim, B. J. (2010). Western views toward Muslims: Evidence from a 2006 cross-national survey. *International Journal of Public Opinion Research*, *22*(1), 4–25.

Wodak, R. (2015). *The politics of fear: What right-wing populist discourses mean*. Los Angeles, London and New Delhi: Sage.

Yang, A., & Self, C. (2015). Anti-Muslim prejudice in the virtual space: A case study of blog network structure and message features of the "Ground zero mosque controversy". *Media, War & Conflict*, *8*(1), 46–69.

Zajonc, R. B. (1980). Feeling and thinking: Preferences need no inferences. *American Psychologist*, *35*(2), 151.

Zanghellini, A. (2012). Are gay rights Islamophobic? A critique of some uses of the concept of homonationalism in activism and academia. *Social & Legal Studies*, *21*(3), 357–374.

Zúquete, J. P. (2008). The European extreme-right and Islam: New directions? *Journal of Political Ideologies*, *13*(3), 321–344.

2

PERSPECTIVES ON THE FAR RIGHT

Introduction

This chapter provides an overview of the main research traditions and concepts, and how they inform our analysis of anti-Islamic mobilization. I engage with these theoretical perspectives, findings, and claims throughout the subsequent chapters. The chapter itself is structured into three main sections. As mobilization against Islam and Muslims is understood as a far-right phenomenon, and ideology is taken as the common denominator which distinguishes the far right from other political phenomena, the first section sets out key perspectives on the various permutations of far-right ideology. These are placed within a taxonomical ladder of abstraction in the tradition of Sartori. "Far right" is used as an umbrella term for the extreme and radical right, whereas fascism is understood as one permutation of the extreme right and ethno-pluralism one permutation of the radical right. I provide an updated taxonomy of the far right in Chapter 8, which includes the anti-Islamic permutation.

The second section deals with the anti-Islamic turn in the wake of 9/11 and how this has been understood. The term Islamophobia is discussed and ultimately rejected in favour of anti-Islam, here conceptualized as *framing Islam as a homogenous, totalitarian ideology which threatens Western civilization*. Opposition to Islam and Muslims is tightly coupled with a defence of Judeo-Christian Western civilization in the shape of Christian heritage, the state of Israel, freedom of speech, democracy, and liberal values (including women's rights and LGBT rights). In the literature, rejection of anti-Semitism is seen as *strategic abandonment*. Muslims are the functional equivalent of Jews, and the inclusion of liberal and progressive positions is seen as a *strategic inclusion*. Strategic is frequently used as a euphemism for deceptive. The emphasis on continuity through theoretical abstraction is one reason why there has been relatively little empirical analysis of claims made by anti-Islamic initiatives that they defend liberal and progressive values.

The third section examines the studies and perspectives on the extra-parliamentary anti-Islamic far right, often understood as a transnational social movement. In line with findings from other fields, some research indicates that the networks are structured along ideological lines. Some, however, contest this position, arguing that the anti-Islamic far right outside party politics is amorphous, loosely connected, and without a unified ideology.

Background

The study of the far right has its roots in the 1930s and immediate period after World War II, focussing on the fascists in Italy and Nazism in Germany. The need to understand exactly how they could come to power in Western, democratic societies – culminating in the devastation of Europe and the attempted extermination of the Jews – was profound. This legacy of mass atrocities, war, and persecution shapes the academic perspectives on the far right to this day.

The first decades of scholarship were dominated by psychoanalytical studies that emphasized the underlying mechanisms for popular participation in what culminated in atrocities, locating the roots in individual and social pathologies. For instance, Wilhelm Reich's study *The Mass Psychology of Fascism* from 1933 [1970] considered fascism to be "the basic emotional attitude of the suppressed man" (p. xiii) and in its purest form "the sum total of all irrational reactions of the average human character" (p. xiv). Similarly, in *The Authoritarian Personality* (1950), Adorno, Frenkel-Brunswik, Levinson, and Sandford argued that the authoritarian politics of fascism and Nazism arose from hierarchical parenting practices which fuelled fear and aggression. More important than repression, however, were the functionalist ideas of social breakdown and anomie expressed by major figures in sociology, such as Emile Durkheim and Talcott Parsons (Useem, 1998, p. 215). These breakdown-theoretical perspectives posit that old social norms and practices dissolve in the face of society-wide change brought about by modernization, industrialization, and capitalism, and later by globalization. Individuals in these societies were thought to be particularly likely to support the far right (e.g. Arendt, 1951).[1]

Theories of social breakdown, of which fascism and Nazism were one supposed outcome, were an integral part social movement studies.[2] The emphasis on collective mobilization driven by irrational, emotional outbursts in response to situations of society-wide crisis, however, eventually led to a decades-long backlash within the social movement field. Scholars shifted their attention from theories of emotions, crisis, and abnormality to perspectives emphasizing rationality and cooperation, such as rational choice (e.g. Olson, 1971), resource mobilization theory (for example, McCarthy & Zald, 1977), political process theory (for example, McAdam, 1982), and subsequently framing theory (see Benford & Snow, 2000). This shift coincides with the almost exclusive focus of social movement literature on leftist movements, whereas the study of the far right became the predominant domain of political scientists and scholars studying party politics.

More precisely, the study of the far right in party politics became a subfield in its own right, whereby the values parties espoused were understood as a perverse inversion of the ideals and procedures of democracy (e.g. Rosanvallon & Goldhammer, 2008, p. 265). A small share of the population was hypothesized as sharing these values based on "structurally determined pathologies" (Scheuch & Klingemann, 1967, p. 18), which become relevant under "extreme conditions" (ibid., p. 86). According to Mudde (2010, p. 1171), this demand-side perspective which fixated on crisis and abnormality dominated the study of the far right in post-war Europe (e.g. Betz & Immerfall, 1998; Grumke, 2004). Concomitantly, there was a lack of studies by political scientists looking at the politics and agency of the far right on the supply side of the equation (Mudde, 2010, p. 1772).

The focus on party-centric scholarship gradually changed from the 1990s onwards, as perspectives from mainstream political science stressing the agency of the far right were applied. For instance, political scientist Elisabeth Carter stated that "parties of the extreme right are to some extent 'masters of their own success'" (2005, p. 12).

Meanwhile, the "groupuscular" world of neo-Nazis, white power, and militant nationalists in the United States and Western Europe won the attention of sociologists, anthropologists, and criminologists who often conducted ethnographic work (e.g. Blee, 1996; Bjørgo, 1997; Fangen, 1998, 1999). In contrast to the demand-side orientation prominent among political scientists, these studies often looked at micro-interactions between individuals within and between groups in order to explain recruitment, activist views, and acts of political violence.

This was followed by a piecemeal reintegration with the broader social movement literature by studying aspects such as political and discursive opportunity structures, framing, diffusion, and networks, spearheaded by Ruud Koopmans (1996, 2004), Jens Rydgren (2003, 2004a, 2005a, 2007), Bert Klandermans and Nonna Mayer (2006), David Art (2011), and Manuela Caiani, Donatella della Porta, and Claudius Wageman (2012).

Organization, strategy, or behaviour cannot be used to delineate the far right from other phenomena, and therefore do not figure in most conceptual definitions (Carter, 2005; Griffin, 2006). Instead, there is now a broad consensus across social scientific disciplines that their ideology is the main factor which distinguishes far right initiatives from others (e.g. Ignazi, 2003; Carter, 2005; Caiani et al., 2012). There is a profusion of concepts such as populist radical right and extreme right, fascist and neo-fascist. Sometimes these concepts are defined in an overlapping manner, or at times they refer to relatively distinct phenomena. Each individual term is in turn often conceptualized in different ways. For instance, as far back as 1996, Cas Mudde identified over 26 different definitions of the term "extreme right". Minkenberg noted that many definitions often "resemble mere shopping lists of criteria" (2003, p. 171). Over time, however, some specific conceptualizations have become dominant over others – meaning that they are frequently cited, endorsed, and applied. This holds for Roger Griffin's definition of fascism, Cas

Muddes' definition of the populist radical right, and Jens Rydgren's conceptualization of extreme right master frames.[3]

The first shared characteristic is that initiatives which are alternately conceptualized as belonging to the fascist, extreme, or radical right primarily tend to be understood as reactionary ideologies, "movements of exclusion" (Rydgren, 2005b, p. 1) and defined by what they are against – and not what they support (Blee, 2017; Durham, 2007; Lo, 1982). Hence the frequent use of the prefix anti – _ anti-immigrant, anti-Semitic, anti-gay, anti-feminist, anti-abortion, anti-communist and so on. Of these it is the opposition to immigration which many claim is the core, defining feature of their ideology and voter appeal in the case of political parties (e.g. van der Brug & Fennema, 2007; Ivarsflaten, 2005; Lucassen & Lubbers, 2012).

Ideologies and master frames

Before moving on to the taxonomy of the far right, the concept of ideology deserves some attention. Converse (1964) used the synonymous term "belief system", defined as a "configuration of ideas and attitudes in which the elements are bound together by some form of constraint or functional interdependence" (p. 3), "logically coherent" (p. 5), and "which consumers come to see as 'natural' wholes" (p. 9). This emphasis on a logically coherent set of ideas has been favoured by some scholars, whereas others have defined ideology in a less restrictive way. For instance, Sainsbury defines it as "a body of normative or normative-related ideas about the nature of man and society as well as the organization and purposes of society" (1980, p. 8) – a definition given by Mudde in his analysis of far-right ideologies (2000, p. 19). Coming from the social movement field, Oliver and Johnston (2005) define ideology as "a system of meaning that couples assertions and theories about the nature of social life with values and norms relevant to promoting or resisting social change" (p. 192).

Ideologies exist at different levels of generality and subdivision. For instance, environmentalist ideology exists in both a conservationist and an ecologist form (Dalton, 1994), while feminism includes several varieties such as liberal, socialist, and radical feminism (Oliver & Johnston, 2005, p. 198).

The concept of collective action framing is a related perspective located below the broad and fixed level of ideology (Snow & Byrd, 2007; Caiani et al., 2012, p. 12). At the meso level, collective action frames can be defined as the dominant worldviews which guide the behaviour of social movement organizations, and which are often produced by the organizational leadership which provides followers and would-be followers with the rationale for participating and supporting them (ibid., p. 13).

Collective action framing by social movements (and political parties) include the articulation of a diagnosis (what is the problem, and who is to blame?), prognosis (what are the solutions?), and motivational framing that articulate calls for action (Snow & Benford, 1988). Ideologies are cultural resources for framing activity, and framing processes involve the emphasis on or amplification of existing beliefs and values (Benford & Snow, 2000, p. 58). Collective action frames often consist of elements of one or more ideologies, where pre-existing ideologies function as both facilitators and constraints on framing processes (Benford & Snow, 2000; Snow & Benford, 1988).

The term master frame is used for collective action frames that have expanded in scope and influence, constraining the activities and orientations of movements both within cycles of protest (Snow & Benford, 1992) and between them (Gerhards & Rucht, 1992; Mooney & Hunt, 1996). They have therefore taken on more of the static nature ascribed to ideologies. Master frames vary according to their potency (salience and resonance), rigidity, and whether blame is directed outward or inward (Snow & Benford, 1988, pp. 139–140). They also have the ability to give rise to families of movements or political parties (Rydgren, 2005a, p. 426). For example, Snow and Benford (1992) defined the collective action framing by the American civil rights movement of the 1950s and 1960s as a "rights" master frame, since their emphasis of equal rights and opportunities was of such a general and inclusive nature that it was usable by other aggrieved groups such as Native Americans, women, and gays and lesbians (ibid., p. 145). Oliver and Johnston (2005), however, argue that master frames differentiate themselves from full-blown ideologies in that they are signifiers which provide an angle and perspective on a problem, and not elaborate social theories and normative systems (pp. 198–199).[4] The "rights" master frame pointed many women in the direction of feminism, but did not necessitate fully embracing feminist ideology (ibid.). In other words, it is precisely because master frames exist at a lower level of internal complexity to ideologies that they are able to diffuse and be incorporated by initiatives (social movement organizations [SMOs] and parties) with different ideologies.

Conceptualizations and levels of abstraction

These terms and the way they are conceptualized guide our analysis in different directions. We can make a rough distinction between lumpers and splitters. The lumpers build broad macro-level categories – some of which tend towards the universalistic, while splitters look for nuances ranging from the micro level of variations within organizations and groups to the meso level between groups and organizations. Generally speaking, lumpers stress historical continuity, while splitters identify discontinuity and novelty. Both approaches carry their own risks.

The lumpers run the risk of what Sartori defined as "the line of least resistance"; namely, conceptual *stretching* (1970, p. 1034). Concepts are made in a specific historical and political context, and when we attempt to expand them beyond their original scope and context, we are in danger of underreporting differences – equating apples with oranges. Splitters, on the other hand, stand in danger of not seeing the forest for the trees, and therefore impair the accumulation of knowledge.

To avoid these pitfalls, Sartori advocates a taxonomical approach to conceptualization. He uses the hierarchical terminology of genus, species, and subspecies to structure scientific inquiry and knowledge aggregation. In the hierarchy of abstraction these concepts are redefined as high-level (HL), medium-level (ML), and low-level (LL) categories. The further down on the ladder of abstraction, the more "adjectives" are added; whereas travelling up on the ladder means that the concepts contain less. In other words, the high-level categories allow for maximal *extension* to the entire universe of cases, but have minimal *intension*. At the opposite end, low-level categories extend to few cases (extension) but have a maximal level of intension, meaning that they contain much more information. These categories are the most "grounded" in the contextual, thick information from the specific cases, and it is the low-level conceptual containers that are put to immediate use and challenged directly (ibid., p. 1043). I apply this approach to build a taxonomy of the far right based on some of the most widely cited perspectives.

Constructing a ladder of abstraction for the far right

Substantially speaking, two terms are most commonly used at the highest level of abstraction; far right and extreme right. We can distinguish between two uses of the term far right – one relative and the other absolute. The relative conceptualization has its roots in the way which the two terms have been used in political science. The term "right" is used as opposed to "left", and denotes a spatial difference between them in terms of socioeconomic and sociocultural politics (Rydgren, 2005b), whereas the prefix "far" is often used to categorize initiatives which differentiate themselves from the mainstream right on the sociocultural dimension (e.g. Art, 2011). That is to say, the far right is more restrictive and exclusionary than the mainstream right. Due to its spatial basis, what the term "far right" actually covers can differ from country to country and over time, depending on the level of analysis. If two initiatives are labelled far right, this does not necessarily denote any kind of kinship in the organizational, historical, or even ideological sense. This has led some to reject the term far right as too diffuse (e.g. Carter, 2005).

Another usage has emerged, however, which is partially unmoored from the spatial origins laid out previously. In this second usage, "far right" is used as a conceptual container at the highest level of abstraction for initiatives whose ideology fulfil two criteria. First, it is nativist. Nativism, in Mudde's definition, is the combination of xenophobia and nationalism whereby the nation-state should only consist of members from the native group, making non-natives a threat by default (2007, p. 17). Second, it is either anti-systemic in the sense that it seeks to replace the current system of democracy in toto, or fundamentally challenges some core dimensions of the liberal democratic system (and not just procedural democracy). As already stated, the far right is an umbrella term (Fielitz & Laloire, 2016, p. 8) that implies a certain fixed nature, subsuming the myriad of initiatives and ideological positions which the literature define as fascist, extreme, radical, and so on. If an initiative's ideological platform or collective action framing does not incorporate anti-systemic positions or a rejection of some core dimension of liberal democracy, then it falls outside the scope of what far right entails. By implication, far-right ideologies can become both "mainstream" and "moderated", but never "moderate".

In much the same way, the term "extreme right" has been used two different ways. The first way, which has a long pedigree in Germany and France, is to use it as a vague high-level container for everything that is understood as different from the mainstream right on the sociocultural dimension. In this way, extreme right become synonymous with the relative understanding of the far right – a moving target depending on the context, and therefore equally open for the critique of conceptual stretching and vagary.[5] The other approach is to narrow it down to those initiatives and ideologies which are directly opposed to democracy and the social and political rights which are embodied by the various political institutions and norms that dominate Western Europe today; namely, the anti-systemic. This places the extreme right below the far right on the level of abstraction. In both cases, it the second conceptualizations of far right and extreme right that allows us to rank them hierarchically, which therefore holds more merit, according to Sartori's taxonomical logic. It is this logic I adhere to in the remainder of this book.

Fascism

Fascism is another key concept in the study of the far right. Roger Griffin's definition of fascism as "a political ideology whose mythic core in its various permutations is a palingenetic form of populist ultra-nationalism" (2006, p. 41) has become the standard reference. Unlike many other approaches, Griffin argues that the ideology of fascism is not primarily negative in the sense of anti-liberalism, anti-Semitism or anti-Marxism, but constituted by their positive identification of remedies to the crises which beset society – the idea that a heroic elite will intervene and enable the national community to regenerate and resurrect "from the ashes of the decadent old order" (ibid., p. 42). In this sense, however, fascism is anti-systemic and can therefore be understood as a subset of the extreme right. This also allows us to recognize Nazism as one historical permutation of fascism at the lowest level of abstraction, which Griffin defines as "a form of ultra-nationalism deeply imbued with notions of imperialism, anti-Semitism, Aryan supremacy, racial hygiene and eugenics" (ibid., p. 44). Although fascism first emerged in the interwar period, he is highly critical of those that say it is also (largely) limited to this period of European history. In the Griffinian sense, fascism is a heuristic tool applicable to cases across time and culture, and which allows us to delimit it from other forms of far right and subsequently extreme right ideology.

Thus conceptualized, fascism has more or less died out as a party-political phenomenon in Western Europe and North America. It continues to exist as a subcultural, groupuscular phenomenon carried by neo-Nazi and white power groups with a transnational orientation, and also has a moderated intellectual tradition in France (the so-called *nouvelle droite*, or new right) (ibid., pp. 59–61). In contrast, the world of party politics in these countries has become "post-fascist".[6] This is not the case in all of Europe, however, as shown by the rise of Golden Dawn in Greece and Jobbik in Hungary.

(Populist) radical right

Another distinction at the intermediate level of abstraction within the far right is between the extreme and radical right. Etymologically speaking, radical is derived from the word "radix" or root. It has often been used, however, in the same spatial and relative way as both extreme and far right. In the most widely used definitions, however, an essential and qualitative difference between the extreme and radical right is identified in their approach to democracy. Whereas extreme right ideology includes an anti-systemic rejection of democracy which opens up for violent revolution, the radical right does not want to overthrow democracy per se, and therefore rejects violence (e.g. Bornschier, 2010b). It does, however, include a strong anti-establishment critique of, for instance, representative democratic institutions as an obstacle to the will of the majority, which they claim to represent. Because of this, the radical right is often understood as "semi-loyal" (Capoccia, 2005). Cas Mudde's definition of radical right ideology incorporates this qualitative change with the term "populism", which has won over a large number of adherents. Populist radical right ideology is defined as a combination of three elements; nativism, authoritarianism and populism (Mudde, 2007, 2016, p. 1).

Whereas nativism refers to the belief that the nation-state should only consist of members from the native group (regardless of how the native group is defined), authoritarianism refers to the belief in a society which is strictly ordered and where all infringements on this order are be punished severely (ibid., p. 23). Finally, populism is the belief that society is separated into two homogenous and mutually hostile groups, the "pure people" versus "the corrupt elite" (ibid., p. 23). The populist radical right opposes phenomena that are perceived as detrimental to "the people", but caters to the interests of the minority. As such, populism channels "elite protest" rather than "system protest". In Mudde's perspective, all three features combined is what identifies an initiative as populist radical right (p. 34). On their own, these ideological components are necessary, but not sufficient.

Even though this approach identifies anti-establishment populism as the main distinction between the radical and extreme right, nativism is the most salient feature of radical right ideology. Whereas nativism is generally understood to be the exclusive terrain of the radical and extreme right, the two other dimensions of radical right ideology are not. Populism, as a thin-centred ideology, can also be found on the left as well as the right (Mudde & Kaltwasser, 2017), while authoritarianism is a core part of conservatism (Layton-Henry, 1982, p. 1; Pilbaum, 2003). Furthermore, as nativism in the form of ethnic nationalism is the principal ideological feature for the radical right, the inclusion of populism in the terminology has criticized for being misleading (e.g. Rydgren, 2007).

A new master frame

The re-emergence of the far right as a prominent phenomenon in Western Europe is partly connected to the changing salience of economic and cultural issues. In the post-war era, politics was structured by the traditional left-right economic cleavage (Budge, Robertson, & Hearl, 1987). The cultural cleavage grew in salience with the rise of the so-called new social movements on the left which mobilized on issues such as minority rights, feminism, and environmental protection. This created political opportunities for counter-forces, but the extreme right in the fascist tradition was unable to fill the void. It is commonly argued that the defeat and destruction of Nazi Germany and the fascist state in Italy during World War II explain why. The destruction of these regimes is also understood as the death knell for fascism as a mass movement or viable ideology for an electorally successful party in Western Europe. Not only was fascism defunct as an ideology, so were aspects most particularly connected to Nazism, which nonetheless were prevalent among broader swathes of society during the interwar period, such as the belief in biologically based racial hierarchies of worth and virulent anti-Semitism (Rydgren, 2005a, p. 413). Rydgren argues that the resurgence of the far right from the 1980s and onwards is partly due to the innovation and diffusion of a new set of ideas to replace these – a new master frame unhampered by the legacy of war and mass extermination, and therefore able to fill the space left by left-wing mobilization on cultural issues.

The innovation consisted of two parts which circumvented the social stigma and burden associated with fascism. First, the anti-systemic antagonism to democracy was replaced with an anti-establishment critique (ibid., p. 428). Second, biological racism was replaced by "cultural racism" (ibid.). More specifically, the master frame which emerged during the interwar period included an explicit and racialized hierarchy, whereas the second master frame is based on the notion of ethno-pluralism. In the ethno-pluralist perspective, the cultures of different ethnicities or races are not formally placed in a hierarchical order, but are nonetheless seen as distinct entities requiring their own states in order to survive. The generalized form of nativism which Mudde and others include in the definition of radical right ideology, is in this perspective not detailed enough as it masks the vital distinction between the fascist extreme right and the ethno-pluralist radical right. Although explicitly biologically racist notions is the purview of the extreme right, it may however be more correct to conceptualize the ethno-pluralist line as one of several possible nativist permutations for the radical right, such as the more inclusive form of civic nationalism (Mudde, 2000, p. 17). The ethno-pluralist, anti-establishment master frame should therefore be seen as a subset of radical right ideology, which means that it is at a lower level of abstraction, akin to how fascism is a subset of the extreme right.

Rydgren identifies the French Front National as the genesis of the new master frame, and its electoral breakthrough in 1984 and subsequent media coverage inspired other nascent radical right parties to adopt the two core elements of populism and ethno-pluralism. The ideological roots for the ethno-pluralist line of reasoning come from the French *nouvelle droite* (Rydgren, 2005a, pp. 416, 427), which Griffin described as a permutation of the fascist extreme right.

A far-right taxonomy

In this overview of far-right ideology, I have made the case that the different concepts can be systematized and placed in a taxonomical ladder of abstraction under the common umbrella rubric of far right. This is systematized in Figure 2.1, operating with distinct categories at the high level, mid-level and low level of abstraction.

The two constituent elements in extreme right ideology are nativism and the rejection of democracy, whereas radical right ideology is constituted by nativism and the rejection of the political establishment. At this level of abstraction, the distinction therefore consists of the radical right's shift towards anti-establishment populism. Moving down a level, the differences become clearer. What Rydgren describes as the ethno-pluralist and anti-establishment master frame is best understood as one possible permutation of radical right ideology, which means that we can place it at the same level of abstraction as fascism. Fascism is fundamentally opposed to democracy as a political system, seeking a national rebirth facilitated by a select elite and including notions of racial superiority and inferiority, whereas ethno-pluralism combines opposition to the political establishment with claims of ethno-cultural uniqueness rather than superiority. Griffin identified German Nazism as the prototypical case of fascism, although the Italian fascist party which the term is derived from was the genesis for the first cycle of ideological diffusion.

Levels of abstraction	Far right	
High level	*Nativist*	
	Radical right	**Extreme right**
	Anti-establishment	*Anti-democratic*
Mid-level	**Ethnopluralism**	**Fascism**
	Against the political establishment and emphasizing ethno-cultural difference between people, necessitating expulsion	*Against procedural democracy as political system and emphasizing a biological hierarchy among people based on race, necessitating extermination, expulsion and subordination*
Low level prototype	**Front National (FN)**	**National Socialist German Workers' Party (NSDAP)**

FIGURE 2.1 A taxonomical hierarchy of abstraction for far-right ideologies and master frames

In the case of the ethno-pluralist radical right, Rydgren identifies the French Front National as genesis (2005a) and also as the prototype for this ideology.[7]

Islam and new directions for the far right

During the early 2000s, scholars began to note the increased antagonism towards Islam and Muslims by far-right parties and other initiatives (e.g. Rydgren 2008, p. 761). In comparison to the focus on populism, however, this was treated tangentially. Two of the first notable exceptions are José Pedro Zúquete's "The European extreme-right and Islam: New directions?" (2008) and Hanz-Georg Betz and Susi Meret's "Revisiting Lepanto: the political mobilization against Islam in contemporary Western Europe" (2009). Zúquete argued that the *Islam-as-a-threat-to-European-security-and-values frame* (p. 223) went from being intermittently and sporadically used during the 1990s to a basic ideological feature for the European far right after 9/11 (2008, p. 322), defining it as an ideological reorientation (p. 215) of parties with diverse roots (p. 212). Betz and Meret see this antagonism as a continuation of the ethno-pluralist master frame identified by Rydgren (2009, p. 314; see also Jackson, 2011, p. 12), which is built on confounding Islam with radical "Islamism" (p. 319). By now, the far right in Western Europe is almost exclusively focussed on the perceived threat of Islam (e.g. Deland Minkenberg & Mays, 2014, p. 12; Mudde, 2016, p. 32).[8] Nonetheless, it is common to raise the level of abstraction and define them as, for instance, hostile to migrants and minorities – thereby stressing the continuity between current and older iterations of the far right. Studies that either explicitly deal with or acknowledge opposition to Islam and Muslims as the primary nativist sentiment of the current far right in Western Europe use the terms Islamophobia (e.g. Allen, 2010, 2011; Bangstad, 2014, 2016; Bleich, 2011), anti-Islamic (e.g. Zúquete, 2008; Sedgwick, 2013; Berntzen & Sandberg, 2014), and anti-Muslim (e.g. Bail, 2012, 2014; Busher, 2013, 2015). Of these, Islamophobia has become the most widely used term.

Islamophobia, anti-Islam, and anti-Muslim

The term Islamophobia was coined in 1918 by two French researchers, novelists, and converts to Islam.[9] Highly critical of their compatriots' work in North Africa and the Middle East, they devised the concept of Islamophobia as a way to classify what they saw as a political, colonial struggle to undermine Islam. The term resurfaced in Britain in the 1990s, when Muslim rights groups attempted to put discrimination against Muslims on the political agenda. In 1997, a commission of the left-wing think-tank the Runnymede Trust issued a report on British Muslims and Islamophobia (CBMI) (1997) entitled "Islamophobia: A Challenge for Us All". They defined Islamophobia as "an unfounded hostility towards Islam, and therefore fear or dislike of all or most Muslims" (ibid., p. 4). It has subsequently seen widespread use, and entered into academic discourse – especially in the Anglo-Saxon sphere. The term came into use for two different reasons, one analytical and one normative/operational. It was meant to capture a "new reality" which needed naming, and be a tool to identify precisely what should be acted against (Sayyid & Vakil, 2008, p. 40).

As with the term "extreme right", it has been common to use Islamophobia without defining it explicitly (e.g. Bunzl, 2007; Halliday, 1999; Kaplan, 2006; Betz & Meret, 2009). Of the explicit conceptualizations, Erik Bleich's (2011) definition of Islamophobia as "indiscriminate negative attitudes or emotions directed at Islam or Muslims" (2011, p. 1585) has won most ground. This and several other definitions have three elements in common. First, Islamophobia is used as a container for prejudice and hostility towards both Islam and Muslims in general. The inclusion of both anti-Muslim prejudice and anti-Islamic sentiment recalls the Runnymede definition, and has subsequently been proposed by other researchers (Allen, 2010) who have tended to opt for a scale-based approach, which is radial and "how much?" oriented. Radial categories are structured in a diametrically opposite fashion to taxonomic categories (Collier & Mahon, 1993). In the taxonomical approach, we leave out information, or adjectives, the higher we go up the ladder of abstraction, and conversely begin with a dense conceptualization at the high level (many adjectives) and drop them as we move down the ladder using a radial approach (ibid., p. 851). Second, they tend to understand Islamophobia in terms of emotional *reactions* (primarily fear), a subset of cognitive responses (e.g. Abbas, 2004; Lee, Gibbons, Thompson, & Timani, 2009). Third, the main focus is directed towards the individual, attitudinal level and not towards the meso level of ideology or the collective action framing of social movement organizations.

Leaving aside its use as a polemical tool to castigate political opponents and stigmatizing any critique of Islam,[10] a strong case can be made against the uses of Islamophobia. I mention four key points. First, the term *phobia* means morbid fear, and is commonly used to classify mental illnesses where the fear of something is both irrational and impossible to control. The focus on irrational reactions mirrors the influential studies of fascism between the 1930s and 1970s. This approach has been rejected as analytically unfruitful in the broader field of social movement studies. Second, it has been used to conflate very different phenomena, such as French state secularism with hatred of Muslims, a fuzziness which is subject to "conceptual stretching". This is because most previous studies have not used Islamophobia as an umbrella term containing two different phenomena, but actually *conflated* prejudice against Muslims and anti-Islamic positions. Studies of far-right initiatives indicate that they primarily focus on Islam (e.g. Betz & Meret, 2009), whereas hostility towards Muslims flows causally from this, and not all Muslims are portrayed in an unequivocally antagonistic manner (Berntzen & Sandberg, 2014). This suggests that we should treat hostility towards Islam and hostility towards Muslims as two analytically distinct categories. Empirical studies at the individual level also show that an aversion to Islam does not does not necessarily translate into negativity towards Muslims (Kühnel & Leibold, 2007; Leibold, Kühnel, & Heitmeyer, 2006). Finally, even though the conceptualizations refer to irrational or unbased fear of both Islam and Muslims, the term Islamophobia itself is misleading since it only suggests an irrational fear of Islam.

Bearing in mind that anti-Islam and anti-Muslim refer to two analytically distinct, but causally linked issues, the dominant antagonism should be reflected in the labelling. Anti-Islam is therefore the correct term to use if these initiatives primarily mobilize on messages against Islam. This is in line with the taxonomical logic and Rydgren's argument that the term "populist" should not be included on equal footing to radical right. The term anti-Islam makes the implicit primacy of hostility towards Islam over Muslims in the term Islamophobia explicit. It also lets us move away from the focus on irrationality and fear as constitutive elements.[11] Moving from the label to the conceptualization, these initiatives portray Islam as a totalitarian ideology akin to Nazism, and the Quran as equivalent to Hitler's *Mein Kampf* (Betz & Meret, 2009, p. 320). In line with this logic, anti-Islam can be defined as framing Islam as a homogenous, totalitarian ideology which threatens Western civilization.

Conceptualizing anti-Islam in terms of framing also shifts the theoretical focus from reaction to action, in line with the agency-oriented perspective dominant in social movement analysis today. Anti-Muslim prejudice at the individual, cognitive level can be conceptualized through a simple recalibration of Rydgren's definition of prejudiced stereotypes (2004b, p. 129)[12] into an attitude or set of attitudes held regarding Muslims, encompassing over-simplified beliefs and a set of negative feelings and evaluations. In terms of framing, Christopher Bail identified a commonly recurring "Muslim as Enemy" frame, which "depicts all Muslims as potentially violent radicals who have a religious obligation to overthrow Western governments" (2012, p. 863). When speaking of the relational, meso level of parties/social movement organizations, the choice of anti-Muslim or anti-Islam as label should be driven by which "perspective" takes pre-eminence.

Naturally, the term "anti-Islam" is open to some of the same critiques as "Islamophobia". It can, for instance, be claimed that anti-Islam blurs the lines between antagonistic views of Islam and Muslim culture on the one hand, and secular criticism of religion on the other. While anti-Islamic framing in the case cited has some family resemblances to the secular criticism of religion, the latter is neither singularly focussed on Islam, nor does it require an essentialized view of Islam as a homogenous entity or more dangerous than other religious manifestations in the public sphere.

Strategic abandonment and strategic inclusion

A frequent argument, especially prominent in the Islamophobia literature building on the old perspectives of fascism, is that Muslims have taken the place of Jews; anti-Semitism has been replaced by Islamophobia (Williams, 2010; Fekete, 2012; Meleagrou-Hitchens & Brun, 2013). Exemplifying this dominant position, Bunzl (2007) argues that it is because there is no debate on the legitimacy of the Jewish presence in Europe. One approach is to understand Jews and Muslims as functional equivalents by their nature of being the targeted out-group. Another is that traditional anti-Semitism is simply dormant, or "off-stage" (see Jackson, 2011, p. 9), shelved for strategic purposes (Betz, 2013, p. 80). For instance, Fleischer argues that the radical right reject anti-Semitism and use support for Israel as a tactic to disassociate themselves from the stigma of neo-Nazism (2014, p. 54), and that there are no contradictions between anti-Muslim and anti-Semitic prejudice (ibid., p. 55).[13] This implies that anti-Islamic far right is compatible with other variations, such as neo-Nazism (see Kundnani, 2012). This means that who they say the enemy is has little real significance when it comes to the rest of their ideology or the political alliances that far-right initiatives form.

From a historical perspective, the most striking development is the inclusion of liberal and progressive positions by the anti-Islamic far right. Betz and Meret (2009, p. 319) argue that it is precisely their antagonism towards Islam and Muslims which has allowed them to define themselves as defenders of liberal values of individualism, secularism, and gender equality (ibid.). This stands in stark relief compared to the older far-right versions and concurrent neo-Nazi and white power focus on gender, which emphasizes (white) male domination and women as subordinate non-political mothers and wives who nurture their family, race, and nation (Bedi, 2006; Lesselier, 2002; Anahita, 2006; Vertigans, 2007).

The inclusion of liberal positions is understood as emanating from their hostility towards Islam (Zúquete, 2008, p. 224). In other words, the far right has co-opted issues that mainstream politicians find it hard to disagree with, such as the rights of women in Muslim communities and the rights of women in general (Akkerman & Hagelund, 2007; Betz, 2013, p. 73), arguments that were formerly the exclusive domain of progressive and feminist groups (Zúquete, 2008, p. 222). The notion that one ideological "exchange" – Jews for Muslims – is causally connected to the inclusion of new positions and stands in opposition to the aforementioned perception of the enemy as interchangeable, and thereby to a certain extent inconsequential.

Betz and Meret identify the Danish Peoples Party (FP) as among the first to make the question of Islam's incompatibility with liberal democracy and rights an issue (2009, p. 319), and other far right (nativist) parties adopted this position following Pim Fortuyn's success in the Netherlands (ibid., p. 322). This has been conceptualized as a form of liberalism turned inwards and driven by fear (Akkerman, 2005; Betz & Meret, 2009, p. 423). It has also meant that these initiatives emphasize a supranational, Western identity and belonging over the strictly national by stressing the common heritage of Judeo-Christian religion and culture. Mirroring these claims, Brubaker argues that the populist radical right has shifted from nationalism to "civilizationalism", which builds on an identitarian Christianism (to wit not a belief in Christ, but adherence to Christian culture) and a liberal defence of gender equality, gay rights, and freedom of speech (2017, p. 1191). Takis Pappas describes this as "liberalism for the natives" (2016, p. 27).

A majority position within the literature is that the championing of Western civilization, and liberal and progressive values, is a strategic attempt to shield themselves from accusations of racism while still pursuing their standard goal of ethnic homogeneity by excluding Muslims (e.g. Zúquete, 2008; Scrinzi, 2017; Lentin & Titley, 2012). For instance, in their analysis of the Swedish far-right website Flashback, Törnberg and Törnberg argue that "gender equality seems to be used as a discursive strategy in order to criticize Islam" (2016, p. 2), whereas others define it as exploitation of feminism (e.g. Mayer, Ajanovic, & Sauer, 2014). In much the same way, Deland, et al. define anti-Islamic activist claims of supporting LGBT as a "pinkwashing" strategy (2014, p. 12). The exception is Betz and Meret, who do not see it as a strategic consideration but as one which reflects their identity-oriented ideological core (2009, p. 334).

It is not uncommon to use the terms tactical or strategic in a wide array of social scientific fields that emphasize rational agency. When it pertains to the far right, however, the examples mentioned indicate that it is frequently used as a euphemism for being disingenuous and manipulative.

To summarize, even though ideology is seen as the constitutive element that distinguishes the far right from other political initiatives, there is a common understanding that elements distinguishing "newer" varieties of the far right from the old extreme should not be taken at face value. Rejecting anti-Semitism is seen as strategic abandonment, whereas the inclusion of liberal and progressive positions is seen as a strategic inclusion. The inherent duality in emphasizing ideology but rejecting select elements as "strategic" has a long pedigree. For instance, Hainsworth states that "nominal commitment to democracy and constitutionalism should not simply be taken as evidence of its actual realization" (2000, p. 8). The following perspective on political parties such as the Front National and the Danish and Norwegian Progress parties by Griffin succinctly illustrates this widespread position:

> their axiomatic rejection of multi-culturalism, their longing for "purity", their nostalgia for a mythical world of racial homogeneity and clearly demarcated boundaries of cultural differentiation, their celebration of the ties of blood and history over reason and a common humanity, their rejection of *ius soli* for *ius sanguinis*, their solvent-like abuse of history represent a reformist version of the same basic myth. It is one which poses a more serious threat to liberal democracy than fascism because it is able to disguise itself, rather like a stick insect posing as a twig to catch its prey.
>
> *(Griffin, 2000, p. 174)*

Networks and mobilization

The far right is defined by its ideology and not by its organizational form, but ideologies and collective action frames have their structural carriers (Klandermans & Mayer, 2006, p. 11). Whereas some of the literature on the mobilization of the far right against Islam and Muslims included the use of social movement perspectives, most focus almost exclusively on political parties. This has begun to change. In recent years, the party-centric work has been joined by a growing body of studies which focus on the broad range of extra-parliamentary initiatives that create, carry, and disseminate anti-Islamic frames. Prominent examples include websites such as the Gates of Vienna, Atlas Shrugs and Document.no, as well as activist groups such as Act! For America, the English Defence League, PEGIDA, and others. Modern anti-Islamic initiatives have their roots in the "political soil" of post-9/11 North America and Western Europe (Ekman, 2015, p. 1990). These initiatives have been described as forming a far-right movement (Meleagrou-Hitchens & Brun, 2013, p. 1), "sharing an anti-Islamic identity and rhetoric, and have overlapping and close ties" (Berntzen & Sandberg, 2014, p. 761).

The term "movement" is often used uncritically, but among scholars of movements, Mario Diani's synthetic definition, which stresses the constitutive role of networks, is now widely accepted. Specifically, Diani defines a movement as "a network of informal interactions between a plurality of individuals, groups and/ or organizations, engaged in political or cultural conflict, on the basis of a shared collective identity" (1992, p. 165). In other words, a movement is not a single initiative such as an activist group, which often consists of a group of people without a clearly defined structure, or an organization with an internal structure and hierarchy. Instead, a movement consists of several initiatives which have ties to each other, and which take part in a mutually recognized common struggle.

Whereas a majority of studies of extra-parliamentary anti-Islamic initiatives examine individual activist groups such as the EDL (e.g. Allen, 2011; Jackson & Feldman, 2011; Kassimeris & Jackson, 2015; Busher, 2015; Pilkington, 2016) and PEGIDA (Daphi et al., 2015; Dostal, 2015), some also look at the networks between anti-Islamic initiatives. In the United States, initiatives such as Act! For America and Stop Islamization, together with prominent individuals, constitute a deeply intertwined core which "manufacture and exaggerate threats of 'creeping Sharia'" (Ali et al., 2011, p. 2). Anti-Islamic initiatives have grown in influence in the United States and become agenda-setters who have been able to dominate the news cycle using emotionally charged language (Bail, 2012, 2014).

Ideological homophily

Several websites, blogs and communities disseminate anti-Islamic frames and the idea that the West is being colonized (Ekman, 2015, p. 1987). Many of these online initiatives refer to themselves as "counter-jihadists", and researchers use this term for the networks they form (e.g. Fekete, 2012).

Ideology and framing are interconnected with networks, but the causal relationship is difficult to untangle. Research indicates that networks are structured by ideological affiliation among non-government organizations (Murdie, 2014, p. 20), as well as online on Facebook (Thorson & Wells, 2015) and Twitter (Yardi & Boyd, 2010; Himelboim, McCreery, & Smith, 2013, p. 41; Conover et al., 2011). Some studies have found that the degree of ideological segregation online largely reflects the offline mobilization (Gentzkow & Shapiro, 2011; Halberstam & Knight, 2016). Online links are considered good indicators of ideological affinity, common objectives, or shared interests between the groups (Burris, Smith, & Strahm, 2000; Tateo, 2005; Caiani et al., 2012).

Findings indicate that ideological homophily is also predominant within far-right initiatives. In a comparative study of hyperlinks between far-right initiatives in the United States, Italy, and Germany, Caiani et al. (2012) found that that the Italian (ibid., p. 60) and American (ibid., p. 64) networks were strongly fragmented, mirroring the ideological divisions which were more prominent than in Germany (ibid., p. 62). For instance, Christian identity groups were quite disconnected from neo-Nazi, white power, and other extreme groups in the United States (ibid., p. 64). Furthermore, a study of transnational ties between far-right websites online found both ideological and strategic closeness by combining the tracing of hyperlinks with semantic content analysis (Wiederer, 2014, p. 48). The websites identified exhibited a small-world structure, which the author argued meant that national boundaries have become less important for the far right (ibid., p. 49).

Turning to the anti-Islamic far right, Lee uncovered a network of 46 anti-Islamic websites by tracing hyperlink connections starting from five anti-Islamic sites (2015, p. 256). A network analysis starting with the prominent blog Atlas Shrugs primarily found that it had connections to other far-right sites (Yang & Self, 2015) – thereby exhibiting ideological homophily. Contrary to Wiederer's findings, however, this network was geographically contained within the United States.

Whether or not the anti-Islamic far right has ties to initiatives that represent the progressive and liberal positions which the "new" far right claim to defend remains unexplored. This can partly be explained by the limited scope of the network analyses, but it may also reflect the common position that it is a strategic turn.

An amorphous nebula in decline

Whether the anti-Islamic far right in Western Europe and North America is actually one or several movements at all, is directly and indirectly contested by some of these studies. The terminology often indicates that we cannot speak of a social movement per se. For instance, the extra-parliamentary anti-Islamic far right has been described as a "an *amorphous* network of think-tanks, bloggers and activists" (Goodwin, 2013, p. 1; emphasis added) and a "loose global fraternity" (Denes, 2012, p. 295), whereas Lee speaks of a nebula – meaning a cloud of gas in space – to "evoke the indistinct character of the online wing of the counter-jihad scene" (Lee, 2015, p. 249). Both Goodwin (2013) and Busher (2015) call it an "embryonic" phenomenon, whose future direction and possible influence remains to be seen. Speaking to the future direction of the anti-Islamic far right, Fleischer argued that the "counter-jihad" network is fading because the far right began shifting their hostility towards the Roma minority and the European Union (Fleischer 2014, p. 69). Others go a step further. For instance, Önnerfors argues that the European counter-jihad movement is "without a consistent world view, dominant leaders and prolific ideologues" (2017, p. 159).[14]

Activist mobilization

Whether we can speak of a coherent movement and worldview matters a great deal for the mobilizing potential of the anti-Islamic far right. Mobilization refers to the process which brings demand and supply together, and which transforms people into activists (Klandermans, 2003). Both resource mobilization theory and political process theory emphasize social networks as mobilizing structures (Diani, 1997; Diani & McAdam, 2003; Kitts, 2000; McCarthy & Wolfson, 1996). Social movement research has stressed that online networks are important resources for the mobilization of transnational movements, as information can be disseminated almost instantaneously (Petit, 2004), overcoming problems of leadership and decision-making (Castells, 2000) and creating transnational solidarity (Chase-Dunn & Boswell, 2002). Networks facilitate the joint construction of meaning, acting both as a resource and a constraint (Caiani & Wagemann, 2009; Caiani et al., 2012, p. 30). In the study of online networks, web links between organizations are understood as "potential means of co-ordination" (Burris et al., 2000, p. 215).

Having an online presence is obviously not a prerogative of the far right, but online platforms and communication is thought to be particularly important to these initiatives because they face repression and stigmatization in other arenas (Caiani et al., 2012, p. 57; Simi & Futrell, 2009). For instance, Art (2011) showed that the actions of counter-protesters and social sanctions were a deterrent for regular activists. In some ways, however, online platforms can be more vital to the extreme right than the new anti-Islamic far right, as the former risk prosecution (Futrell, Simi, & Gottschalk, 2006).

The ability to mobilize also hinges on the frame alignment between (potential) activists and the initiative or movement (Snow, Benford, McCammon, Hewitt, & Fitzgerald, 2014), meaning that those who join already share some part of their ideology (Klandermans & Mayer, 2006). Frame alignment is defined as "linkage of individual and SMO interpretive orientations, such that some set of individual interests, values and beliefs and SMO activities, goals, and ideology are congruent and complementary" (Snow, Rochford, Worden, & Benford, 1986, p. 464).

Research indicates that people join white supremacist and other extreme right groups without having a solid grasp of their key ideological tenets, including anti-Semitism (Blee, 2017). Instead, they are primarily attracted to opportunities to engage in violence, access to drugs and alcohol, sexual relationships, profit, and links to criminal networks (Simi & Futrell, 2009; Simi, Sporer, & Bubolz, 2016; Fangen, 1998). Turning to studies of anti-Islamic activist groups, Joel Busher identified personal networks and moral shocks as two of the main factors driving EDL recruitment (2015, pp. 42–43), whereas only a minority was already well versed in their anti-Islamic views. Moral shocks have consistently been found to propel people into action (e.g. Jasper, 1998).

This does not mean that ideology and collective action framing are without meaning. Both networks and shocks work as conduits for ideological compatibility and frame alignment. For instance, when a traumatic event occurs to a person and this fits into the narrative of a far-right initiative, that person becomes more susceptible to the rest of the ideological package.

Finally, emotions and "hot cognition" have played a vital mobilizing role. The previously dominant perspectives with the explicit or implicit assumption that emotions stood in contrast to rationality has been repudiated (Aminzade & McAdam, 2002; Emirbayer & Goldberg, 2005; Gould, 2009). In particular, social movement literature points to negative emotions as powerful mobilizers (Jasper, 1998, p. 414), with anger as the prototypical protest emotion (Van Stekelenburg & Klandermans, 2017). It is an approach-oriented emotion which boosts to protest participation (Van Zomeren, Spears, Fischer, & Leach, 2004; van Troost et al., 2013), promoting action against the responsible agent (diagnosis) – promoting a corrective response (prognosis). In other words, frames are tailored to elicit specific emotions. Whereas emotions have been under-analyzed when it comes to far-right mobilization as a whole, research shows that the anti-Islamic far right in the United States managed to use emotionally charged frames to mobilize and to become dominant actors in the public debate in the years following 9/11 (Bail, 2012, 2014).

Conclusion

This chapter gives an overview of the main concepts and positions of far-right ideology, the anti-Islamic turn, and their extra-parliamentary activism. It argues that anti-Islam is a more suitable label than Islamophobia, offering a definition of anti-Islam as the framing of Islam as *a homogenous, totalitarian ideology which threatens Western civilization*. Whereas some describe the anti-Islamic worldview as a continuation of the ethno-pluralist master frame described by Rydgren, others point to the novelty of the inclusion of liberal and progressive positions – a sort of "civic nativism". Some describe it as liberalism turned inwards, driven by fear. Their inclusion of liberal and progressive positions is thought to flow causally from viewing Islam as an existential threat. However, this is commonly depicted as a strategic façade. I return to these theoretical perspectives and claims in Chapters 5–8. Several studies describe an anti-Islamic far right outside party politics which is transnational in scope and prominent online; their online networks seem to be structured on an ideological basis. Yet, whether it is a coherent phenomenon in terms of ideology and relations between initiatives remain contested, with some arguing that it is actually in decline. We shall see how these findings compare to my own in Chapters 6–8.

Finally, none of the studies that examine anti-Islamic organizational networks online discuss ties to other initiatives on the basis of their civilizational perspective, which includes the defence of Christianity, Jews and progressive ideals with their associated minorities, such as LGBT persons. I deal with this absence in the network analyses in Chapter 6.

Notes

1 For a thorough overview, see Jens Rydgren's article "The Sociology of the Radical Right" (2007).
2 Social movement scholarship is dominated by sociology, but includes the work of social psychologists, historians, political scientists, and social anthropologists (van Troost, van Stekelenburg, & Klandermans, 2013).
3 As of June 2017, going by Google Scholar, Roger Griffin's article "The Nature of Fascism" (1993) was cited 910 times, Cas Mudde's "Populist Radical Right Parties in Europe" (2007) 1,800 times, and Jens Rydgren's "Is Extreme Right-wing Populism Contagious? Explaining the Emergence of a New Party Family" (2005a) 408 times.
4 This understanding of master frames shares some similarities with what some call "thin-centered" ideology.
5 Others, such as Elisabeth Carter (2005) use the term "right-wing extremism" as the overarching conceptual container in which she combines both spatial and absolute reasoning. Carter identifies five subsets of extreme right parties from the 1980s onwards: neo-Nazi, neo-fascist, authoritarian xenophobic, neo-liberal xenophobic, and neo-liberal populist.
6 Although Griffin's definition allows us to delimit "fascism" from other forms of far-right ideology, many of those who use the term include the very political actors which Griffin himself excludes. These works are perhaps the most easily identifiable as the lumpers committing the sin of conceptual stretching.
7 The anti-democratic position is a necessary factor to designate a political initiative under the rubric of right-wing extremism, but the biological racism which defines fascist nativism (at least of the Nazi variety) can be exchanged with ethno-pluralist or other forms of nativism.
8 Mudde uses the term "Islamophobia". See conceptual discussion of this term ahead.
9 Dinet and Ibrahim (1918).
10 See, for example, Halliday (1999, p. 899), and Zúquete (2008, p. 324). This is an issue common to all terminology used to describe the far right, however, and outside the control of academia.
11 Instead of making theoretical assumptions about irrationality and fear as constitutive elements, concepts need to be built (and tested) from the ground up.
12 While Rydgren includes negative and positive feelings and evaluations in his definition of prejudice, positive evaluations and feelings are a priori excluded from anti-Muslim prejudices: "A prejudiced stereotype can be defined as an attitude or set of attitudes held toward a group or members of a group, encompassing over-simplified beliefs and a set of negative or positive feelings and evaluations" (2004b, p. 129).
13 Although Fleischer uses the word "prejudice", which commonly refers to individual-level attitudes, his analysis and discussion actually revolves around ideology.
14 Clearly, the conceptualization and delimitation of what a social movement is and what it is not has a big impact for our understanding of the anti-Islamic far right. This is highlighted by the fact that several studies which look at initiatives such as the EDL and PEGIDA define them as movements unto themselves, and not social movement organizations which are part of a wider movement.

Bibliography

Ali, W., Clifton, E., Duss, M., Fang, L., Keyes, S., & Shakir, F. (2011). Fear, Inc. *The roots of the Islamophobia network in America.* Washington, DC: Center for American Progress.
Abbas, T. (2004). After 9/11: British South Asian Muslims, Islamophobia, multiculturalism, and the state. *American Journal of Islamic Social Sciences, 21*(3), 26–38.
Adorno, T. W., Frenkel-Brunswik, E., Levinson, D. J., & Sanford, R. N. (1950). *The authoritarian personality.* New York: Harper & Row.

Ajanovic, E., Mayer, S., & Sauer, B. (2016). Spaces of right-wing populism and anti Muslim racism in Austria. *Politologický časopis-Czech Journal of Political Science, 23*(2), 131–148.

Akkerman, T. (2005). Anti-immigration parties and the defence of liberal values: The exceptional case of the list Pim Fortuyn. *Journal of Political Ideologies, 10*(3), 337–354.

Akkerman, T., & Hagelund, A. (2007). "Women and children first!" Anti-immigration parties and gender in Norway and the Netherlands. *Patterns of Prejudice, 41*(2), 197–214.

Allen, C. (2010). *Islamophobia*. Ebook. Farnham: Ashgate Publishing, Ltd.

Allen, C. (2011). Opposing Islamification or promoting Islamophobia? Understanding the English Defence League. *Patterns of Prejudice, 45*(4), 279–294.

Allen, C. (2014). Anti-social networking: Findings from a pilot study on opposing Dudley Mosque using Facebook groups as both site and method for research. *Sage Open, 4*(1), doi:10.1177/2158244014522074

Aminzade, R., & McAdam, D. (2002). Emotions and contentious politics. *Mobilization: An International Quarterly, 7*(2), 107–109.

Anahita, S. (2006). Blogging the borders: Virtual skinheads, hypermasculinity, and heteronormativity. *Journal of Political and Military Sociology, 34*(1), 143.

Arendt, H. (1951). *The origins of totalitarianism*. New York: Schocken Books.

Art, D. (2011). *Inside the radical right: The development of anti-immigrant parties in Western Europe*. Cambridge: Cambridge University Press.

Bail, C. A. (2012). The fringe effect: Civil society organizations and the evolution of media discourse about Islam since the September 11th attacks. *American Sociological Review, 77*(6), 855–879.

Bail, C. A. (2014). *Terrified: How anti-Muslim Fringe organizations became mainstream*. Princeton, NJ: Princeton University Press.

Bangstad, S. (2013). Eurabia comes to Norway. *Islam and Christian – Muslim Relations, 24*(3), 369–391.

Bangstad, S. (2014). *Anders Breivik and the rise of Islamophobia*. London: Zed Books.

Bangstad, S. (2016). Islamophobia: What's in a name? *Journal of Muslims in Europe, 5*(2), 145–169.

Bedi, T. (2006). Feminist theory and the right-wing: Shiv Sena women mobilize Mumbai. *Journal of International Women's Studies, 7*(4), 51–68.

Benford, R. D., & Snow, D. A. (2000). Framing processes and social movements: An overview and assessment. *Annual Review of Sociology, 26*(1), 611–639.

Berntzen, L. E., & Sandberg, S. (2014). The collective nature of lone wolf terrorism: Anders Behring Breivik and the anti-Islamic social movement. *Terrorism and Political Violence, 26*(5), 759–779.

Betz, H. G. (2013). Mosques, minarets, burqas and other essential threats: The populist right's campaign against Islam in Western Europe. In R. Wodak, B. Mral, & M. Khosravinik (Eds.), *Right-wing populism in Europe: Politics and discourse* (pp. 71–88). London: A&C Black.

Betz, H. G., & Immerfall, S. (Eds.). (1998). *The new politics of the right: Neo-populist parties and movements in established democracies*. London: Macmillan.

Betz, H. G., & Meret, S. (2009). Revisiting Lepanto: The political mobilization against Islam in contemporary Western Europe. *Patterns of Prejudice, 43*(3–4), 313–334.

Bjørgo, T. (1997). *Racist and right-wing violence in Scandinavia: Patterns, perpetrators and responses*. Oslo: Tano Aschehoug.

Blee, K. M. (1996). Becoming a racist: Women in contemporary Ku Klux Klan and neo-Nazi groups. *Gender & Society, 10*(6), 680–702.

Blee, K. M. (2017). How the study of white supremacism is helped and hindered by social movement research. *Mobilization, 22*(1), 1–15.

Bleich, E. (2011). What is Islamophobia and how much is there? Theorizing and measuring an emerging comparative concept. *American Behavioral Scientist, 55*(12), 1581–1600.

Bornschier, S. (2010a). *Cleavage politics and the populist right.* Philadelphia, PA: Temple University Press.

Bornschier, S. (2010b). The new cultural divide and the two-dimensional political space in Western Europe. *West European Politics, 33*(3), 419–444.

Brubaker, R. (2017). Between nationalism and civilizationism: The European populist moment in comparative perspective. *Ethnic and Racial Studies, 40*(8), 1191–1226.

Budge, I., Robertson, D., & Hearl, D. (Eds.). (1987). *Ideology, strategy and party change: Spatial analyses of post-war election programmes in 19 democracies.* Cambridge: Cambridge University Press.

Bunzl, M. (2007). *Anti-semitism and Islamophobia: Hatreds old and new in Europe* (Vol. 28). Chicago, IL: Prickly Paradigm.

Burris, V., Smith, E., & Strahm, A. (2000). White supremacist networks on the Internet. *Sociological Focus, 33*(2), 215–235.

Busher, J. (2013). Grassroots activism in the English Defence League: Discourse and public (dis) order. In M. Taylor, P. M. Currie, & D. Holbrook (Eds.), *Extreme right wing political violence and terrorism* (pp. 65–84). Bloomsbury Publishing.

Busher, J. (2015). *The making of anti-Muslim protest: Grassroots activism in the English Defence League.* London: Routledge.

Caiani, M., Della Porta, D., & Wagemann, C. (2012). *Mobilizing on the extreme right: Germany, Italy, and the United States.* Oxford: Oxford University Press.

Caiani, M., & Wagemann, C. (2009). Online networks of the Italian and German extreme right: An explorative study with social network analysis. *Information, Communication & Society, 12*(1), 66–109.

Capoccia, G. (2005). *Defending democracy: Reactions to extremism in interwar Europe.* Baltimore, MA: JHU Press.

Carter, E. (2005). *The extreme right in Western Europe: Success or failure?* Oxford: Oxford University Press.

Castells, M. (2000). Toward a sociology of the network society. *Contemporary Sociology, 29*(5), 693–699.

Chase-Dunn, C., & Boswell, T. (2002). *Transnational social movements and democratic socialist parties in the semiperiphery.* The Institute for Research on World-Systems. Riverside, CA: University of California, unpublished manuscript.

Collier, D., & Mahon, J. E. (1993). Conceptual "stretching" revisited: Adapting categories in comparative analysis. *American Political Science Review, 87*(4), 845–855.

Collier, R. B., & Collier, D. (1991). *Shaping the political arena: Critical junctures, the labor movement, and regime dynamics in Latin America.* Notre Dame: University of Notre Dame Press.

Conover, M., Ratkiewicz, J., Francisco, M. R., Gonçalves, B., Menczer, F., & Flammini, A. (2011). Political polarization on twitter. *ICWSM, 133*, 89–96.

Converse, P. E. (1964). Ideology and discontent. In D. Apter (Ed.), *Ideology and discontent* (pp. 206–261). New York: Free Press.

Dalton, R. J. (1994). *The green rainbow: Environmental groups in Western Europe.* New Haven: Yale University Press.

Daphi, P., et al. (2015). *Protestforschung am Limit. Eine soziologische Annäherung an PEGIDA.* Retrieved from www.wzb.eu/sites/default/files/u6/pegida-report_berlin_2015.pdf

Deland, M., Minkenberg, M., & Mays, C. (Eds.). (2014). *In the tracks of Breivik: Far right networks in Northern and Eastern Europe* (Vol. 37). Münster: LIT Verlag.

Denes, N. (2012). "Welcome to the Counterjihad": Uncivil networks and the narration of European public spheres. *Journal of Civil Society, 8*(3), 289–306.

Diani, M. (1992). The concept of social movement. *The Sociological Review, 40*(1), 1–25.

Diani, M. (1997). Social movements and social capital: A network perspective on movement outcomes. *Mobilization: An International Quarterly, 2*(2), 129–147.

Diani, M., & Bison, I. (2004). Organizations, coalitions, and movements. *Theory and Society, 33*(3), 281–309.

Diani, M., & McAdam, D. (Eds.). (2003). *Social movements and networks: Relational approaches to collective action.* Oxford: Oxford University Press.

Dinet, E., & Ibrahim, E. H. S. B. (1918). *La Vie de Mohammed Prophéte d'Allah.* Paris: Piazza.

Dostal, J. M. (2015). The PEGIDA movement and German political culture: Is right-wing populism here to stay? *The Political Quarterly, 86*(4), 523–531.

Durham, M. (2007). *White rage: The extreme right and American politics.* New York: Routledge.

Ekman, M. (2015). Online Islamophobia and the politics of fear: Manufacturing the green scare. *Ethnic and Racial Studies, 38*(11), 1986–2002.

Emirbayer, M., & Goldberg, C. A. (2005). Pragmatism, Bourdieu, and collective emotions in contentious politics. *Theory and Society, 34*(5), 469–518.

Fangen, K. (1998). Right-wing skinheads-Nostalgia and binary oppositions. *Young, 6*(3), 33–49.

Fangen, K. (1999). On the margins of life: Life stories of radical nationalists. *Acta Sociologica, 42*(4), 357–373.

Fekete, L. (2012). The Muslim conspiracy theory and the Oslo massacre. *Race & Class, 53*(3), 30–47.

Fielitz, M., & Laloire, L. L. (Eds.). (2016). *Trouble on the far right: Contemporary right-wing strategies and practices in Europe* (Vol. 39). Bielefeld: Transcript Verlag.

Fleischer, R. (2014). Two fascisms in contemporary Europe? Understanding the ideological split of the radical right. In M. Deland, M. Minkenberg, & C. Mays (Eds.), *In the tracks of Breivik: Far right networks in Northern and Eastern Europe* (pp. 53–70, 54). Vienna and Münster: LIT.

Futrell, R., Simi, P., & Gottschalk, S. (2006). Understanding music in movements: The white power music scene. *The Sociological Quarterly, 47*(2), 275–304.

Gentzkow, M., & Shapiro, J. M. (2011). Ideological segregation online and offline. *The Quarterly Journal of Economics, 126*(4), 1799–1839.

Gerhards, J., & Rucht, D. (1992). Mesomobilization: Organizing and framing in two protest campaigns in West Germany. *American Journal of Sociology, 98*(3), 555–596.

Goodwin, M. J. (2013). *The roots of extremism: The English Defence League and the Counter-Jihad Challenge.* London: Chatham House.

Gould, D. B. (2009). *Moving politics: Emotion and ACT UP's fight against AIDS.* Chicago, IL: University of Chicago Press.

Griffin, R. (1993). *The nature of fascism.* London: Routledge.

Griffin, R. (1995). *Fascism: A reader.* Oxford: Oxford University Press on Demand.

Griffin, R. (2000). Interregnum or endgame? The radical right in the "post-fascist" era. *Journal of Political Ideologies, 5*(2), 163–178.

Griffin, R. (2006). Fascism's new faces (and new facelessness) in the "post-fascist" Epoch. In W. Laqueur (Ed.), *Fascism past and present, West and East: An international debate on concepts and cases in the comparative study of the extreme right* (Vol. 35). New York: Columbia University Press.

Grumke, T. (2004). Take this country back! In *Die Neue Rechte – eine Gefahr für die Demokratie?* (pp. 175–185). Wiesbaden: VS Verlag für Sozialwissenschaften.

Hainsworth, P. (2000). *The politics of the extreme right: From the margins to the mainstream*. London: Pinter.

Halberstam, Y., & Knight, B. (2016). Homophily, group size, and the diffusion of political information in social networks: Evidence from Twitter. *Journal of Public Economics, 143*, 73–88.

Halliday, F. (1999). Islamophobia' reconsidered. *Ethnic and Racial Studies, 22*(5), 892–902.

Himelboim, I., McCreery, S., & Smith, M. (2013). Birds of a feather tweet together: Integrating network and content analyses to examine cross-ideology exposure on Twitter. *Journal of Computer-Mediated Communication, 18*(2), 40–60.

Ignazi, P. (1992). The silent counter-revolution. *European Journal of Political Research, 22*(1), 3–34.

Ignazi, P. (2003). *Extreme right parties in Western Europe*. Oxford: Oxford University Press on Demand.

Ivarsflaten, E. (2005). The vulnerable populist right parties: No economic realignment fuelling their electoral success. *European Journal of Political Research, 44*(3), 465–492.

Jackson, P., & Feldman, M. (2011). *The EDL: Britain's "new far right" social movement* (NECTAR, the Northampton Electronic Collection of Theses and Research). The University of Northampton, Northampton.

Jackson, P., & Feldman, M. (2014). *Doublespeak: The framing of the far-right since 1945*. Stuttgart: Ibidem-Verlag.

Jackson, S. (2011). Muslims, Islam (s), race, and American Islamophobia. In J. L. Esposito & I. Kalin (Eds.), *Islamophobia: The challenge of pluralism in the 21st century* (pp. 93–108). Oxford: Oxford University Press.

Jasper, J. M. (1998). The emotions of protest: Affective and reactive emotions in and around social movements. *Sociological Forum, 13*(3), 397–424. Springer Netherlands.

Kaplan, J. (2006). Islamophobia in America? September 11 and Islamophobic hate crime 1. *Terrorism and Political Violence, 18*(1), 1–33.

Kassimeris, G., & Jackson, L. (2015). The ideology and discourse of the English Defence League: "Not racist, not violent, just no longer silent". *The British Journal of Politics and International Relations, 17*(1), 171–188.

Kitts, J. (2000). Mobilizing in black boxes: Social networks and participation in social movement organizations. *Mobilization: An International Quarterly, 5*(2), 241–257.

Klandermans, B. (2003). Collective political action. *Oxford Handbook of Political Psychology*, 670–709.

Klandermans, B., & Mayer, N. (2006). *Through the magnifying glass: The world of extreme right activists*. London: Routledge.

Koopmans, R. (1996). Explaining the rise of racist and extreme right violence in Western Europe: Grievances or opportunities?. *European Journal of Political Research, 30*(2), 185–216.

Koopmans, R. (2004). Movements and media: Selection processes and evolutionary dynamics in the public sphere. *Theory and Society, 33*(3–4), 367–391.

Kundnani, A. (2012). Blind spot-security narratives and far-right violence. *Security & Human Rights, 23*, 129.

Kühnel, S., & Leibold, J. (2007). *Islamophobie in der deutschen Bevölkerung: Ein neues Phänomen oder nur ein neuer Name? Ergebnisse von Bevölkerungsumfragen zur gruppenbezogenen Menschenfeindlichkeit 2003 bis 2005* (pp. 135–154). Baden-Baden: Nomos Verlagsgesellschaft mbH & Co. KG.

Layton-Henry, Z. (1982). Introduction: Conservatism and conservative politics. In *Conservative politics in Western Europe* (pp. 1–20). London: Palgrave Macmillan.

Lee, B. (2015). A day in the "swamp": Understanding discourse in the online counter-Jihad nebula. *Democracy and Security, 11*(3), 248–274.

Lee, S. A., Gibbons, J. A., Thompson, J. M., & Timani, H. S. (2009). The Islamophobia scale: Instrument development and initial validation. *The International Journal for the Psychology of Religion, 19*(2), 92–105.

Leibold, J., Kühnel, S., & Heitmeyer, W. (2006). Abschottung von Muslimen durch generalisierte Islamkritik? *Aus Politik und Zeitgeschichte, 1.*

Lentin, A., & Titley, G. (2012). The crisis of "multiculturalism" in Europe: Mediated minarets, intolerable subjects. *European Journal of Cultural Studies, 15*(2), 123–138.

Lesselier, C. (2002). Far-right women in France: The case of the national front. In P. Bacchetta & M. Power (Eds.), *Right-wing women: From conservatives to extremists around the world* (pp. 127–140). London: Routledge.

Lo, C.Y. (1982). Countermovements and conservative movements in the contemporary US. *Annual Review of Sociology, 8*(1), 107–134.

Lucassen, G., & Lubbers, M. (2012). Who fears what? Explaining far-right-wing preference in Europe by distinguishing perceived cultural and economic ethnic threats. *Comparative Political Studies, 45*(5), 547–574.

Mayer, S., Ajanovic, E., & Sauer, B. (2014). Intersections and inconsistencies: Framing gender in right wing populist discourses in Austria. *NORA-Nordic Journal of Feminist and Gender Research, 22*(4), 250–266.

McAdam, D. (1982). *Political process and the development of black insurgency, 1930–1970.* Chicago, IL: University of Chicago Press.

McCarthy, J. D., & Wolfson, M. (1996). Resource mobilization by local social movement organizations: Agency, strategy, and organization in the movement against drinking and driving. *American Sociological Review,* 1070–1088.

McCarthy, J. D., & Zald, M. N. (1977). Resource mobilization and social movements: A partial theory. *American Journal of Sociology, 82*(6), 1212–1241.

Meleagrou-Hitchens, A., & Brun, H. (2013). *A neo-nationalist network: The English Defence League and Europe's counter-Jihad movement.* London: International Centre for the Study of Radicalisation and Political Violence.

Minkenberg, M. (2003). The West European radical right as a collective actor: Modeling the impact of cultural and structural variables on party formation and movement mobilization. *Comparative European Politics, 1*(2), 149–170.

Mooney, P. H., & Hunt, S. A. (1996). A repertoire of interpretations: Master frames and ideological continuity in US agrarian mobilization. *The Sociological Quarterly, 37*(1), 177–197.

Mudde, C. (1996). The war of words defining the extreme right party family. *West European Politics, 19*(2), 225–248.

Mudde, C. (2000). *The ideology of the extreme right.* Manchester: Manchester University Press.

Mudde, C. (2007). *The populist radical right in Europe.* Cambridge: Cambridge University Press.

Mudde, C. (2010). The populist radical right: A pathological normalcy. *West European Politics, 33*(6), 1167–1186.

Mudde, C. (2016). *The study of populist radical right parties: Towards a fourth wave.* C-REX Working Paper Series, 1.

Mudde, C., & Kaltwasser, C. R. (2017). *Populism: A very short introduction.* Oxford: Oxford University Press.

Murdie, A. (2014). The ties that bind: A network analysis of human rights international non-governmental organizations. *British Journal of Political Science, 44*(1), 1–27.

Oliver, P. E., & Johnston, H. (2005). What a good idea! Ideologies and frames in social movement research. *Frames of Protest: Social Movements and the Framing Perspective,* 185–204.

Olson, M. (1971). *The logic of collective action* (Vol. 124). Cambridge, MA: Harvard University Press.

Önnerfors, A. (2017). Between Breivik and PEGIDA: The absence of ideologues and leaders on the contemporary European far right. *Patterns of Prejudice, 51*(2), 159–175.

Pappas, T. S. (2016). Distinguishing liberal democracy's challengers. *Journal of Democracy, 27*(4), 22–36.

Petit, C. (2004, August). *Social movement networks in Internet discourse.* Annual meetings of the American Sociological Association, San Francisco, Vol. 17.

Pilbaum, B. (2003). *Conservatism in crisis? Anglo-American conservative ideology after the cold war.* Houndmills: Palgrave Macmillan.

Pilkington, H. (2016). *Loud and proud: Passion and politics in the English Defence League.* Manchester: Manchester University Press.

Rosanvallon, P., & Goldhammer, A. (2008). *Counter-democracy: Politics in an age of distrust* (Vol. 7). Cambridge: Cambridge University Press.

Reich, W. (1970). *The mass psychology of fascism.* New York: Macmillan.

Runnymede Trust, L. U. K. (1997). *Islamophobia: A challenge for us all.* London: Runnymede Trust.

Rydgren, J. (2003). Meso-level reasons for racism and xenophobia: Some converging and diverging effects of radical right populism in France and Sweden. *European Journal of Social Theory, 6*(1), 45–68.

Rydgren, J. (2004a). Explaining the emergence of radical right-wing populist parties: The case of Denmark. *West European Politics, 27*(3), 474–502.

Rydgren, J. (2004b). The logic of xenophobia. *Rationality and Society, 16*(2), 123–148.

Rydgren, J. (2005a). Is extreme right-wing populism contagious? Explaining the emergence of a new party family. *European Journal of Political Research, 44*(3), 413–437.

Rydgren, J. (2005b). *Movements of exclusion: Radical right-wing populism in the Western world.* New York: Nova Publishers.

Rydgren, J. (2007). The sociology of the radical right. *Annual Review of Sociology, 33*, 241–262.

Rydgren, J. (2008). Immigration sceptics, xenophobes or racists? Radical right-wing voting in six West European countries. *European Journal of Political Research, 47*(6), 737–765.

Sainsbury, D. (1980). *Swedish social democratic ideology and electoral politics 1944–1948: A study of the functions of party ideology.* Stockholm: Almqvist and Wiksell International.

Sartori, G. (1970). Concept misformation in comparative politics. *American Political Science Review, 64*(4), 1033–1053.

Sayyid, S., & Vakil, A. (2008). *Thinking Thru' Islamophobia*, Symposium, University of Leeds.

Scheuch, E. K., & Klingemann, H. D. (1967). *Theorie des Rechtsradikalismus in westlichen Industriegesellschaften.* Hamburg: JCB Mohr (P. Siebeck).

Scrinzi, F. (2017). A "new" national front? Gender, religion, secularism and the French populist radical right. In M. Köttig, R. Bitzan, & A. Petö (Eds.), *Gender and far right politics in Europe* (pp. 127–140). Springer International Publishing. DOI: 10.1007/978-3-319-43533-6

Sedgwick, M. (2013). Something varied in the state of Denmark: Neo-nationalism, anti-Islamic activism, and street-level thuggery. *Politics, Religion & Ideology, 14*(2), 208–233.

Simi, P., & Futrell, R. (2009). Negotiating white power activist stigma. *Social Problems, 56*(1), 89–110.

Simi, P., Sporer, K., & Bubolz, B. F. (2016). Narratives of childhood adversity and adolescent misconduct as precursors to violent extremism: A life-course criminological approach. *Journal of Research in Crime and Delinquency, 53*(4), 536–563.

Snow, D. A., & Benford, R. D. (1988). Ideology, frame resonance, and participant mobilization. *International Social Movement Research, 1*(1), 197–217.

Snow, D. A., & Benford, R. D. (1992). Master frames and cycles of protest. *Frontiers in Social Movement Theory*, *133*, 155.

Snow, D. A., Benford, R. D., McCammon, H., Hewitt, L., & Fitzgerald, S. (2014). The emergence, development, and future of the framing perspective: 25+ years since "frame alignment". *Mobilization: An International Quarterly*, *19*(1), 23–46.

Snow, D. A., & Byrd, S. (2007). Ideology, framing processes, and Islamic terrorist movements. *Mobilization: An International Quarterly*, *12*(2), 119–136.

Snow, D. A., Rochford, E. B., Jr., Worden, S. K., & Benford, R. D. (1986). Frame alignment processes, micromobilization, and movement participation. *American Sociological Review*, 464–481.

Tateo, L. (2005). The Italian extreme right on-line network: An exploratory study using an integrated social network analysis and content analysis approach. *Journal of Computer-Mediated Communication*, *10*(2).

Thorson, K., & Wells, C. (2015). Understanding media effects in an era of curated flows. In T. Vos & F. Heinderyckx (Eds.), *Gatekeeping in transition* (pp. 25–44). London: Routledge.

Törnberg, A., & Törnberg, P. (2016). Combining CDA and topic modeling: Analyzing discursive connections between Islamophobia and anti-feminism on an online forum. *Discourse & Society*, *27*(4), 401–422.

Useem, B. (1998). Breakdown theories of collective action. *Annual Review of Sociology*, *24*(1), 215–238.

van der Brug, W., & Fennema, M. (2007). Causes of voting for the radical right. *International Journal of Public Opinion Research*, *19*(4), 474–487.

Van Stekelenburg, J., & Klandermans, B. (2017). Individuals in movements: A social psychology of contention. In *Handbook of social movements across disciplines* (pp. 103–139). New York: Springer.

Van Troost, D., Van Stekelenburg, J., & Klandermans, B. (2013). *Emotions of protest* (pp. 186–203). New York, NY: Palgrave Macmillan.

Van Zomeren, M., Spears, R., Fischer, A. H., & Leach, C. W. (2004). Put your money where your mouth is! Explaining collective action tendencies through group-based anger and group efficacy. *Journal of Personality and Social Psychology*, *87*, 649–664.

Vertigans, S. (2007). Beyond the Fringe? Radicalisation within the American far-right. *Totalitarian Movements and Political Religions*, *8*(3–4), 641–659.

Wiederer, R. (2014). Mapping the right-wing extremist movement on the Internet – structural patterns 2006–2011. In M. Deland, M. Minkenberg, & C. Mays (Eds.), *In the tracks of Breivik: Far right networks in Northern and Eastern Europe* (pp. 19–51). Münster: LIT Verlag.

Williams, M. H. (2010). Can Leopards change their spots? Between xenophobia and trans-ethnic populism among West European far right parties. *Nationalism and Ethnic Politics*, *16*(1), 111–134.

Yang, A., & Self, C. (2015). Anti-Muslim prejudice in the virtual space: A case study of blog network structure and message features of the "ground zero mosque controversy". *Media, War & Conflict*, *8*(1), 46–69.

Yardi, S., & Boyd, D. (2010). Tweeting from the town square: Measuring geographic local networks. *ICWSM*, 194–201.

Zúquete, J. P. (2008). The European extreme-right and Islam: New directions? *Journal of Political Ideologies*, *13*(3), 321–344.

3

MAPPING A MOVEMENT

Introduction

The aim of this book is two-fold. The first aim is to expand our knowledge about the ongoing anti-Islamic turn of the far right by mapping and exploring the anti-Islamic movement and subculture. The second aim is to investigate their entanglement with liberal and progressive ideals and their ramifications. In this chapter, I outline the methodologies and data sources used to that end.

In the previous chapter, I discussed how ideology is seen as the defining characteristic which distinguishes the far right from other initiatives.[1] Nonetheless, it is common to argue that ideological elements which break with the legacy of the extreme right should not be taken at face value. For instance, whereas rejecting anti-Semitism is seen as a strategic abandonment driven by historical necessity, the adoption of liberal and progressive positions is seen as a strategic inclusion, sometimes described as a frontstage façade. The notion of a front stage and back stage is derived from the social interactionist and constructivist tradition of Erving Goffman (1959). Theoreticians in this vein talk of social interactions and the relational construction of reality in general. In contrast, when used to describe and understand the far right, the frontstage/backstage division is not conceived of as something which permeates all social life, but rather to indicate that the far right covers up their "true", anti-democratic, anti-Semitic, and homophobic beliefs. Substantially speaking, this assumed frontstage/backstage division stands in stark contrast to Goffman's mundane example of the waiter who behaves differently with customers (front stage) than with the other waiters and chefs in the kitchen (back stage).

In order to reconcile the focus on ideology with the predominant scepticism toward ideological content which breaks with the extreme right, we need to go beyond the front stage of official statements made by figureheads, spokespersons, and leaders. Before getting beyond the front stage, however, we have to come to

TABLE 3.1 Overview of cases, focus, methods, data, and time span in Chapters 4 and 5

Chapter	Cases	Focus	Methods and data	Time span
4	Strongholds of anti-Islamic activism: Norway, Denmark, Britain, Germany, Netherlands, and United States	Historical evolution of anti-Islamic expansion and the biographies of leaders, representatives, and ideologues	Qualitative tracing drawing on newspaper articles and online material from the initiatives themselves	2000–2017
5	Eleven anti-Islamic initiatives in Norway, Britain, and Germany	A comparison of their collective action framing and diagnosis, prognosis, and motivational framing, in addition to women's rights	Qualitative content analysis of framing, drawing on manifestos and official material in addition to public statements by initiative spokespersons and leaders	2010–2017

grips with what their platform actually consists of, and whether it has the semblance of a coherent worldview, or if their ideas are strongly fractured along organizational, regional, and national lines.

This chapter provides an overview of the methodological choices and data sources that are employed to map the (extra-parliamentary) anti-Islamic far right, both the frontstage worldview formulated and expressed by their leaders and spokespersons, and their possible entanglement with liberal and progressive positions beyond this. It begins with the qualitative analyses provided in Chapters 4–5, which rely on a wide range of written sources to trace the evolution of the anti-Islamic far right, the background of their leaders and ideologues, and, finally, their framing (Table 3.1). It then moves on to discuss the gathering and analysis of "big data" used to explore their organizational networks (Chapter 6) and the contents of their online discussions, as well as which messages drive their online mobilization (Chapter 7) (Table 3.2). It finally concludes with a discussion of anonymity.

Laying the groundwork

The anti-Islamic turn of the far right is clarified by distinguishing between two processes; the anti-Islamic reorientation of pre-existing far right initiatives and the anti-Islamic expansion of the far right with new initiatives. While the reorientation predominantly occurred among political parties (see e.g. Betz & Meret, 2009), the expansion is largely an extra-parliamentary affair. Chapter 4 is dedicated to mapping the evolution of the anti-Islamic expansion and the political legacies of the initiators and key figures. This forms an important preamble to Chapter 5, where I investigate their worldviews.

TABLE 3.2 Overview of the cases, focus, methods, data, and time span in Chapters 6 and 7

Chapter	Case(s)	Focus	Methods and data	Timespan
6	Global anti-Islamic network at two points in time consisting of 3,654 and 4,594 groups, respectively	Composition and evolution of anti-Islamic network between initiatives	One-mode network analysis of like links between initiatives on Facebook. Snowball tracing from 27 anti-Islamic initiatives (two-step)	March 2015 versus March 2016
7	A total of 298 anti-Islamic initiatives	1) Comparing activist framing to official platform, and 2) emotions and messages driving mobilization	Posts, comments, likes, and reactions analyzed using automated sentiment analysis, key words in context, word networks around key words, and multilevel regression analysis	12–18 August 2016

Tracing the expansion

The evolution of the "new" anti-Islamic far right is traced through the use of publicly available material from a wide collection of sources: newspaper articles, "about us" statements, and overviews available from the initiatives' own websites, in addition to secondary research material. It covers initiatives and key figures responsible for the anti-Islamic expansion of the far right from the United States, Britain, the Netherlands, Germany, Denmark, and Norway. These are all strongholds of anti-Islamic activism, countries where a wave of anti-Islamic activism began or the home of prominent and well-established initiatives which underpin these waves. Austria, Sweden, Belgium, and France have also witnessed a large and durable mobilization against Islam and Muslims, but they are excluded as it has been channelled through pre-established radical right parties that underwent an ideological reorientation: the French FN, the Freedom Party of Austria (*Freiheitliche Partei Österreichs*, FPÖ), and SD in Sweden. Of the countries included, Norway and Britain also have pre-existing parties which have undergone a reorientation and transformation towards anti-Islam: the Norwegian FrP, and the British UKIP and BNP. Again, these parties are not included in the analysis. The overview of the anti-Islamic expansion is followed by a structured comparison of their leaders, representatives and ideologues based on publicly available biographical data. The time period of anti-Islamic mobilization detailed in this chapter stretches from 9/11, which is widely seen as the critical event preceding both the anti-Islamic reorientation and expansion of the far right, up until 2017.

Collective action framing – worldviews

When looking at the worldviews promoted by the official platforms of anti-Islamic initiatives, I narrow them down to 11 cases in three countries between 2010 and 2017: Britain, Germany, and Norway. Organizationally speaking, the 11 cases extend from small political parties and think-tanks to protest groups and websites dealing with alternative news. The list is not exhaustive of all the anti-Islamic initiatives which have been operational in the three countries, but they include the largest and perhaps most influential in the anti-Islamic expansion. Unlike the preceding chapter that traced the evolution of the anti-Islamic expansion and the most prominent figures' backgrounds, notable individuals that are not leaders or representatives for a collective entity are excluded.

Data consist of a wide selection of manifestos and public statements printed in newspapers and on their websites. This is supplemented by interviews with the leaders and representatives in Norway.[2] Their positions were first coded and systematized for each initiative, and then compared. Both coding and analysis was theoretically guided and structured applying Snow and Benford's (1988, 2000) distinction between diagnostic, prognostic, and motivational framing on a sentence-based level. In addition, the cross-cutting issue of how they frame women's rights was coded on a similar basis. The issue of women's rights was chosen as it is one of the most prominent and academically contentious issues of the concomitant liberal and progressive turn which is thought to flow from their mobilization against Islam. Describing their shared collective action framing over a long period involves simplifying for analytical reasons, and rationalization of texts that are sometimes ambiguous.

Digital traces – networks and messages

When combined with computational resources, the availability of massive amounts of social media data has given rise to a growing body of work using machine learning, natural language processing, network analysis, and statistics for measuring human behaviour and social structure on a previously unprecedented scale (Ruths & Pfeffer, 2014, p. 1063). In this regard, the two last empirical chapters build on large amounts of online activity in order to grasp the substantial scope and structure of the anti-Islamic turn and overall entanglement with progressive and liberal positions. It is argued that the internet is particularly important for the far right (e.g. Castells, 2012), but that we nonetheless know little about how they actually use the internet for political communication and mobilization (Caiani & Parenti, 2013).

In this book, I shed light on their online political communication and mobilization, but investigating the online dimension is not a primary goal per se. It offers no empirical comparison between online and offline communication among anti-Islamic initiatives. Instead, their online presence and activity are a source for "naturally occurring" information (Shah, Cappella, & Neuman, 2015, p. 7) which would otherwise prove difficult to gather. Our digital lives leave traces that can be "compiled into comprehensive pictures of both individual and group behavior, with the potential to transform our understanding of our lives, organizations, and societies" (Lazer et al., 2009, p. 721).

The online data stems exclusively from Facebook. Globally, Facebook is the most prominent online platform for activism and information dissemination with over 2 billion members as of June 2016, exceeding the more studied Twitter by 1.7 billion. By 2015, six out of ten Americans aged 18–33 and five out of ten of those aged 34–49 got their political news on Facebook, and close to one in three were members of issue-based groups (Duggan, 2015, pp. 8–12). The data were gathered using the web scraper Netvizz, which is accessible as an application on Facebook (Rieder, 2013). Netvizz lets us gather content from specific Facebook groups and pages, as well as connections between groups. In order to circumvent limits on data gathering set by Facebook, I operated with 12 different Facebook accounts connected to an equal number of unique email accounts.

Networks

The network analysis started with the purposive sampling of the Facebook pages of 11 anti-Islamic initiatives in Norway, Britain, and Germany, and 16 of their offshoots across the world, which in network terminology are described as seeds. Prominent groups include the English Defence League, Stop Islamization of Europe and PEGIDA Deutschland. These are key actors that undisputedly belong to the category under scrutiny. See endnote for the full list.[3] The subsequent boundaries of the network were not defined a priori, but were discovered through a "snowball saturation" approach which extended two steps out from each individual Facebook page, capturing three subsets. The first step traces the connection between the 27 seeds in subset 1 and newly discovered nodes, which form subset 2. The second step identifies all ties between the nodes in subset 2 and the ties they have back to the seeds in subset 1, as well as the other nodes they connect to in the third subset. In the final step, we see whether nodes in subset 3 have ties which connect them back to subsets 1 and/or 2. At no point are ties between initiatives assumed; they are only empirically found. In sum, all possible interrelations between the groups contained in the universe of cases are accounted for. The two-step snowball approach provides data which can tell us the scope, geographical distribution, and configuration of relations between anti-Islamic initiatives. Crucially, it also lets us empirically identify relations to groups that have a different ideological orientation. As Christopoulos and Aubke state, the merit of this approach is that it gives us a comprehensive overview of a network when the boundaries are difficult to predefine (2014, p. 17). Peripheral groups that tie in, but whose ties are not reciprocated, however, are not captured in the analysis. The network structure is also influenced by "where we start the ball rolling" (Hanneman & Riddle, 2005), unless our analysis extends to all the potential subsets.

Ties between the initiatives are identified through likes. Moderators can like another page or group on Facebook on behalf of their own group or page, just as individual users can. See Chapter 6 for an elaboration on the functions and qualitative meaning of Facebook likes between pages and groups.

Data was collected in March 2015 and March 2016. While not truly longitudinal, it allows for a comparison between the network configuration at two points in time. The same 27 initiative pages were used as starting points at both intervals, capturing a network of 3,654 and 4,594 groups and pages, respectively.

Different measures are used to describe and analyze networks. The analyses in this book include measures of centrality and modularity, as well as block models to describe the structure of the network.

Centrality measures characterize the position of a node in the network, with degree, centrality, and closeness centrality being the most common (see e.g. Freeman, Roeder, & Mulholland, 1979). Degree centrality gives us the normalized sum of row and column degrees, which means that an individual node with a high degree of centrality is connected with many others. This should give them an easier access to resources – ranging from financial to ideological (Walther & Christopoulos, 2015). Betweenness centrality tells us a group's relative position as a broker or gatekeeper between other nodes in the network, whereas closeness centrality measures the inverse of the average distance from one node to other nodes in the network. Nodes with a high score in closeness centrality are closer to others, and should therefore be able to spread information with relative ease. In addition to these measures, I operate with "honest brokerage measures" to pinpoint actors who provide unique connections or exclusive control of resources between other actors (Christopoulos & Quaglia, 2009). These distinguishes between pure brokerage, weak brokerage, and no brokerage. Pure brokerage means that there are no

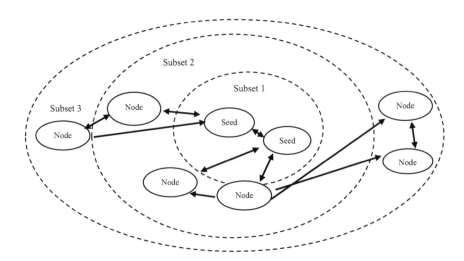

FIGURE 3.1   Illustration of the three subsets within the network analyses

other ties between any pair of alters joined by a broker, whereas weak brokerage means that one directed tie is allowed between pairs of alters joined by a broker. Non-brokerage means that alters who have ties to a broker also have two-way ties with each other (Walther & Christopoulos, 2015, p. 13).

Modularity reflects the concentration of edges (connections) within a given module, which is a subset of the entire network, compared with a random distribution of edges between all the given nodes, regardless of clustering. The ability to locate local substructures is one of the most interesting features of network analysis. Not only can we say something about the whole network and the individual groups, but we can also see the way a network divides into different cliques (Hanneman & Riddle, 2005). Here, I use the modularity scores to create aggregates, where individual nodes in a graph represent entire communities of groups according to the modularity scores they have been awarded. This means that instead of showing like-ties between specific initiatives on Facebook (where the maximum is 1–1), ties can vary in strength according to the number of aggregate likes that flow between the specific communities.

Supplementing this, block modelling is a key approach for uncovering tie strength both within and between network segments (Hanneman & Riddle, 2005), allowing us to say something about the structural connectivity for the various segments. Block modelling is particularly useful when it comes to identifying whether the network exhibits a strong core-periphery structure. I include density matrices which show us the correlation between observed scores and scores which should be present if each node had ties to the other within a segment, and between segments (block).

In all of these cases, the network analyses are used to describe and analyze the transnational anti-Islamic networks in their entirety, not on a comparative country-by-country basis.

Text as data

Whereas textual information was primarily analyzed qualitatively, with quantitative social scientists focussing on numerical data, the massive amounts of textual data and advances in computational techniques allow us to treat and analyze text as text on a large scale. Today, much of the data being compiled and analyzed in the social sciences is in textual form (Shah et al., 2015, p. 12).

The concluding empirical section of the book consists of a multi-pronged analysis of the contents in 298 of the anti-Islamic initiatives which were identified in the network analysis from 2016. They form the subset of anti-Islamic initiatives where the members were active – posting and commenting – in August 2016. The data from these initiatives amounts to 1,799,970 observations consisting of posts, shares, likes and comments between the period of 12–18 August 2016. The posts and comments are rich sources of textual data.

The analysis consists of two main sections. In the first section, I investigate how "regular" activists write about the issues which are included in the anti-Islamic initiatives collective action framing (Chapter 5) through triangulation. In the second section, I investigate which emotions and messages drive internal mobilization and the diffusion of messages. Computational analyses of big data provides new means of triangulation in multimethod confirmation (Shah et al., 2015, p. 7). I use automated sentiment analysis and word network analysis supplemented by qualitative analysis of associated text. As a counter-point to my approach, which employs "an interdisciplinary skill set that draws from traditional social sciences, statistics, and computer science" (Miller, 2011, p. 1815), some scholars have argued that qualitative analysis, and indeed hypothesis testing, is made obsolete by massive amounts of data and computational analyses (Anderson, 2008, p. 108), such as natural language processing, sentiment, and network analysis.

Keywords such as "Muslim", "women", "democracy", "violence" form the backbone and starting point for the tools used to investigate the corpus of text in the first section. The keywords form what I describe as "seeds" for one-mode word networks. These identify the co-occurrence of the selected keyword alongside others in a sentence after filtering out stop words (e.g. "so", "that", "to", "go"). The third approach used to qualitatively investigate and validate the patterns which emerge from the sentiment analysis and word networks is keywords in context (KWIC). KWIC transcripts provide the entire sentences in which the key words are embedded.

Research shows that emotional states can be transferred to others via emotional contagion through personal networks (Fowler & Christakis, 2008). An ethically controversial experimental study conducted on Facebook users indicates that this is also the case with online networks without in-person contact (Kramer, Guillory, & Hancock, 2014). The impact of emotions and sentiments can also be studied without experimental interference. Automated sentiment analysis is the most novel, and in some regards advanced, approach used. I use automated sentiment analysis as one of the tools to scrutinize the contents in the anti-Islamic activist groups, as well as identifying which emotions and associated messages drive mobilization and diffusion. I use the Canadian National Research Council's (NRC) Word-Emotion Association Lexicon (Mohammad & Turney, 2010, 2013), available as a package for the open software R. The NRC-Canada system ranked first in several competitions at the annual international Conference on Semantic Evaluation Exercises (Mohammad, Kiritchenko, & Zhu, 2013; Zhu, Kiritchenko, & Mohammad, 2014; Kiritchenko, Zhu, & Mohammad, 2014). The lexicon contains association connections between words and positive and negative sentiments, as well as eight emotions divided into four pairs: 1) joy–sadness; 2) trust–disgust; 3) fear–anger; 4) surprise–anticipation. The lexicon has valence and emotion associations for about 25,000 words, coded using paid respondents on Amazon Turk. The more words there are in a piece of text, the higher the validity.

To investigate which emotions and messages drive mobilization and diffusion, I use multilevel regression analysis. This is used because the data has an inherent multilevel structure, such that comments, likes, shares, and reactions are nested within – or, more precisely, attached to – posts. For an overview of multilevel regression analysis and modelling, see for instance Snijders and Bosker (2011).

Data collection ethics

As this overview has shown, I draw on a broad range of data and methodologies to map the anti-Islamic social movement and the expansion of the far right. The material for Chapters 4–5 consists of publicly available and publicly *intended* statements, in addition to interview material from some of the leaders and representatives in Norway. Shortly after the interviews were conducted, the transcriptions were sent to those leaders with the offer of anonymity, redaction, and retraction.

In the second part, the network analysis is at an organizational level and does not reveal information about individuals. In the subsequent analysis of the content, individual activists (users) are anonymized prior at the point of download using the Netvizz application. That means that the names of those who post, comment, like, share, and react have never been a part of any data examined by me. In addition, the data from these pages is treated as an aggregate corpus of text. In other words, the contents of a post or comment is not traced back to the specific pages where they were posted.

Notes

1 I use the word initiative(s) as a generic term referring to the broad panoply of collective actors that engage in anti-Islamic activism, ranging from street-based activist groups, think-tanks, political parties, websites, and online communities.
2 I conducted semi-structured interviews with the leader of the activist group Stop Islamization of Norway (SIAN), the alternative news site Document.no and spokesperson for the self-described think-tank Human Rights Service (HRS). The interviewees were selected and approached due to the central position their respective organizations hold within the anti-Islamic scene in Norway. The interviews were carried out in October 2010.
3 List of the 27 initial anti-Islamic Facebook pages used as seeds for the two-step network analyses:

  1) Document.no, 2) Human Rights Service, 3) Pegida Norway, 4) Pegida Norge, 5) Pegida Bergen og Vestlandet, 6) Pegida United Kingdom, 7) PEGIDA, 8) PEGIDA Deutschland, 9) Pegida – BW Stuttgart, 10) Pegida BW – Heilbronn, 11) PEGIDA France, 12) PEGIDA Iceland, 13) Pegida in Poland, 14) Pegida Spain, 15) English Defence League, 16) Norwegian Defence League, 17) March For England, 18) Liberty Great Britain, 19) Stopp islamiseringen av Norge, 20) Partiet Stop Islamiseringen Af Danmark, 21) Stop Islamization of India, 22) Stop Islamization of Nations, 23) Stop Islamization of America, 24) Stop Islamization of Myanmar, 25) Stop Islamization of Canada, 26) Stop the Islamization in Spain, 27) Stop Islamization of Europe Deutschland.

Bibliography

Anderson, C. (2008). The end of theory: The data deluge makes the scientific method obsolete. *Wired Magazine, 16*(7), 16–17.

Benford, R. D., & Snow, D. A. (2000). Framing processes and social movements: An overview and assessment. *Annual Review of Sociology, 26*(1), 611–639.

Betz, H-G., & Meret, S. (2009). Revisiting Lepanto: The political mobilization against Islam in contemporary Western Europe. *Patterns of Prejudice, 43*(3–4), 313–334.

Caiani, M., & Parenti, L. (2013). 8 extreme right organizations and online politics. *Politics and the Internet in Comparative Context: Views from the Cloud, 11*, 135.

Castells, M. (2012). *Networks of outrage and hope: Social movements in the Internet age.* Oxford: John Wiley & Sons.

Christopoulos, D., & Aubke, F. (2014). Data collection for social network analysis in tourism research. In *Knowledge networks and tourism* (pp. 126–142). New York: Routledge.

Christopoulos, D., & Quaglia, L. (2009). Network constraints in EU banking regulation: The capital requirements directive. *Journal of Public Policy, 29*(2), 179–200.

Fowler, J. H., & Christakis, N. A. (2008). Dynamic spread of happiness in a large social network: Longitudinal analysis over 20 years in the Framingham heart study. *British Medical Journal, 337*, a2338.

Freeman, L. C., Roeder, D., & Mulholland, R. R. (1979). Centrality in social networks: II. Experimental results. *Social Networks, 2*(2), 119–141.

Goffman, E. (1959). *The presentation of self in everyday life.* Edinburgh: University of Edinburgh Social Sciences Research Centre.

Goffman, E. (1974). *Frame analysis: An essay on the organization of experience.* New York: Harper & Row.

Hanneman, R. A., & Riddle, M. (2005). *Introduction to social network methods.* Published online. Retrieved from http://faculty.ucr.edu/~hanneman/nettext/

Kiritchenko, S., Zhu, X., & Mohammad, S. M. (2014). Sentiment analysis of short informal texts. *Journal of Artificial Intelligence Research, 50*, 723–762.

Kramer, A. D., Guillory, J. E., & Hancock, J. T. (2014). Experimental evidence of massive-scale emotional contagion through social networks. *Proceedings of the National Academy of Sciences, 111*(24), 8788–8790.

Lazer, D., Pentland, A. S., Adamic, L., Aral, S., Barabasi, A. L., Brewer, D., & Jebara, T. (2009). Life in the network: The coming age of computational social science. *Science, 323*(5915), 721.

Miller, G. (2011). Social scientists wade into the tweet stream. *Science, 333*(6051), 1814–1815.

Mohammad, S. M., Kiritchenko, S., & Zhu, X. (2013c). *NRC-Canada: Building the state-of-the-art in sentiment analysis of tweets.* arXiv preprint arXiv:1308.6242.

Mohammad, S. M., & Turney, P. D. (2010, June). *Emotions evoked by common words and phrases: Using mechanical Turk to create an emotion lexicon.* Proceedings of the NAACL HLT 2010 workshop on computational approaches to analysis and generation of emotion in text. Association for Computational Linguistics, pp. 26–34.

Mohammad, S. M., & Turney, P. D. (2013a). Crowdsourcing a word – emotion association lexicon. *Computational Intelligence, 29*(3), 436–465.

Mohammad, S. M., & Turney, P. D. (2013b). *NRC emotion lexicon.* NRC Technical Report. Ottawa, Canada: National Research Council Canada.

Rieder, B. (2013, May). *Studying Facebook via data extraction: The Netvizz application.* Proceedings of the 5th annual ACM web science conference, pp. 346–355.

Ruths, D., & Pfeffer, J. (2014). Social media for large studies of behavior. *Science, 346*(6213), 1063–1064.

Shah, D. V., Cappella, J. N., & Neuman, W. R. (2015). Big data, digital media, and computational social science: Possibilities and perils. *The ANNALS of the American Academy of Political and Social Science, 659*(1), 6–13.

Snijders, T. A., & Bosker, R. J. (2011). *Multilevel analysis: An introduction to basic and advanced multilevel modeling.* London: SAGE.

Walther, O. J., & Christopoulos, D. (2015). Islamic terrorism and the Malian rebellion. *Terrorism and Political Violence, 27*(3), 497–519.

Zhu, X., Kiritchenko, S., & Mohammad, S. (2014, August). *NRC-Canada-2014: Recent improvements in the sentiment analysis of Tweets.* SemEval@ COLING, pp. 443–447.

4

EXPANSION AND LEGACY

Introduction

The overarching turn on the far right from focussing on ethnicity and national-ity to focussing on Muslims and Islam is driven by two factors. First, there is an anti-Islamic *reorientation* among pre-existing far-right initiatives and an anti-Islamic *expansion* of the far right with the creation of new initiatives. As with the other empirical chapters, this chapter focuses on the anti-Islamic expansion. Although a variety of populist radical right parties such as Lega Nord (LN), Belgian Vlaams Belang (VB), French Front National (FN), Norwegian Progress Party (FrP), and Sweden Democrats (SD) have undergone an ideological reorientation,[1] the expan-sion is predominantly a story of extra-parliamentary activism. Organizationally, anti-Islamic activism outside of party politics takes many forms, from think-tanks, blogs, and alternative news sites to street-oriented protest groups. Several of the street-oriented protest groups such as Stop Islamization of Denmark (SIAD) and the English Defence League (EDL) have tried to enter party politics, but failed to get above electoral thresholds. The expansion also includes some successful political parties, however, such as the Dutch List Pim Fortuyn and Geert Wilders' Party for Freedom.

Older populist radical right parties have intermittently mobilized by explicitly targeting Islam and Muslims for several decades. The former leader of the Norwe-gian Progress Party, Carl I. Hagen, was probably one of the first politicians to push an anti-Islamic agenda when he toured the country in the run-up to the 1987 elec-tions with a fictitious letter from "Muhammed" which stated that Muslims would take over Norway and replace the cross in the flag with the star and crescent moon (Bangstad, 2013). However, the anti-Islamic positions for which these far-right ini-tiatives are the carriers did not really coalesce into a salient and relatively coherent worldview before the turn of the century, informed by the works of the late historian Bernard Lewis and political scientist Samuel Huntington. Both scholars came to see Islam as the main challenge to the West, articulated in Bernard's article "The Roots of Muslim Rage" (1990) and Samuel Huntington's "The Clash of Civilizations?" (1993). In his oft-quoted article, Huntington argues that civilizations are fundamentally different and durable products of centuries, and that Islamic civilization is a particular challenge to the West because of its insurgence and demographic growth; something which would inevitably lead to a bloody clash.

While the importance of these intellectual treatises should not be overstated, some regarded them as prophetic after Al-Qaeda's attacks on the United States on 11 September 2001 (9/11). In contrast, it is no overstatement to say that increased politicization of hostility towards Muslims and the anti-Islamic expansion of the far right has been profoundly impacted by events such as 9/11 (Bail, 2012), other jihadist terror attacks, and political assassinations in the name of Islam, as well as public controversies such as the Muhammed cartoon crisis. These have contributed to creating what Swidler (1986, p. 282) calls "unsettled times". These are rare historical periods when large-scale crises or unprecedented events generate cultural change (McAdam, 1982; Sewell, 1996; Wagner-Pacifici, 2010). Historical turning points of this kind have three features in common (Abbott, 1997). First, they create widespread public uncertainty because very few people anticipated these events (Kurzman, 2004), undermining the legitimacy of the political establishment. This helps explain precisely why the clash of civilizations narrative became so potent. Second, this creates political and discursive opportunities for challengers to alter the cultural trajectory of a society (e.g. Amenta, Caren, Chiarello, & Su, 2010; Meyer & Minkoff, 2004; Soule & Olzak, 2004). Finally, these dramatic events have triggered strong emotional reactions – moral shocks – which propel people into action (Jasper, 1998). Almost all the instances of anti-Islamic mobilization and the establishment of activist initiatives cited in this chapter can be traced to one such event or another. Not all moral shocks stem from dramatic events that affect all of society or dominate the public debate. Some of the people who went on to establish an anti-Islamic initiative were shocked into action by local demonstrations of Islamists and others *they* associated with Islam and political violence. This was the case with the EDL in Luton, Britain and PEGIDA in Dresden, Germany.

This chapter begins with an analysis of the expansion of anti-Islamic activism between 2001 and 2017, before moving on to a comparative analysis of the biographical backgrounds of the leaders and representatives behind the groups, think-tanks and parties.

The four waves of expansion

Starting with the creation of the online counter-jihadi community, the anti-Islamic expansion of the far right has undergone four waves between 2001 and 2017 (Table 4.1). Each wave is defined by the creation of a new activist group which managed to establish offshoots in several countries. This first counter-jihadi wave

TABLE 4.1 The four waves of transnational anti-Islamic expansion from 2001 to 2017

Time period	First wave (2001–2005)	Second wave (2005–2009)	Third wave (2009–2014)	Fourth wave (2014–)
Starting point	United States, the Netherlands	Denmark, Britain	Britain	Germany
Main initiative	Little Green Footballs, List Pim Fortuyn	Stop Islamization, Act!	Defence Leagues	PEGIDA
Primary arenas	Traditional websites, party politics	Traditional websites and streets	Facebook and streets	Facebook and streets
Moral shock	11 September 2001 terror attacks	Muhammed cartoon crisis	Islamist picketing of soldier funerals	German Salafists clash with protesting Kurds, *Charlie Hebdo* terror attack

was followed by the spread of Stop Islamization groups, and offshoots and affiliates of the EDL and finally PEGIDA. Online activism has been a crucial factor in all four waves. The first wave stands out for its two parallel genesis points – both online and within party politics. The three latter waves have also been visible on the streets. Each subsequent wave of activism has led to the solidification of transnational, organizational networks between the myriad of anti-Islamic initiatives. Major initiatives such as the EDL and PEGIDA have continued to add to the online fauna after dwindling away from the streets. They each are notable in their own right, but also because they have reinvigorated think-tanks, blogs, and alternative news sites established during previous waves. More than specific forms activism, these waves of expansions are processes of ideological diffusion.

These four waves of anti-Islamic expansion and ideological diffusion are proof that organized opposition to Islam, and Muslim culture and immigration, exists across Europe and the West. Since the outset, it has been a transatlantic affair with cooperation between American and European initiatives. Nonetheless, some countries stand out as strongholds of anti-Islamic activism – countries where a wave of anti-Islamic activism began, or are home to prominent and long-lasting initiatives which undergird these waves. These stronghold countries are the United States, the Netherlands, Britain, Norway, Denmark, and Germany.

First wave – online and party politics

The organized, explicitly anti-Islamic far right outside of mainstream party politics started in 2000 with Arne Tumyr's Norwegian Forum against Islamization (*Forum mot islamisering*).[2] At that time, it stood out as an isolated anomaly with its singular focus on Islam and Muslims, but not for long. On 11 September 2001, Al-Qaeda struck the United States with four coordinated attacks in New York and Washington, D.C., killing 2,996. It was the largest attack on American soil since Pearl Harbor.[3] These attacks triggered the transformation of the website Little Green Footballs (LGF) from a predominantly non-political forum led by a self-proclaimed liberal into a hotbed of agitation against "Islamic fascism" and the creation of the self-defined counter-jihadist[4] scene (Munksgaard, 2010, p. 48). This marked the first wave of anti-Islamic activism, and at its peak in 2004, the blog was listed as the sixth most popular worldwide.[5] The success of LGF inspired the growth of several other, now more prominent counter-jihadist blogs such as Jihad Watch by Robert Spencer and Gates of Vienna (GoV) in 2003, and Atlas Shrugs by Pamela Geller in 2004.[6] GoV eventually took over the mantle as the dominant counter-jihadi web community, placing their struggle against Islam in a historical context:

> The roots of the movement [Islam, sic.] can be traced back to antiquity, since the first violent *razzia* against Christian civilization in the seventh century, under Mohammed and the early Caliph.
>
> *(Gates of Vienna, 24 November 2011)*

They took their name from the Ottoman siege of Vienna in 1683, an event the counter-jihadists portray as a turning point for Western civilization. On their website, they present a list of points they claim to be fighting for: civil liberties, the rights of women and homosexuals, religious freedom, and opposition to religiously sanctioned violence. They frame their struggle in stark terms, stating "To oppose the Counterjihad is, in a sense, to support jihad". Their most prominent contributor has perhaps been the Norwegian blogger known by the alias Fjordman, otherwise known as Peder Nøstvold Jensen. GoV has since become notorious due to the use of texts from many of their key contributors, not least from Fjordman (Gardell, 2014), by the terrorist Anders Behring Breivik.

The newly formed counter-jihadi community found a unifying narrative in Bat Ye'or's (Gisele Littman) Eurabia thesis, first publicized in 2002.[7] Ye'or claimed that the European Union had entered into a conspiratorial alliance with Muslim states to create a single unified region – Eurabia. This collaboration has supposedly been ongoing since the petroleum crisis of 1973, marking the European Union as "spiritual heirs of the 1930s Nazism and anti-Semitism".[8]

In parallel with the establishment of the online counter-jihad emanating from the website LGF, the Lebanese-born activist Brigitte Gabriel set up the organization American Congress for Truth, to inform the American public about "Islamofascism" in the wake of the 9/11 attacks.[9] Gabriel describes herself as a Christian "survivor of Islamic terror", claiming that she does not want the United States to share the fate of Lebanon.

In the wake of the 9/11 terror attacks, and partially interwoven with them, the Netherlands witnessed a development in anti-Islamic activity when it burst onto the stage of party politics in earnest. It began with the openly homosexual and public intellectual Pim Fortuyn, who published a pamphlet entitled "The Islamization of our Culture: Dutch identity as foundational" in 1997, inspired by the likes of Huntington and Lewis. Dutch media picked up Fortuyn's message after the terror attacks against the United States (Eyerman, 2008). Shortly after this surge in media attention, Fortuyn founded his own party, LPF. The main issues were stricter immigration and asylum policy, a complete halt to immigration from Muslim countries, and assimilation rather than integration.[10] Fortuyn's arguments cemented the idea of Islam as a civilizational threat to Dutch culture, represented as a unified entity with four core elements: the separation of church and state, respect between the genders and between adults and children, and individual rather than collective responsibility (Eyerman, 2008, p. 104).

On 6 May 2002, Pim Fortuyn was assassinated. The murderer claimed he had committed the act on behalf of the country's Muslim population. A week after Fortuyn's death, his party won 24% of the vote and 26 seats in the Dutch Parliament (ibid., p. 45). The party fell victim to bickering and infighting not long after, but had by then contributed to a fundamental shift in the political debate on Islam, immigration and multiculturalism.

Two years later, the Netherlands was rocked by the murder of Theo van Gogh, a high-profile film director who had just released a film entitled *Submission* about women and Islam, together with the Somali-born politician, author, and activist Ayan Hirsi Ali. After killing van Gogh, the murderer left a note pinned to his body with a knife. It contained a diatribe against the West, addressed to Hirsi Ali. The fact that the killer, Mohammed Bouyeri, was a 26-year-old Dutch-Moroccan further polarized the debate about Islam and the position of Muslims in Dutch society. At around the same time, the politician Geert Wilders took up Fortuyn's anti-Islamic mantle, and set up his own party, PVV. Ever since, Wilders has waged a continuous political campaign against Islam and what he perceives as the Islamization of the Netherlands. He has compared the Quran with Hitler's *Mein Kampf*, drawing clear parallels between Islam and Nazism. The party's outspoken goal has been to stop all Muslim immigration, to halt the building of mosques, to ban the Quran, and to outlaw hijabs. Wilders is portrayed as a hero by anti-Islamic activists across Europe and in the United States for his stand against Islam and Muslims in spite of an unknown number of death threats and having to live with police protection.[11]

Outside the Netherlands, Al-Qaeda sympathizers bombed commuter trains in Madrid on 11 March 2004, killing 191 and wounding 1,800. A little over a year later, Muslim extremists set off three bombs on separate underground trains in London during the morning rush hour 7 July 2005 (7/7). An hour later, a fourth bomb went off on a bus. The attacks in London cost the lives of 52 travellers and four suicide bombers, with 7,001 injured. Together with the Dutch developments, these attacks formed the backdrop for what turned out to be a long-lasting international crisis.

Second wave – streets and alliances

On 30 September 2005, Denmark's biggest newspaper, *Jyllands-Posten*, printed 12 cartoons of the prophet Mohammed. These ranged from relatively benign to provocative, the most famous being one of Mohammed with a bomb in his turban.[12] In November 2005, the cartoons received a lot of negative attention in several Muslim majority countries, among them Egypt, where the government played a leading role as agitator (Hjärpe, 2006, p. 165). On 9 January 2006, the Norwegian Christian conservative newspaper *Magazinet* printed a replica of the cartoons. Shortly thereafter, the conflict escalated. A long list of organizations and prominent figures, mostly in the Middle East, condemned the publications as blasphemous. By 4 February, the Danish and Norwegian embassies in Damascus had been set on fire. In the days that followed, large demonstrations took place in a long list of countries with a Muslim majority and in front of Danish embassies in major European cities. The protesters chanted slogans against Norway, Denmark, and the United States. For the first time, Danish and Norwegian flags were burnt in demonstrations in other countries – scenes closely associated with anti-war and anti-colonial activism towards the United States and major European powers with a recent colonial past.

In turn, these reactions by Muslim citizens and states spurred a great expansion of organized, anti-Islamic mobilization in Western Europe and North America. The clarion call was free speech. It propelled the counter-jihadist community to mobilize in the streets for the first time, with rallies for free speech held in London and Copenhagen.[13] After these demonstrations, participants from GoV got together and formed the 910 Group. Their goal was "organizing a movement that could actually initiate action against the encroachment of sharia in Western Society".[14] In Denmark, Anders Gravers Pedersen set up the organization Stop Islamization of Denmark (*Stop Islamiseringen af Danmark*, SIAD) inspired by the Danish resistance to Nazi occupation during World War II. Shortly thereafter Gravers Pedersen established the pan-European umbrella organization Stop Islamization of Europe (SIOE) together with Stephen Gash, who ran a small initiative called No Sharia Here (later Stop Islamization in Britain). With this, the anti-Islamic protest scene started to gain traction. Stop Islamization offshoots were subsequently set up in several Western European countries and have remained a fixture among the anti-Islamic and counter-jihadi community since.[15]

In the United States, anti-Islamic activism also solidified with the establishment of the organization Act! For America in 2007 by Brigitte Gabriel. Act! is dedicated to combatting "islamofascism" for the "survival of our nation, the protection of the United States of America and the Western values upon which our nation was built, and the preservation of the freedom of religion and speech".[16] Act! members have been described as predominantly "evangelical Christian conservatives, hardline defenders of Israel (both Jews and Christians) and Tea Party Republicans".[17] As of 2017, they claim to have 750,000 members in the United States. They focus on lobbying state and federal officials, and have initiated a drive for so-called anti-Sharia bills in state legislatures. Besides Gabriel, the leadership includes Guy Rodgers, a former consultant for John McCain's 2008 presidential campaign and director for Ralph Reed's Christian Coalition. Several prominent conservatives have served on Act! For America's board, including Michael T. Flynn, who worked as United States National Security Advisor in the first months of Donald Trump's presidential administration.

Besides triggering the formation of new initiatives, the crisis increased the traffic on counter-jihadi websites such as Atlas Shrugs and GoV. In addition, it caused a number of pre-existing initiatives and alternative news outlets to adopt the anti-Islamic cause, much in the same way that Little Green Footballs did after 9/11. This was the case for the German website Politically Incorrect (PI), the Norwegian Document.no, Human Rights Service (HRS), and the Danish Snaphanen.dk, Uriasposten and Trykkefrihedsselskabet (TFS). These initiatives' websites have large readerships in their respective countries, and have intermittently collaborated with each other over the years.[18] With the exception of PI, however, they do not define themselves as counter-jihadists. This is in contrast to the protest groups and the blog community spawned from LGF after the first "moral shock" of 9/11.

In 2001, Rita Karlsen established HRS as a politically independent think-tank, and have since been granted government funding. The journalist Hege Storhaug joined HRS a year later. With Storhaug on board, HRS initially worked with the plight of Muslim girls and female genital mutilation as their primary issues, but became outspokenly anti-Islamic over the years, with the cartoon crisis marking the tipping point. In 2015 Storhaug's book *Islam. The 11th Plague (Islam. Den 11. Landeplage)* became a bestseller. In it, she argues that mosques should be banned and that anti-Semitism in the Quran is worse than what is expressed in Hitler's *Mein Kampf*. As of 2017, HRS are among most widely shared on Norway's social media[19] articles.

Journalist Hans Rustad set up Document.no in 2003 as a conservative counter-weight in the Norwegian public debate. Initially much of the coverage was about the American war on terror and the invasions of Afghanistan and Iraq with a more favourable perspective on President George W. Bush and the Republicans. As the cartoon crisis escalated, it retained the international outlook, but almost exclusively focussed on (un)covering issues related to Islam and Muslims. By 2017, it had become one of the most read online news outlets in Norway.

Meanwhile in Denmark, the blog Uriasposten (2003) was established by the historian Kim Møller. This was followed by the prominent blog Snaphanen.dk by Steen Raaschou and TFS, co-founded by the journalist Lars Hedegaard, historian David Gress, philosopher Kai Sørlander, priest and politician Søren Krarup, priest, journalist and politician Jesper Langballe and Max Stugbgaard in 2004. Both Snaphanen and Uriasposten have consistently been among the top-ranked blogs in Denmark, whereas TFS has had significant influence in the public debate in general.

Like the Norwegian Document.no, the German teacher Stefan Herre founded PI in 2004 after the re-election of George W. Bush. When the cartoon crisis unfolded, PI went from being a conservative and pro-American blog to a fully-fledged anti-Islamic initiative. In 2006, and concomitant with its adoption of anti-Islamic agitation, it became one of the most popular blogs in Germany and has retained a large readership since.[20] Beyond the online sphere, the crisis also marked the start of anti-Islamic protests in Germany. The activist group and self-proclaimed human rights organization Federal Association of Citizens' Movements (*Bundesverband der Bürgerbewegungen*)[21] was established in 2003 to combat Turkish accession to the EU, and became explicitly anti-Islamic during the onset of the cartoon crisis.

In 2006, another German anti-Islamic activist group, calling itself Pax Europa, was also established. Together with the Danish SIAD and the British No Sharia Here, Pax Europa planned a demonstration against the alleged Islamization of Europe in Brussels on 11 September 2007, but was barred by government officials. In 2008, Pax Europa and the Federal Association of Citizens' Movements merged, changing their name to Citizens' Movement Pax Europa (*Bürgerbewegung Pax Europa*, BPE).

BPE's attempts to mobilize were partly inspired by the successful "UK and Scandinavia Counterjihad Summit" in Copenhagen on 14 April 2007, which came about through the collaboration of the Stop Islamization community and 910 Group from GoV. The main organizer, SIAD, stated that they chose the location as a direct consequence of the cartoon crisis. This was followed up with a second gathering in Brussels in October the same year. The conference was hosted by the Flemish populist radical right Vlaams Belang, with prominent speakers such as Lars Hedegaard (TFI), and the originator of the Eurabia thesis, Bat Ye'or.[22] The close cooperation with Vlaams Belang and the presence of Kent Ekeroth from the Swedish radical right Sweden Democrats (SD) caused a rupture among the originators of the online counter-jihadist community. For instance, the founder of the, until then, most prominent counter-jihadi site LGF attempted to distance himself and his blog from the scene, which he saw as increasingly influenced by right-wing "kooks", extremists and racists (Munksgaard, 2010, p. 50).

In the following years, the Stop Islamization and GoV community dominated the anti-Islamic activist scene, convening counter-jihadi conferences in Vienna (2008), Copenhagen (2009), and Zurich (2010). The conferences were an important platform for building ties between established populist radical right parties and the broader fauna of anti-Islamic activist initiatives. In Zurich, the Swiss People's Party (*Schweizerische Volkspartei*, SVP) showcased their successful campaign to ban the building of minarets in Switzerland. One of the key events was a workshop, by a French organization called Alliance to Stop Sharia, on how to stop any alleged Islamization and the introduction of Sharia by fighting for the rights guaranteed by the Universal Declaration of Human Rights and several Western constitutions. Alongside these gatherings, the Stop Islamization community continued to grow. The Norwegian activists joined the umbrella organization SIOE in 2008, taking the name Stop Islamization of Norway (SIAN). Their stated goal was to "counteract, stop and reverse the Islamization of Europe".[23] In this period, Stop Islamization initiatives never managed to mobilize a large number of activists for street demonstrations, however, and remained mostly active in other forms. For instance, the Norwegian group SIAN also arranged reading groups, where they discussed the Quran and other books on Islam. It was not before the advent of the EDL in 2009 that we saw large-scale anti-Islamic street activism.

Third wave – British reinvigoration and transnational solidification

The EDL began as a local initiative calling themselves the United People of Luton, protesting against a gathering of extreme Islamists from the (banned) group

Al-Mahajiroun. The Islamists were themselves staging a demonstration against the British military, with slogans such as "Anglian Soldiers: cowards, killers, extremists" (Gable, Cressy, & Woodson, 2009).

Like the other counter-jihadi and anti-Islamic initiatives that came before them, they claimed to be fighting for democracy and freedom of speech. Like the Norwegian HRS, the Stop Islamization groups, and BPE, they also explicitly labelled themselves as a human rights organization protecting against the infringement of human rights, including the right to "to protest against radical Islam's encroachment into the lives of non-Muslims".[24] In a short time, the EDL became one of the most active protest groups in Europe, staging over 50 demonstrations between 2009 and 2011, regularly gathering between 1,000 and 3,000 activists.[25] In doing so, they rapidly managed to establish a national media profile and more than 80 local divisions, amassing over 80,000 Facebook supporters by 2010 (Goodwin, 2013). In an ongoing attempt to counter the stigma of racism, they also established a Jewish division and a Sikh division. In their marches, they carried both the rainbow flag used by the LGBT community and the Israeli flag. An issue on which they campaigned heavily was the alleged abuse and grooming of non-Muslim women.

Their "success" and media attention drew admiration from the older counter-jihadi and anti-Islamic community. For instance, GoV called them "the most significant anti-sharia movement in Europe".[26] In 2011, GoV arranged a London summit together with Stop Islamization[27] and other well-known public figures to build ties with the EDL. The main goal was to form a political party based on opposition to Islam. This led to the creation of the short-lived British Freedom Party (BFP) headed by Paul Weston, and supported by the EDL. In 2012, Tommy Robinson was named deputy leader of the BFP,[28] whereas Weston remained the chair until January 2013, when he was replaced by Kevin Carroll from the EDL. By then, the British Electoral Commission had already decommissioned the BFP two months earlier for failure to return the annual registration form.[29] The decommissioning of the BFP was shortly followed by the establishment of Liberty Great Britain (LGB), also headed by Weston.

These attempt to establish a party and run for elections was preceded by the Danish Anders Gravers Pedersen's SIAD in 2005, and subsequently the Freedom Party (*Die Freiheit − Bürgerrechtspartei für mehr Freiheit und Demokratie*, DF) in 2010. The German DF was headed by René Stadtkewitz, a local Christian Democratic Union (CDU) politician and leader of the activist group BPE. Stadtkewitz set up DF after he was expelled from the conservative CDU because he invited Geert Wilders to speak in Berlin. Wilders later gave his support to the German counterpart, and intended to include them in his own transnational anti-Islamic organization (International Freedom Alliance).[30]

The EDL made vigorous attempts to build offshoots and mobilize street activism in other countries, coordinating 18 Defence Leagues across Europe and North America.[31] They staged the first rally outside the United Kingdom on 30 October 2010, travelling to Amsterdam to show their support for Geert Wilders during his trial.[32] They held a second rally outside the United Kingdom in Denmark together with SIAD, SIAN, the Danish Defence League (DDL), and Norwegian Defence League (NDL) in Aarhus, 31 March 2012.[33] Despite these efforts and the willingness to travel abroad, Defence League groups outside the United Kingdom never managed to mobilize large numbers of on-the-street activists on their own. For instance, the NDL's first attempts to mobilize were an abject failure and only drew a handful of activists, swamped by journalists.[34]

Perhaps more importantly, the rapid rise of the EDL in the United Kingdom contributed the ongoing establishment of transnational, organizational connections among anti-Islamic initiatives at the top level. This process was already prominent during the second wave, and continued in 2010 when Pamela Geller and author Robert Spencer set up Stop Islamization of America (SIOA) at the request of Anders Gravers Pedersen.[35] In October 2010, representatives from BPE, Act! For America, and Stadtkewitz from the German DF travelled to Tel Aviv to speak at the Alliance of the European Freedom and National Parties Conference alongside Geert Wilders and other prominent populist radical right politicians.[36]

In 2011, the counter-jihadi and anti-Islamic community gathered in Stockholm to establish the umbrella organization Stop Islamization of Nations (SION). Their so-called President's Council consisted of Anders Gravers from SIAD/SIOE, Tommy Robinson and Kevin Carroll from the EDL, Debbie Robinson from the Australian Liberty Alliance, and Robert Spencer and Pamela Geller from SIOA/ Atlas Shrugs/Jihad Watch.[37] Their board included figures such as the far-right Swiss politician Oskar Freysinger and Stefan Herre of Politically Incorrect.

A year later, EDL figures attended the SION free speech conference in New York on 11 September 2012, where they co-founded the European Freedom Initiative. The trip proved unfortunate for Robinson, who was imprisoned after entering the United States illegally using a friend's passport.[38] American backers such as Pamela Geller and Robert Spencer attempted to help him and the EDL through fundraising. Robinson was later sentenced to ten months in prison.[39] The trip and subsequent imprisonment marked the beginning of a downward spiral driven by internal organizational troubles and increased police and state intervention. During the period of imprisonment, Robinson's close friend Kevin Carroll took over. Both, however, resigned in October 2013,[40] and Tommy Robinson joined the anti-radicalization think-tank Quilliam Foundation. The decline of the EDL in 2013 marked a two-year lull in anti-Islamic activity across Western Europe.

Fourth wave – PEGIDA and Eastward expansion

The rise and spread of PEGIDA is the fourth wave of anti-Islamic activism. Similarly to the establishment of the EDL in Luton, the moral shock leading to the creation of PEGIDA was a local event. It began when the founder, Lutz Bachmann, personally witnessed Kurdish supporters of the Kurdistan Workers Party (PKK) demonstrating against the Islamic State in Iraq and Syria (ISIS) in Dresden.[41] This was followed by clashes between Salafists and Kurds in Hamburg, something which garnered broad news coverage. Angered by the spread of what he saw as terrorism and extremism, Bachmann turned to Facebook, where he created a page entitled Peaceful Europeans against the Islamization of the West (later exchanging Peaceful for Patriotic).[42] Bachmann used this page as a platform to rally people for weekly marches through the city of Dresden. The marches and their slogan, "We are the people!", hark back to the demonstrations against the former DDR regime in East Germany. Initially only drawing a handful of participants, PEGIDA marches quickly ballooned in size. Within a month, it had become one of the biggest protest phenomena in East Germany since the fall of the Berlin Wall. The number of people marching under PEGIDA's banner reached a peak with approximately 25,000 participants in the week after the terror attacks on 7 January 2015 when two jihadists struck the offices of the French satirical magazine *Charlie Hebdo* in Paris, killing 13 and wounding 11.

Not long after, PEGIDA became beset by infighting which began when Bachmann resigned under mounting pressure after a photo of him posing with a "Hitler mustache" was leaked online.[43] On the advice of Frauke Petry, leader of AfD (*Alternative für Deutschland*, Alternative for Germany), several prominent figures also withdrew in the wake of Bachmann's resignation, establishing a competing group calling themselves Direct Democracy for Europe (*Direkte Demokratie für Europa*, DDE).[44]

Bachmann was quickly reinstated, but the internal leadership struggles continued. Following the wave of resignations, Tatjana Festerling became the new spokesperson alongside Bachmann. Before she became a leader in PEGIDA, Festerling had been active in AfD. Some months later, Festerling ran as a candidate for mayor in Dresden, where she received 9.6% of the vote in the first round. Festerling received the backing of key figures in the anti-Islamic movement, with Geert Wilders travelling to Dresden to speak on her behalf. Not long after she ran for mayor, however, she was expelled from PEGIDA. She has since been staging counter-protests against Bachmann by way of retaliation.[45]

At a more general level, there have also been informal relations between PEGIDA and AfD, but Petry and Bachmann shared a mutual dislike of each other. Bachmann has stated that he was open for the two initiatives to join forces and merge into one political party, as long as Petry resigned as AfD leader. On her part, Petry got the Saxonian AfD board to decree that AfD members should not appear as speakers or with party symbols at PEGIDA events.[46] Indicative of the strained relationship between the two, Bachmann established his own political party in 2016 – the Liberal Direct Democratic People's Party (*Freiheitlich Direktdemokratische Volkspartei*).[47] Despite the conflict with Petry and ongoing infighting, PEGIDA have been able to stage weekly marches through Dresden more or less unabated since the inception in October 2014 until the summer of 2017.

PEGIDA led to a revitalization of the anti-Islamic far right across Western Europe, drawing both older activists from the Stop Islamization and Defence League communities and new participants. Between January and June 2015, PEGIDA groups marched in Britain, Denmark, Austria, the Netherlands, and Belgium. PEGIDA Netherlands was one of the first offshoots, holding their first rally in the city of

Utrecht on 11 October 2015. Headed by Edwin Wagensveld, the rally was attended by Bachmann as well as Tommy Robinson.[48] They held several rallies between 2015 and 2016 in Amsterdam, Rotterdam and Apeldoorn.[49] On 18 March 2016, they held a protest in support of Geert Wilders during his second trial for inciting racism.[50]

After speaking at PEGIDA rallies in Utrecht, Dresden, and Cologne, the former EDL leader Robinson staged a return to the anti-Islamic activist scene in Britain by creating PEGIDA UK.[51] Unlike the heyday of the EDL between 2009 and 2011, with marches drawing up to 3,000 protesters, PEGIDA UK reached its peak with 400 participants during a rally in Newcastle.[52] In terms of street mobilization, the British offshoot drew numbers equivalent to the first round of protests in 2005, when the counter-jihadi community first took their activism offline. In Denmark, a PEGIDA offshoot was first set up by the Social Democrat Carsten Thrane, later replaced by Nicolai Sennels, a former parliamentary representative for the radical right DF. In Norway, PEGIDA was headed by the teacher and shop owner Max Hermansen and supported by prominent figures from SIAN and the former NDL. As in the British case, the revitalization of the anti-Islamic far right in Norway and Denmark did not lead to mass demonstrations.[53] Instead of large numbers of demonstrators, the wave of expansion and revitalization in Western Europe is notable because it happened within a very short time span, indicative of the small but determined pool of activists which have accumulated during the three preceding waves of anti-Islamic activism. Most offshoots were set up by mid-January, attracting large numbers of online followers and members (Berntzen & Weisskircher, 2016).

PEGIDA's success in Germany also triggered the establishment of anti-Islamic initiatives across Central and Eastern Europe. The eastward expansion was partly facilitated by the shock of the so-called refugee crisis, in which previously unprecedented numbers of migrants entered Europe during the summer of 2015. A Czech group calling itself the Bloc Against Islam (*Blok proti islámu*, BPI), led by Martin Konvicka, became the most influential, organizing a joint rally in Prague in June 2016, where Bachmann and Robinson spoke to the crowds alongside the Czech president Miloš Zeman.[54]

In January 2016, Czech BPI arranged a meeting of representatives from PEGIDA offshoots around Europe, the Italian populist radical right party, the Italian Northern League (*Lega Nord*, LN) and other anti-Islamic initiatives in the town of Roztoky. There they signed the so-called "Prague Declaration", where they affirmed their common goal of saving Western civilization from being destroyed by an Islamic conquest of Europe. At the behest of Bachmann, they called out "We are Fortress Europe" in English and German, before signing the treaty and formalizing their collaboration using under the banner of Fortress Europe.[55] According to one participant, the decision to collaborate was in response to the sexual assaults on New Year's Eve in Cologne, which had sent shockwaves of anger and indignation through the German public just a week before.

Two weeks later, PEGIDA, Bloc Against Islam and several other initiatives who flocked to the banner of Fortress Europe staged protest marches across Europe, ranging from Ireland to Estonia.[56] The ability to orchestrate simultaneous demonstrations across Europe was something which had eluded the counter-jihadi, Defence League, and Stop Islamization groups before them. The "Fortress Europe" marches were met by anti-racist and far-left counter-demonstrations in most countries, but in the Polish city of Wroclaw organizers cancelled after receiving threats from the extreme right Radical Nationalist Camp (*Oboz Narodowo-Radykalny*, ONR). This demonstrates the fraught and often hostile relationship between extreme right initiatives of the older kind and anti-Islamic initiatives.

In sum, the four waves of anti-Islamic expansion have transformed the far-right activist scene. Starting from a relatively disjointed position with a couple of websites, a lone activist group in Norway and a single anti-Islamic party in the Netherlands, the anti-Islamic far right is now an established presence with transnational ties across Europe, North America, and beyond. This expansion has been propelled by a long list of moral shocks, ranging from terror attacks to Islamist demonstrations on the streets of European cities.

Legacies and identities

Klandermans and Mayer write that "social movements never emerge from nothing: They are a combination of old and new elements; it is a cumulative process" (2006, p. 270). They point to ideological continuity *through* activist continuity. The question they pose is whether the radical right, between the 1980s and early 2000s, were the heirs of the fascist and Nazi organizations of the 1930s, or whether they were what McGann and Kitschelt (1995) call the New Radical Right.[57]

As continuity of personnel is an important factor for understanding the far right (e.g. Klandermans & Mayer, 2006; Art, 2011), providing an overview of the organizational legacies and known affiliations is therefore an important part of grappling with whether the anti-Islamic turn and expansion represents a "new" far right phenomenon or not.

In this section, I compare the backgrounds and political affiliations of 30 figureheads – leaders, representatives and ideologues – from the six strongholds that have been prominent in the four waves of anti-Islamic expansion. Besides their political background, several other dimensions are of interest; gender and (openly professed) sexual identity, religion and class. Brief biographies for each figure are given in Appendix I, on a country-by-country basis. I start with their political backgrounds before becoming active in the anti-Islamic struggle and then move on to gender, sexual identity, religion and class.

Beyond establishing the extent to which their affiliations represent a direct link with older forms of the radical and extreme right, their individual backgrounds matter in two clear ways.

First, if they have a background that clearly sets them apart from open fascists, neo-Nazis, and so forth, this can impact their authenticity and public appeal. Elisabeth Ivarsflaten argued that a far right party's success depended on their "reputational shields" (2005, p. 2). If a party started out as, say, focussed on economic liberalization before picking up anti-immigration as an issue, then that afforded them and their electorate a shield against accusations of being racist. An individual figurehead's background can function in a synonymous way. Second, studying their backgrounds can provide an agency-oriented avenue to explain why certain ideas have become widespread among anti-Islamic initiatives, and not others.

Many former leftists

Of the 30 figureheads, 22 were politically active before they became engaged in anti-Islamic activity. Their political activities span a broad range of activities, from participating in single-issue groups such as Free Tibet to having been prominent members of political parties. An equal number had a history of left-wing activism (11) as right-wing activism (ten).

Those with a left-wing background have been central in the four waves of anti-Islamic expansion. For instance, Hans Rustad of Document.no has been influential from the second wave onwards and has a background as an active member of the Norwegian Socialist Youth Organization, whereas the newcomer Anne Marie Waters of Sharia Watch UK, PEGIDA, and UKIP was a Labour member and activist who stood twice as a party candidate. Pim Fortuyn, who altered the dynamics of Dutch politics, going on to become the most important figure in the first wave, began as a communist before migrating to the Dutch Labour Party and then Livable Netherlands before forming his own explicitly anti-Islamic party. Another prominent example, Lars Hedegaard of TFS, was an active member of the Danish Socialist Workers Party in his younger days. It is worth noting that Charles Johnson, an American with no former far-right affiliations and with centre-left leanings, was the most acclaimed figure among the "cadre" of anti-Islamic activist leaders during the two first waves of anti-Islamic expansion.

Peripheral extreme right, prominent centre-right, and radical right

Among those with a right-wing background prior to becoming engaged in anti-Islamic activism, the numbers are equally distributed between the centre right and the far right. The major Dutch figures, Geert Wilders and Ayaan Hirsi Ali, were both parliamentary members of the centre-right People's Party for Freedom and Democracy (VVD), whereas René Stadtkewitz, chairman of the German BPE was a member of the centre-right CDU and was a local councillor for ten years in Berlin, before being expelled in 2011 after inviting Geert Wilders to speak at a rally, at which point he formed a German sister-party to Wilders'.

Of those that have an identifiable far-right background, only Ronny Alte, former leader of NDL, activist in PEGIDA Norway, and subsequent leader of Sons of Odin, has a known history of right-wing extremism. Alte was a member of a local neo-Nazi group for several years during his youth, and has never been affiliated with left-wing parties or organizations. Furthermore, he can be described as a peripheral figure among the anti-Islamic activists. In Britain, Tommy Robinson,[58] co-founder and leader of the EDL between 2009 and 2013, and PEGIDA UK from 2015, had been a low-ranking member of the BNP for one year in his youth. Stephen Gash, a vehement opponent of the BNP and former leader of SIOE, who was an active figure in the anti-Islamic movement during the second wave of expansion, was a member of the nationalist English Democrats Party (EDP) and the National Council of the Campaign for an English Parliament before that. In Denmark, the founder of SIAD and co-founder of SIOE, Anders Gravers Pedersen, was a member of the nationalist Danish Association (*Den Danske Forening*, DDF) prior to founding SIAD and co-founding SIOE with Stephen Gash. Although not an official member, former leader of SIAN, Arne Tumyr consistently expressed support for the nationalist anti-immigration organization the Peoples' Movement against Immigration (*Folkebevegelsen mot innvandring*, FMI), the Norwegian sister organization to DDF. This despite the fact that FMI's former leader, Arne Johannes Myrdal, had been sentenced to one year's imprisonment for planning to blow up a refugee centre on the island of Tromøy in 1990 (on Myrdal, see Bjørgo, 1997, p. 283).

The older nationalist anti-immigrants – a bridging function?

In sum, the extreme right legacy among the leaders, spokespersons, and activists is not a prominent feature, but some connections do exist. In his study of the Scandinavian radical and extreme right outside party politics, Bjørgo noted that the anti-immigrant nationalists and neo-Nazi communities had contact and some personnel overlaps (1997, p. 288). Despite the fact that only one activist leader has a neo-Nazi background, the affiliations between some anti-Islamic figureheads and militant nationalist communities facilitate a certain degree of interaction between the anti-Islamic and neo-Nazi side. I exemplify this in a diagram which expands on Bjørgo's findings and the ideological typology of the anti-immigrant nationalists (or "national democrats") and the extreme right neo-Nazis (ibid., p. 64).

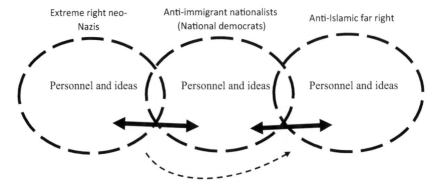

FIGURE 4.1 The potential bridging function of the older anti-immigrant nationalists between neo–Nazi and anti-Islamic personnel and ideas

The anti-immigrant nationalists are analogous to what is otherwise described as ethno-pluralists.

In this sense, the nationalist groups, which have a longer organizational history, can act as a bridge between the anti-Islamic far right and the neo-Nazi extreme right, and therefore meaning that neo-Nazi activists and ideas have the potential to gain influence. This potential for extreme right influence has led to splits within the anti-Islamic movement, most prominently when Johnson of LGF denounced the self-described counter-jihad which he himself had helped set up.

It is important to note, however, that the anti-Islamic far right portrays Islam as an equivalent to Nazism and often expresses clear disdain for neo-Nazis. Similarly, scattered evidence indicate that contemporary neo-Nazis see anti-Islamic activists as traitors. For instance, on the Danish neo-Nazi blog Hammersmeden (Hammersmith), anti-Islamic activists and their ideas are denigrated as "globalists", "feminists", and "gay lovers" who are blinded by their opposition to Islam, when the true enemy is the Jew.[59]

Few, but prominent, women and LGBT

Turning to the issue of gender and sexual identity, two things stand out. First, there is a noticeable gender gap in the top cadre of anti-Islamic activists, with only six women against 24 men. Four of the six women are self-professed feminists. For instance, Hege Storhaug of HRS anchors and legitimizes her antagonism to Islam as a struggle for gender equality, women's rights, and against female gender mutilation, much in the same vein as the Somali-born Dutch-American, Ayaan Hirsi Ali. Second, some leaders have been outspoken about being gay/lesbian, and including it in their public platform. Pim Fortuyn is the first and most prominent example, who based much of his arguments against Islam and Muslim immigration around the notion that Muslims threatened the rights of homosexuals. British Anne Marie Waters also bases her activism on opposition to Sharia law as a danger to women's rights and as well as religious homophobia from Muslims.

The prominent role of women and people with an overt LGBT identity is not unique to the initiatives that have been part of the anti-Islamic expansion. It is also evident among the radical right parties which have undergone a reorientation. For instance, the French FN has been led by Marine Le Pen since 2011, and the Norwegian FrP has been led by Siv Jensen since 2006, whereas Pia Kjærsgaard led radical right DF until 2012 (for an analysis of gender issues and the role of women leader's in these parties, see e.g. Meret & Siim, 2013). More recently, the openly lesbian Alice Weidel was nominated as AfD's Chancellor candidate for the 2017 elections.

Religion and class

When it comes to religious identity, half of the 30 leaders have incorporated their affiliation in their public identity and mobilization activity. Ten are Christian, and four identify as atheist or agnostic. The latter have a history of left-wing activism. In terms of class, a majority can be characterized as coming from a middle-class background. Furthermore, eight have worked in journalism or publishing and four as programmers, and several of them hold university degrees in history.

A minority come from working-class backgrounds. Some of them have become small entrepreneurs, and others work in manual jobs. These are also predominantly engaged in street-oriented initiatives, have no clear religious affiliation, and represent the subset of leaders who have an extreme right legacy or expressed affinity with militant nationalists.

Conclusion

The all-encompassing turn of the far right from focussing on ethnicity to Muslims and Islam on the far right consists of two processes: an anti-Islamic *reorientation* among pre-existing far-right initiatives; and an anti-Islamic *expansion* of the far right with the creation of new initiatives. This book is a study of the latter. In this chapter, I have provided an overview of the waves of anti-Islamic expansion anchored in the anti-Islamic strongholds of the United States, Britain, Germany, the Netherlands, Denmark, and Norway. I have made an analytical distinction between four waves of anti-Islamic expansion. The initial wave is traced back to two different starting points; the US-based website LGF and the Dutch party LPF. The second wave marks the turn towards street-oriented activism, co-originating in Britain and Denmark called Stop Islamization. The third wave began in Britain with the formation of the EDL, whereas the fourth wave started off with PEGIDA in Germany. Furthermore, I trace these waves to critical events and moral shocks ranging from the "international" – such as the 9/11 terror attacks and Muhammed cartoon crisis – to "local" events of Muslim picketing soldiers' funerals outside Luton and Kurds marching on the streets of Dresden.

In the second section, I analyzed the biographies of the 30 main anti-Islamic leaders, spokespersons, and ideologues active in these countries during the four waves of expansion. Four aspects stand out. First, political left-wing backgrounds are more common than far right or extreme right-wing backgrounds – yet the older ethno-nationalist groups can serve as a bridge between the anti-Islamic far right and the neo-Nazi extreme right, and thereby provide the extreme right with some potential for influence. Second, while men are in the clear majority, women also play a prominent role – as do people with an outspoken LGBT identity. Several of the women are self-professed feminists. Third, half of the leaders, spokespersons and intellectuals incorporate their Christian or non-religious (atheist and agnostic) identity into their public persona and mobilization activity. Whereas a majority of the Christians have a right-wing background, the non-religious have a left-wing background. Fourth, a majority have what can be described as a middle-class background with careers in journalism, publishing, and programming.

The presence or collaboration with self-professed progressives and liberals has been noted in other cases. For instance, pointing to the Belgian journalist Claude

Demelenne, Liberal MP Alain Destexhe, and the feminist Nadia Geerts, Fekete writes that they have gained allies among dogmatic secularists and identity-bound feminists through the idea of Islamo-fascism (2012, p. 42).

There is no lack of historical figures and leaders who have moved from one end of the ideological spectrum to the other during the course of their political lifetime. Historically, Benito Mussolini is the perhaps the most prominent and pertinent example. Mussolini started his career as a socialist before becoming a nationalist, and later founded the fascist movement. Whether or not a person's legacy creates an ideological path dependency is disputable. Yet just as Mussolini carried with him and mutated socialist ideas, it is certainly plausible that people with a past political background as left-wing activists and politicians at least carry with them some – if not all – of the ideas which they previously professed. The left-wing legacy among several of the key figureheads is a possible channel for the dissemination and adoption of nominally left-wing, progressive and liberal ideas in the broader anti-Islamic movement.

Notes

1 See Zúquete (2008) and Betz and Meret (2009) for an analysis of the anti-Islamic reorientation of several populist radical right parties.
2 Briefly called *Aksjonskomiteen mot bønnerop*.
3 In the wake of these attacks, President George W. Bush launched what he called a Global War on Terror, drawing in allies from across the globe. After having approached the Afghani Taliban and then the Pakistani military ruler, Pervez Musharraf, he went on the world stage saying, "You are either with us or against us in the fight against terror" on 6 November 2001; CNN (2006, 6 November). "You are either with us or against us", *Cable News Network*. Retrieved 16 August 2014, from http://edition.cnn.com/2001/US/11/06/gen.attack.on.terror/.
4 Or anti-jihadist, the terms are used interchangeably.
5 IsraelNN.com. (2004, May 11). "At Israel's Right". Article is no longer accessible online, screen dump provided by Daniel Munksgaard through personal correspondence.
6 Geller was a frequent poster on LGF. The LGF forum and its host later became one of the most ardent critics of the counter-jihadi scene.
7 Available online in French at: http://obs.monde.juif.free.fr/pdf/omj04-05.pdf (accessed 26 June 2015). The outspoken Italian journalist and feminist Oriana Fallaci later popularized the Eurabia theory in her book *The Force of Reason* (La Forza della Ragione), published in 2004 (Bangstad, 2013, p. 145).
8 http://archive.frontpagemag.com/Printable.aspx?ArtId=12077fa
9 Later named Act! For America Education
10 In an interview with the Dutch newspaper *Volkskrant*, Fortuyn was asked "why he hated Islam", to which he replied "I don't hate Islam. I consider it a backward culture. I have travelled a lot and wherever Islam rules, it's just terrible. All the hypocrisy. It's a bit like those old reformed Protestants. The Reformed lie all the time. And why is that? Because they have standards and values that are so high that you can't humanly maintain them. You also see that in that Muslim culture. Then look at the Netherlands. In what country could an electoral leader of such a large movement as mine be openly homosexual? How wonderful that that's possible. That's something that one can be proud of. And I'd like to keep it that way, thank you very much". (*Volkskrant*, 9 February 2002).
11 In an interview with *The Guardian* in 2008, Wilders was asked if his "provocative rhetoric fermented hatred", to which he replied "I don't create hate. I want to be honest.

I don't hate people. I don't hate Muslims. I hate their book and their ideology". Source: https://www.theguardian.com/world/2008/feb/17/netherlands.islam (accessed 2 September 2014).

12 The raison d'etre given for publishing them was that the Danish author Kåre Bluitgen had trouble finding an illustrator willing to draw Mohammed in his children's book (Kapelrud, 2008).

13 The free speech rally in London was attended by around 300 protesters, who stated they were not against Muslims and that they feared infiltration from the fascist British National Party. Source: http://news.bbc.co.uk/2/hi/uk_news/england/london/4844634.stm (accessed 2 September 2014).

14 Quote from the text "A Brief History of the Transatlantic Counterjihad by the Counterjihad Collective", available online: http://gatesofvienna.blogspot.co.uk (accessed February 2013). The group formalized in 2007, calling itself the Center for Vigilant Freedom (CVF). They later merged with other activists, rebranded as the International Civil Liberties Alliance, taking their name from a quote by Thomas Jefferson saying that "the price of liberty is eternal vigilance". www.libertiesalliance. org/about-2/ Today, they continue as a Swiss-based NGO called the Center for Vigilant Freedom.

15 Gravers Pedersen first tried to enter politics with Stop Islamization of Denmark, which received a total of 11,172 votes in the municipal elections in Aalborg, 2005.

16 www.actforamerica.org/policy

17 www.nytimes.com/2011/03/08/us/08gabriel.html?pagewanted=all

18 These initiatives share each other's stories, participate in joint celebrations, and have established formal collaboration. For instance, HRS and Hege Storhaug participated in the ten-year anniversary celebration of Trykkefrihedsselskabet in Denmark alongside Hans Rustad from Document.no and Raaschou from Snaphanen.dk. TFS and Document.no have also provided funding to Snaphanen. For a short time in 2016, Uriasposten was shut down and Kim Møller headed up *Document.dk* in collaboration with Hans Rustad and Document.no. www.trykkefrihed.dk/trykkefrihedsselskabet-pa-mosbjerg-folkefest.htm

19 www.klassekampen.no/article/20170609/ARTICLE/170609967 (accessed 13 June 2017).

20 By 2017, PI was ranked as the 389th most visited website in Germany www.alexa.com/siteinfo/pi-news.net (accessed 13 June 2017).

21 Headed by Willi Schwend.

22 Lars Hedegaard has become a well-known figure internationally after a failed attempt on his life by a jihadist in 2013 (the perpetrator later joined ISIS).

23 Quote from SIAN's 'about us' webpage section (in Norwegian), http://sian.no/om-sian (accessed 12 March 2014). Norwegian group later split when a moderate faction split off following a heated general assembly meeting early 2014, forming a group called Core Values (*Verdier i Sentrum*, ViS).

24 "The English Defence League: About us", available online: http://englishdefenceleague. org/about-us (accessed 20 June 2012).

25 "Policing EDL demo in Bristol cost force £495,000", *BBC News*, 10 August 2012.

26 "A Brief History of the Transatlantic Counterjihad", available online: http://gatesofvienna.blogspot.co.uk (accessed February 2013).

27 http://gatesofvienna.blogspot.no/2011/10/slouching-towards-london.html (accessed 2 May 2016).

28 www.theguardian.com/uk/2012/apr/28/britain-far-right-anti-islamic (accessed 4 February 2015).

29 Carroll went on to found Liberty GB, which fielded three candidates for the 2014 European elections: www.bbc.com/news/uk-england-hampshire-27186573 (accessed 4 February 2015).

30 See www.zeit.de/2010/40/Geert-Wilders-Berlin/seite-2 (accessed 5 February 2015), and www.rnw.org/archive/wilders-sets-international-alliance-against-islam (accessed 5 February 2015).

31 In January 2013, the European Freedom Initiative listed affiliated defence leagues in Britain, the United States, Norway, Denmark, Finland, Italy, Sweden, Germany, Australia, Serbia, Greece, Indonesia, Poland, the Philippines, Belgium, Czech Republic, Romania, and Luxemburg. Website no longer available.

32 Wilders was on trial for hate speech and inciting racism: www.theguardian.com/world/2010/oct/08/far-right-geert-wilders-protest (accessed 4 February 2015).

33 http://cphpost.dk/news/international/racist-network-to-hold-rally-in-aarhus.html (accessed 4 February 2015).

34 www.nrk.no/norge/takket-de-10-frammotte-1.7587515

35 https://query.nytimes.com/gst/fullpage.html?res=9E05EEDB113CF933A25753C1A9 669D8B63&scp=3&st=cse&pagewanted=all (accessed 23 September 2014).

36 www.reuters.com/article/us-europe-islam-far-right-idUSTRE6BJ37120101220 (accessed 4 February 2015).

37 http://pamelageller.com/2012/08/announcing-the-sion-presidents-council-the-fruit-of-stockholm.html/ (accessed 12 May 2015).

38 This was likely because he was refused entry to the United States to attend a protest against building a mosque on the "Ground Zero" site two years before.

39 www.channel4.com/news/edl-leader-stephen-lennon-jailed-for-10-months (accessed 19 May 2016).

40 www.bbc.com/news/uk-politics-24442953 (accessed 19 May 2016).

41 "KURDEN DEMO DRESDEN", YouTube: www.youtube.com/watch?v=d6aFr9GVE2c (accessed 1 December 2016). In the video description, Bachmann wrote "They are demanding weapons for the PKK. This is a terrorist organization, which is banned in Germany, and they demand weapons on our streets! Where's the police?" (author's translation).

42 PEGIDAs symbol is a man throwing flags carrying the emblems of the Kurdish PKK, Nazi Germany, Anti-Fascist Action (AFA), and ISIS into a trash bin. www.independent.co.uk/news/world/europe/pegida-leader-lutz-bachmann-steps-down-over-hitler-photograph-9993425.html (accessed 1 December 2016).

43 www.independent.co.uk/news/world/europe/pegida-leader-lutz-bachmann-steps-down-over-hitler-photograph-9993425.html (accessed 1 December 2016)

44 www.theguardian.com/world/2015/feb/23/pegida-head-lutz-bachmann-reinstated-hitler-moustache-photo (accessed 1 December 2016); www.spiegel.de/politik/deutschland/afd-beriet-pegida-in-der-hitler-affaere-von-lutz-bachmann-a-1014623.html (accessed 1 December 2016)

45 www.thelocal.de/20160927/pegida-take-to-dresden-streets-to-march-against-pegida (accessed 1 December 2016).

46 www.tagesspiegel.de/politik/plaene-fuer-gemeinsame-kundgebung-afd-und-pegida-planen-schulterschluss/19743318.html (accessed 25 June 2017)

47 www.faz.net/aktuell/politik/inland/lutz-bachmann-hat-angeblich-eine-pegida-partei-gegruendet-14348098.html (accessed 25 June 2017)

48 www.independent.co.uk/news/world/europe/dead-pigs-reportedly-dumped-outside-refugee-site-following-dutch-pegida-rally-a6891556.html (accessed 2 December 2016).

49 www.independent.co.uk/news/world/europe/dead-pigs-reportedly-dumped-outside-refugee-site-following-dutch-pegida-rally-a6891556.html (accessed 12 January 2017).

50 www.rtlnieuws.nl/nieuws/binnenland/grote-demonstratie-van-pegida-tijdens-wilders-proces&usg=ALkJrhhWRNYgwOUkj39wcqol0h3YwHZ6AA (accessed 12 January 2017).

51 www.huffingtonpost.co.uk/2015/12/03/tommy-robinson-launch-pegida-uk_n_8710610.html (accessed 01.12.2016); www.bbc.com/news/magazine-35432074 (accessed 1 December 2016).

52 www.bbc.com/news/uk-england-tyne-31657167 (accessed 2 December 2016).

53 In Norway, PEGIDA held 19 marches across the country between January and June 2015. The largest drew 200 participants, with an average of 40 participants across the marches (Berntzen & Weisskircher, 2016).
54 www.breitbart.com/london/2015/11/17/eastern-europe-rising-czech-president-speaks-anti-islam-rally-pegida-leaders-tommy-robinson/ (accessed 10 June 2016).
55 www.dw.com/en/pegida-meets-with-european-allies-in-the-czech-republic/a-19000895 (accessed 7 May 2017).
56 www.jpost.com/Breaking-News/Thousands-protest-in-Poland-against-Islamisation-of-Europe-444083 (accessed 7 May 2017); www.independent.co.uk/news/world/europe/thousands-take-part-in-anti-islam-pegida-protests-across-europe-a6857911.html (accessed 2 December 2016); www.baltictimes.com/pegida_to_hold_anti-islamic_march_in_estonia/ (accessed 7 May 2017).
57 On organizational or ideological continuity, see also Ignazi (1992, 2003), Rydgren (2007), and Carter (2005).
58 Whose true name is Stephen Christopher Yaxley-Lennon.
59 https://hammersmeden.wordpress.com/2015/10/25/hvorfor-moderat-indvandringsmodstand-altid-taber/ (accessed 30 August 2016).

Bibliography

Abbott, A. (1997). On the concept of turning point. *Comparative Social Research*, *16*, 85–106.
Amenta, E., Caren, N., Chiarello, E., & Su, Y. (2010). The political consequences of social movements. *Annual Review of Sociology*, *36*, 287–307.
Art, D. (2011). *Inside the radical right: The development of anti-immigrant parties in Western Europe.* Cambridge: Cambridge University Press.
Bail, C. A. (2012). The fringe effect: Civil society organizations and the evolution of media discourse about Islam since the September 11th attacks. *American Sociological Review*, *77*(6), 855–879.
Bangstad, S. (2013). Eurabia comes to Norway. *Islam and Christian – Muslim Relations*, *24*(3), 369–391.
Berntzen, L. E., & Weisskircher, M. (2016). Anti-Islamic PEGIDA beyond Germany: Explaining differences in mobilisation. *Journal of Intercultural Studies*, *37*(6), 556–573.
Betz, H.-G., & Meret, S. (2009). Revisiting Lepanto: The political mobilization against Islam in contemporary Western Europe. *Patterns of Prejudice*, *43*(3–4), 313–334.
Bjørgo, T. (1997). *Racist and right-wing violence in Scandinavia: Patterns, perpetrators and responses.* Oslo: Tano Aschehoug.
Carter, E. (2005). *The extreme right in Western Europe: Success or failure?* Oxford: Oxford University Press.
Eyerman, R. (2008). *The assassination of Theo van Gogh: From social drama to cultural trauma.* Durham: Duke University Press.
Fekete, L. (2012). The Muslim conspiracy theory and the Oslo massacre. *Race & Class*, *53*(3), 30–47.
Gable, G., Cressy, S., & Woodson, T. (2009). A hot August? *Searchlight*, *410*, 8–9.
Gardell, M. (2014). Crusader dreams: Oslo 22/7, Islamophobia, and the quest for a monocultural Europe. *Terrorism and Political Violence*, *26*(1), 129–155.
Goodwin, M. J. (2013). *The roots of extremism: The English Defence League and the Counter-Jihad challenge.* London: Chatham House.
Hjarpe, J. (2006). Jyllands-Postens Muhammedbilder tolkning av en konflikt. *Kirke og Kultur*, (2), 161–180.
Huntington, S. P. (1993). The clash of civilizations? *Foreign Affairs*, 22–49.

Ignazi, P. (1992). The silent counter-revolution. *European Journal of Political Research, 22*(1), 3–34.

Ignazi, P. (2003). *Extreme right parties in Western Europe.* Oxford: Oxford University Press on Demand.

Ivarsflaten, E. (2005). The vulnerable populist right parties: No economic realignment fuelling their electoral success. *European Journal of Political Research, 44*(3), 465–492.

Jasper, J. M. (1998). The emotions of protest: Affective and reactive emotions in and around social movements. *Sociological Forum, 13*(3), 397–424. Springer Netherlands.

Kapelrud, P. E. (2008). *Offerets makt:: En diskursanalyse av karikaturstriden i Norge* (Master's thesis). Oslo: University of Oslo.

Klandermans, B., & Mayer, N. (2006). *Through the magnifying glass: The world of extreme right activists.* London: Routledge.

Kurzman, C. (2004). Can understanding undermine explanation? The confused experience of revolution. *Philosophy of the Social Sciences, 34*(3), 328–351.

Lewis, B. (1990). The roots of Muslim rage. *The Atlantic Monthly, 266*(3), 47–60.

McAdam, D. (1982). *Political process and the development of black insurgency, 1930–1970.* Chicago, IL: University of Chicago Press.

McGann, H. K. A., & Kitschelt, H. (1995). *The radical right in Western Europe: A comparative analysis.* Ann Arbor: University of Michigan Press.

Meret, S., & Siim, B. (2013). Gender, populism and politics of belonging: Discourses of right-wing populist parties in Denmark, Norway and Austria. In B. Siim & M. Mokre (Eds.), *Negotiating gender and diversity in an emergent European public sphere* (pp. 78–96). London: Palgrave Macmillan.

Meyer, D. S., & Minkoff, D. C. (2004). Conceptualizing political opportunity. *Social Forces, 82*(4), 1457–1492.

Munksgaard, D. C. (2010). *Warblog without end: Online anti-Islamic discourses as persuadables* (PhD thesis). City of Iowa: University of Iowa.

Rydgren, J. (2007). The sociology of the radical right. *Annual Review of Sociology, 33,* 241–262.

Sewell, W. H. (1996). Three temporalities: Toward an eventful sociology. *The Historic Turn in the Human Sciences,* 245–280.

Soule, S. A., & Olzak, S. (2004). When do movements matter? The politics of contingency and the equal rights amendment. *American Sociological Review, 69*(4), 473–497.

Swidler, A. (1986). Culture in action: Symbols and strategies. *American Sociological Review,* 273–286.

Wagner-Pacifici, R. (2010). Theorizing the restlessness of events. *American Journal of Sociology, 115*(5), 1351–1386.

Zúquete, J. P. (2008). The European extreme-right and Islam: New directions? *Journal of Political Ideologies, 13*(3), 321–344.

5

WORLDVIEWS

Introduction

As seen in Chapter 4, the anti-Islamic worldview originated and was spread by the online counter-jihadist community, the activists beginning in Norway, and the radical right parties following the rise of LPF in the Netherlands. The diffusion and salience of this rhetoric and worldview closely coincides with key events, first of which was Al-Quaeda's attacks that brought down the World Trade Center in New York, 11 September 2001. This chapter examines the rhetoric and ideas of leaders and representatives from 11 political initiatives in Britain, Germany, and Norway. These actors have all become known for their hostility towards Islam and Muslims, and the selected countries are three of the main epicentres for the following waves of organized opposition to Islam and Muslims.

Several studies define this opposition as a transnational movement, yet most studies looking at their ideology and framing beyond a cursory level study individual organizations or single countries. By conducting a qualitative comparison, my first aim is to provide insight into the degree of transnational alignment. Is this an ideologically homogenous phenomenon? Previous studies have indicated that many of these actors claim to defend liberal values, women's rights and the rights of vulnerable minorities. This apparent paradox lies at the core of understanding the anti-Islamic turn, and the initial process of grappling with the apparent inclusion of liberal values by actors and movements defined as belonging to the far right is the second aim of this chapter. In most instances, these claims are treated very briefly or understood as deceptions. This sometimes resembles tautological reasoning: actors using anti-Islamic rhetoric are defined as far right, and since the far right has historically been consistently illiberal, consequently actors using anti-Islamic rhetoric must by definition still be illiberal through and through – and therefore, it cannot be anything but a masquerade. The previous chapter showed that among the figureheads, it was just as common to have a left-wing political background as a right-wing political background. By making an in-depth comparison of their framing specifically related to these claims, the goal is to go one step further and simultaneously escape tautological reasoning or getting locked into the binary logic of true or false.

My analysis underlines the transnational character of the views found in this movement and subculture. This strengthens the arguments made in the growing body of literature on what is defined as the new Islamophobic or anti-Islamic far right. They share the supranational diagnosis that Islam is a totalitarian ideology and an existential threat to the West and all other groups in society, with the "elites" either co-conspiring or passively allowing this destruction. By and large, they also adopt democracy and non-violent solutions. Nevertheless, some of their solutions are clearly authoritarian. Finally, their motivational framework stresses the need to fight for liberty and "Western" values.

Narrowing down to the way they frame the issue of women's rights vis-à-vis Muslims, this chapter shows that they intermittently rely on male-centric, traditional "protector" frames and female-centric, modern "equality" frames. In particular, the issue of women's rights captures the tension intrinsic to this movement and subculture's framing – straddling the span between the old far-right legacies and positions previously held more exclusively by self-defined liberals and leftists. This intermittent use of these two largely opposing frames is a form of strategic ambiguity which allows those involved to bridge their anti-Islamic collective action framework with a feminist framework. It also allows them to lay the foundations for portraying themselves as the "true" defenders of women's rights and gender equality; those who do not share their view of Islam and Muslims become de facto anti-feminists. This strategic ambiguity is a general pattern in their "adoption" of liberal values and vulnerable minorities. Based on these findings, I argue that anti-Islam constitutes a third master frame for the far right.

This chapter is structured as follows. First, the methods, data and choice of actors are discussed. This is followed by a brief outline of framing theory before the analysis of the actors' diagnostic, prognostic, and motivational framing.[1] Then comes an analysis of the way in which they frame the issue of women's rights vis-à-vis Muslims. Finally, the findings and claims are put in a broader, comparative context by drawing on Jens Rydgren's overview of the far right's ideological evolution.[2]

Methods and actors

Data in this chapter are: 1) a wide selection of literature from eleven anti-Islamic initiatives in Norway, Britain and Germany from 2010 and onwards (Table 5.1): manifestos and statements by leaders in newspapers, on their own websites and in periodicals; and 2) supplemented by interviews with key actors in Norway. As this chapter demonstrates, they share a common identity and rhetoric. The texts are illustrative and not exhaustive, but they capture the general rhetoric of the movement. Describing their shared collective action framing means simplifying for

TABLE 5.1 Number of anti-Islamic initiatives included in the qualitative frame analysis, by country and type

Country	Germany	Britain	Norway
Protest groups and minor parties	2	3	2
Alternative news and think-tanks	1	1	2
Sum	3	4	4

analytical reasons. Even though they are adept at getting their message across, analyzing several actors' statements over a long period entails a certain rationalization of ambiguous text.

The broad spectrum of anti-Islamic initiatives spans from small political parties and think-tanks to protest groups and websites dedicated to alternative news. The list does not include all the anti-Islamic initiatives which have been operational in the three countries, but it does include the largest and perhaps most influential ones. In Britain, the cases included are the activist groups English Defence League (EDL), Stop Islamization of Europe (SIOE, formerly No Sharia Here), and the British Freedom Party (BFP), as well as the website Four Freedoms Community (4F). The German cases include the activist group PEGIDA, the website Politically Incorrect (PI), and the small group Stop Islamization of Europe Deutschland (SIOED). In Norway, the cases included are the activist groups Stop Islamization of Norway (SIAN) and PEGIDA Norway, the alternative news site Document.no, and the self-described think-tank Human Rights Service (HRS).

The frame analysis could have been expanded to the larger populist radical right parties, the Norwegian FrP, British UKIP and German AfD, but these are not included in the analysis. In addition to having undergone an ideological transformation and reorientation towards opposition to Islam, they also mobilize on a different set of issues, not all of which are related to their opposition to Islam or Muslim immigration and culture. For instance, although immigration is the most important issue for FrP voters, the party also receives considerable support for their emphasis on lowering taxes, improved healthcare for the elderly, and broader issues of law and order. Similarly, the AfD includes a broader range of issues and began by mobilizing on the economic dimension, arguing that the Euro should be replaced with the Deutsche Mark. As the frame analysis demonstrates, however, it is a mistake to view the activist groups as strictly single issue. Opposition to Islam and Muslims is the core issue, but they also mobilize against those they see as their internal opponents and propose a wide range of solutions (such as more direct democracy).

When it comes to the issue of internal movement centrality, organizations such as HRS probably hold more sway than UKIP, FrP, or AfD. For these parties, the peripheral status is something they have actively sought, as being too strongly associated with activist groups could undermine their legitimacy in mainstream party politics. This allows them to adopt and refine parts of their message, which is something FrP did in the 2009 elections with the concept of "sneak Islamization".

Movement centrality is built on a qualitative understanding of where individual actors are situated in the web of influence vis-à-vis others. Besides HRS, the core consists of the largest and longest lasting activist groups – the EDL, PEGIDA, and SIAN, as well as the alternative news sites Document.no and PI. This is not a strictly party or non-party distinction, as some of the activist groups also belong to the periphery in terms of intra-movement influence. This primarily holds for the smaller organizations which are offshoots from PEGIDA, SIOE, and the EDL. The various organizations are on a continuum of conspiratorial thinking, which is a relative marker of differentiation. Along this continuum, actors such as HRS and Document.no are at the moderate end of the scale, emphasizing the dichotomy of the people versus the elite, and warning against the "Islamization" of society, but putting little emphasis on hidden agendas and conspiracies. A majority of the agents such as PEGIDA, SIOE, SIAN, and the EDL, by contrast, are at the opposing end, openly embracing conspiracy theories. The most common conspiracy theory is the so-called "Eurabia thesis". This conspiracy theory claims that the political and cultural elites have entered into a covert partnership with the Muslim Brotherhood and other Islamists, and that this collusion has been in effect for decades (Bangstad, 2013). They also consistently define political opponents as cultural Marxists and denigrate the press as liars (*Lügenpresse*), who are conspiring to destroy Western civilization from within.

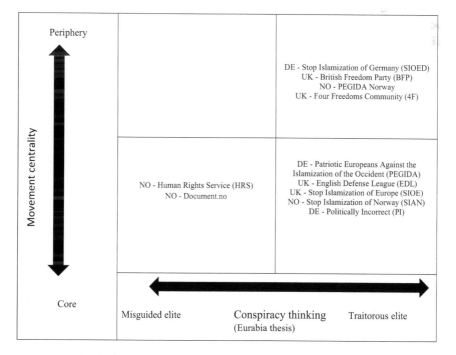

FIGURE 5.1   Anti-Islamic actors divided along the dimensions of movement centrality and conspiratorial thinking

Framing theory

In studies of social movements, framing theory is concerned with rhetoric and language (Snow, Rochford Jr, Worden, & Benford, 1986; Snow & Benford, 1988, 1992; Gamson, 1992). It offers a specific tool for comparing the rhetoric of different political entities. The term "frame" is taken from Goffman, and describes "schemata of interpretation" used by individuals to attach meaning to events and occurrences (1974, p. 21). The basic idea is that one of the major tasks of social movements is to develop and diffuse these inter-subjective frames. In framing theory, the rhetoric of social movements is conceptualized as collective action frames. These can be categorized in different ways, but Snow and Benford's (1992) version, encompasses a diagnosis and a prognosis of a problem, and a call to action for its resolution (Cress & Snow, 2000, p. 1071). Diagnostic framing is concerned with problem identification (who is to blame?), prognostic framing with problem resolution (what can be done about it?), and motivational framing with a rationale for engaging in collective action, or some articulation of a motive (Benford & Snow, 2000, p. 617). These are analytical categories, and all three aspects can be present in an individual sentence.

Anti-Islamic collective action framing

Diagnosis

To construct a common framework for action, the different actors must operate with a unified understanding of what they define as problematic (Benford & Snow, 2000, p. 617). The anti-Islamic initiatives identify a wide range of problems, but their core diagnosis is that "we" are at risk of being "destroyed", culturally and demographically. The survival of their respective countries and the West at large is under threat of becoming subservient to Muslims within a few decades. The key factor is the portrayal of two enemies: one internal, and one external. Conceiving of the political elite as an internal enemy, they vary between including only the parties on the right wing or only those on the left. They portray the external enemy (Muslims) as conspiring, or having fooled or intimidated the "politically correct" internal enemy. The survivalism rhetoric is underlined by linking this overarching frame to facts such as the construction of mosques, which are "hate factories . . . teaching Muslim children the grotesque message from the Q'uran: 'Kill the infidel!' . . . and that they will 'exterminate the unbelievers'".[3]

Even though Islam and Muslims are portrayed as the main threat, most of the carriers of the anti-Islamic collective frames acknowledge the differences between secular, moderate, and fundamentalist Muslims, as exemplified in the EDL mission statement:

> The EDL argues for the rights and ability of all people to protest against Islam's encroachment into the lives of non-Muslims. We also reject the unjust

assumption that all Muslims are complicit in or somehow responsible for the actions of other Muslims. So we stand firm in support of the right of both Muslims and non-Muslims to speak freely about these actions and encroachments.[4]

Nonetheless, all the anti-Islamic initiatives adhere to one central and unifying tenet – that Islam is a political ideology, and not simply a religion. The EDL, for instance, states that: "It is a category mistake to compare Islam with religions such as Christianity or Judaism. Apples and oranges" (EDL Manifesto, 2016). All of them focus on Islam and Muslim cultural norms gaining a foothold, something which they claim to be undermining Western society. The initiatives define the increased accommodation of Muslims as a form of creeping Islamization. Unless something is done, they argue, Islamization will only increase in speed and extent. As examples of what Islamization entails, they mention the introduction of halal products, Sharia laws, Muslim ghettoes, honour killings, gender segregation, rape, female genital mutilation (FGM), and anti-Semitism.[5] All of this is thought to flow directly from the teachings of Muhammed, here exemplified by a statement on the website PI about the legality of rape and enslavement under Islam:

> Islam codifies and legalizes the diabolical evil of rape. God and his messenger Muhammad not only endorsed the institution of slavery but also the raping and sexual molestation of female slaves. The very proposition that God would make rape a divine, holy act and have as his prophet a man who raped, allowed his male followers to attack their female captives is simply outrageous.[6]

The final outcome is either extermination or subjugation and slavery. As a part of this narrative, they make a clear distinction between Islam and Christendom and Christianity. While Christianity is portrayed as a benevolent force for good, Islam is viewed as an alien, backwards, and historically static force that spreads to the detriment of our own culture and religion. By framing Christianity as a central aspect, they can draw upon historical events dating back to the 7th century, thus pointing out that this is but the latest variation of a gruelling conflict.[7]

Islamization is contextualized by arguing that this is either at the behest of, or due to, the failings of what they define as the globalist and multicultural elites within the political arena, academia and mainstream media. For instance, the EDL position is that Britain's leaders are cowards:

> Our political leaders are too cowardly to deal with the problem of Islamic terror at its root; so they make a virtue out of their cowardice. We are not fooled.
> *(EDL mission statement, 2016)*[8]

The respective anti-Islamic initiatives are primarily concerned with their own countries, followed by Europe and the West in general. As such, the dominant

PICTURE 5.1   Anti-Islamic propaganda material

Sources: a. Propaganda picture of Angela Merkel taken from PEGIDA Deutschland's original Facebook page, no longer available. Downloaded November 2016; b. Propaganda picture targeting the Norwegian Labor Party taken from Stop Islamization of Norway's original Facebook page, no longer available. Downloaded November 2016.

Notes: On the right is a white woman dressed in a Norwegian folk dress (*bunad*) with a veil. The picture tells us that Norway will turn into "Norgestan" by the year 2030, and that the slogan for the Norwegian Labour Party (AP) will be "Allah will be included" instead of their current "Everybody will be included". For the German case, the hated figure of Angela Merkel is represented as a Muslim, signalling that she and others belonging to the elite allow themselves to be "Islamized" in the name of tolerance.

centre-left parties are often portrayed as a main opponent enabling the destruction of traditional, Norwegian, English, and Germany society.[9] The CDU and Angela Merkel have recently superseded the Social Democrats as the embodiment of the internal enemy across the cases following the "refugee crisis" of 2015 and her statements about the leaders of PEGIDA having "hatred in their hearts".[10] For instance, then deputy leader of PEGIDA stated that:

> Angela Merkel is the most dangerous woman in the world. She has given up control of the country, the borders and probably also about herself.[11]

This is a marked shift from being portrayed as a saviour early on in 2010 – when Merkel stated that "creating a multicultural society has utterly failed".[12] The elites are framed as having betrayed the people by oppressing and misleading the popular opposition towards immigration, Islamization, and multiculturalism. In their view, this is not only because they collude with Muslims, or they are ideologically blinded or cowards, but because the elite deem both the people and the anti-Islamic initiatives to be racist. It is from this position that the anti-Islamic initiatives frame their struggle.

It is common to point to the education system as one of the main explanations for the dominance of multiculturalist elites. This is done by "selling in self-hatred to generations" towards Western civilization by downplaying Christianity and preaching the evils of colonialism and the Crusades. The result is cravenness and self-dissolution when faced with foreign cultures. This paints a vast and dark picture of a hegemonic elite that actively conspires to undermine the people it governs, so that *we* have to give ground to *them*. In this way we can argue that they are constructing a framework of injustice. The elite and the left wing are oppressing both them and the people at large. This is done proactively or tacitly in league with Islamic organizations and agents.

The role of the elites in what they see as an ongoing Islamization is reinforced by emphasizing immigration and the subsequent demographic shifts associated with it. One of the main arguments is that non-Western immigration is undermining social coherence and trust. Politicians and the media talk about integration in a way which is deceptive and which conceals reality; that it is ethnic Norwegians, Britons, and Germans are being integrated and assimilated into an alien and oppressive culture. Anti-Islamic initiatives actively incorporate arguments about women being oppressed by the Muslim patriarchy, based on the Quran and Islamic cultural norms being the primary example. They see multiculturalism as a failed project leading to the self-destruction of Western civilization. All these factors help cement the three central dichotomies of anti-Islamic initiatives. These are *the people* versus *the elite, Norwegians/British/German* versus *Muslims* and the *West* versus *Islam*. Throughout this framing activity, they create an active delineation where they view themselves as being on the side of the people, and against the elite, Islam, and Islamists. This sharp divide is at the focal point for enmity.

Prognosis

The construction of a solution-based framework implies an articulation of possible solutions and strategies for coping with the issues which the agents view as problematic (Benford & Snow, 2000). The various anti-Islamic initiatives propose a wide range of solutions and strategies to overcome what they view as multicultural dominance and the Islamization of society. This is seen as an existential struggle for democracy, and all the solutions proposed are non-violent. The rejection of violence is linked to their diagnostic framing of Western societies as civilized and rights-based, in contrast to the violent Islamists. They aim to stop the spread of Islam and to halt Muslim immigration through legislation and political power, directed towards mobilizing the people against multiculturalism by disseminating information and thus contributing to their understanding of the democratic process.

To counter what they see as a failed multicultural doctrine, they argue that the state must place a higher emphasis on Western values. Freedom of speech, gender equality and toleration of difference become focal points that define us, cementing the distinction between the civilized West and their portrayal of Islam and (practicing) Muslims. They argue for assimilation of immigrants and relegating any expressions of Islam and the Muslim faith to the private sphere. By continually emphasizing these aspects, they actively cement the framework which juxtaposes Islam and liberal values. The fear is that Islamic influences will lead to a degradation of our democratic institutions. To counteract this, some argue for a "democracy canon", wherein democracy and all the aspects that are connected to it – such as secularism, equality, and freedom of speech – must be promoted far more actively in schools:[13]

> In order to be able to resist this menace, we need a society in which citizens have a firm appreciation of democracy, a knowledge of its history, and a familiarity with its key texts, and a reverence for its fundamental values. Democracy stands or falls on citizens' love and persistence – their fierce loyalty to these fundamental principles and values.[14]

Some initiatives propose intervening directly in Muslim communities, teaching *them* about democracy.[15] They frame this as a fight against totalitarian and oppressive ideologies such as communism and Nazism on the one hand, and Islam and Islamism on the other. This is pivotal to their argument, and highlights the seriousness of the situation. For this matter, they use the historical cooperation of the

PICTURE 5.2 Anti-Islamic propaganda material

Source: Bundesarchiv, Bild 146-1987-004-09A/Heinrich Hoffmann/CC-BY-SA 3.0 [CC BY-SA 3.0 de (https://creativecommons.org/licenses/by-sa/3.0/de/deed.en)]

Note: An historical photograph of the Grand Mufti meeting Adolf Hitler.

Sunni Muslim Grand Mufti of Jerusalem (who was awarded the title of honorary Aryan) with Adolf Hitler. An historical image that is often reproduced to this effect is one showing the Grand Mufti meeting Hitler.

In order to achieve their goals, they place a large emphasis on the judicial system, something which underlines their focus on state-based solutions. All the different actors, whether they belong to a party, a newspaper, or an independent think-tank, are highly focussed on achieving change through the political system. To stop Islam's encroachment, the anti-Islamic initiatives also advocate a complete halt or a drastic reduction of non-Western immigration. This perspective contains a latent assumption that all Muslims are hard to integrate. Therefore, every Muslim immigrant is a potential threat.[16] As the perception that the anti-Islamic actors are being oppressed by the elite is a central theme, they argue that the elites should start discussing these aspects openly, or things will take a turn for the worse. Subsequently, some initiatives also point to the unwillingness of governing parties to apply scientific analyses of the negative consequences of immigration.[17] In so doing, they present themselves as agents for enlightenment, fighting for the common man:

> Yes, but my goal is that this should be a contribution to the democratic process. It has to be channeled within legal forms, within rational and articulated forms. Otherwise it will take extremely unhealthy directions.
>
> "Unhealthy" means that it isn't being articulated. We do live in a democracy after all, with a long tradition of solving problems in a non-violent way – which means that they have to be articulated! The pressure will keep rising if somebody at the top dictates to the people, saying "no, you're not allowed to say that". This will result in very detrimental conditions.[18]

While they do not promote violent solutions, their belief that Islam is a totalitarian ideology and the penultimate threat to Western civilization has propelled them to propose solutions that are clearly authoritarian. It is not that they just want to halt Muslim immigration or contain Islam within the private sphere of life. They also suggest rewriting or banning the Quran, which they portray as equivalent to Hitler's *Mein Kampf*:

> With the National Socialists, a radical minority emerged to overthrow the majority. The same is true in Islam: When jihad is called for, no Muslim can oppose it, otherwise he is regarded as an apostate and must be killed by the order of Mohammed. The similarity of the two ideologies is demonstrated by the close ties they had at the time. . . . Even today *Mein Kampf* is a best-seller in Islamic countries.[19]

Furthermore, it is not uncommon for anti-Islamic activists to propose banning mosques entirely. Mosques are – to their minds – indoctrination centres, which they defend by pointing to statements such as "The mosques are our barracks, the domes our helmets, the minarets our bayonets and the faithful our soldiers" by Turkish President Recep Tayyip Erdogan.[20]

The desire to confront and halt the spread of Islam is part of a joint framework shared by all the initiatives. They place a major emphasis on peaceful solutions, albeit some of them clearly authoritarian. The general view is that they contribute as a moderating force, and thus reduce the possibility of a violent escalation. This stresses the congruence between the way different agents are framed, wherein the solutions match their diagnosis. In this way, their explicit focus on distancing themselves from violence is a consequence of their framing of Western societies as civilized and rights-based, in contrast to the violent Muslims. The coherence with, and limitations set by the diagnostic framing is a tendency that has been noted in several studies that apply a framing theoretical perspective (Benford, 1997). While they frame Islam as an existential threat and political adversary, the primary opponent becomes the "oppressive, multicultural elites".

Motivational framing

The active construction of a motivational framework is something which Benford and Snow characterizes as a central and final component of the creation of meaning in a social movement. Its primary use is to rationalize and legitimize opposition, and to mobilize people in support of their struggle (Benford & Snow, 2000, p. 619). The anti-Islamic motivational framing is an essentialization of their core arguments, coupled with an emphasis on the primacy of action. They do this by arguing that we are all part of this struggle, whether we want to be or not. Implicitly this means that passivity equals condoning a process in which society becomes Islamized. They frame their opposition as a defensive battle for freedom and democracy, a fight in which they are willing to give anything to win. Either you are on the side of freedom and democracy, or you are opposed and on the same side as the jihadists and Islamists and their totalitarian ideology of Islam:

> The time for tolerating intolerance has come to an end: it is time for the civilised world to unite against a truly Global Jihad, in all its forms.[21]

In other words, they portray their struggle as one to safeguard a tolerant society against intolerance, necessitating intolerant and totalitarian approaches to combat Islam. They reinforce their motivational framing with apocalyptic statements such as "our entire civilization is in peril if the developments we see now continue", and war metaphors such as "invasion", "struggle", "fight", and "traitor" occur frequently. Some draw parallels to World War II. The war metaphors are not meant literally, at least not by most actors, but they highlight the severity of the current situation. In this way, they work as effective motivational framing. The anti-Islamic motivational framework is centred on mobilizing people to join in an active struggle to preserve Western society and values against those who seek to undermine it. This is done by delineating between *us* and *them*, whereby one is forced to take a stand. The conflict is heightened to an existential level between *freedom* versus *submission*, *good* versus *evil*. The emphasis on fighting for "what's ours" can be seen as highly rational when seen in light of the adjoining framework, whereby the very foundations for our free societies are under threat.

To summarize, the anti-Islamic movement adheres to a broad, common framework that is relatively uniform across organizations and countries. Their diagnostic framing of the threat can be roughly divided into two: Islam and Islamism as a totalitarian and existential threat; alongside the elites' attempts to cover up this fact or otherwise conspire with Muslims to destroy Western civilization. They operate with a broad, inclusive understanding of who is being threatened – women, LGBT, and Jews, as well as people of different religious, ethnic, and national backgrounds. In short, the rights and liberties of all other groups are threatened by Muslims. Their prognostic framing is anchored in non-violent and state-centric means: they advocate halting or minimizing non-Western immigration, assimilation instead of multiculturalism, and an extended emphasis on Christianity and liberal values, as well as public inquiries into the negative effects of immigration and achieving an open debate on these subjects. They also propose some clearly authoritarian solutions to achieve assimilation, such as banning or rewriting the Quran and making mosques illegal. Their motivational framework is constructed by combining the diagnostic and prognostic elements, calling for people to fight for freedom and democracy.

Women's rights and strategic ambiguity

The distinction between the civilized "us" and the totalitarian and barbaric "them" transcends the diagnostic, prognostic and motivational framing. This apparent inclusion and defence of liberal and progressive values and vulnerable minorities is particularly striking when seen in a historical perspective, as the far and extreme right have been characterized by their ideological opposition to gender equality and their racism, anti-Semitism, and homophobia. This inclusion, which runs across the cases in this chapter, has been understood as a thin veneer masking their true positions, and nothing more than an "exploitation" of gender and LGBT arguments (e.g. Mayer, Ajanovic, & Sauer, 2014) to defend themselves against accusations of racism (Lentin & Titley, 2012, p. 20). The second part of this chapter therefore unravels the use of these liberal and progressive ideals, and how they relate to more traditional perspectives long dominant among the far right. It does so by narrowing down to the issue of women's rights. Issues such as democracy, freedom of speech, conserving the Christian heritage, and so on, play important roles, but women's rights and safety is perhaps the most salient across time and cases. It is one of the most central and recurring themes in the definition of "us", consistently juxtaposed with the threat posed by Muslim men. The issue of women's rights also captures the tension inherent in this movement and subcultures' framing – straddling the span between older far right legacies and positions previously held exclusively by liberals and leftists. To clarify this, we make an analytical distinction between protector frames (PF) and equality frames (EF), both of which are used intermittently by all

TABLE 5.2 The traditional protector frames and modern equality frames used by anti-Islamic initiatives

	Traditional protector frames (PF)	Modern equality frames (EF)
Point of view	Male	Female
Victim	"Our women"	"Oppressed" Muslim women and all non-Muslim women
Perpetrators	Muslim men	Muslim patriarchy
Enablers	The elite	The elite

Note: The frames are broken down by point of view, portrayal of victim, perpetrators and enablers.

anti-Islamic actors. These frames can be broken down into four recurring components: point of view, victim, perpetrators, and enablers. The two frames are distinct on the first three of these, and only overlap on the last.

First, the PF point of view is male, whereas in the modern EF it is female. Second, PF includes the possessive notion of "our women", whereas EF is more expansive and includes "oppressed" Muslim women as well as all non-Muslim women. Third, PF is agency oriented and refers to Muslim men in general as inherently dangerous, just more so because the Quran supposedly legitimizes rape. On the other hand, EF relies on the structural notion of Muslim patriarchy rooted in social traditions. Nonetheless, the consistent depiction of Muslim men as perpetrators remains fixed in both depictions. They are systematically portrayed as depraved sexual predators, and Islam as an ideology of the penultimate embodiment of male dominance. Within this framework, anti-Islamic initiatives talk about "Western" women being harassed, assaulted, and raped by Muslim men, but also portray Muslim women as the biggest victims, highlighting their inferiority under Sharia law and Islam in general. Finally, both frames overlap in the portrayal of the elite as the enablers of (male) Muslim sexual violence and predatory behaviour.[22] Protector frames are in line with the older extreme right and ethno-pluralist far right, insomuch as it is about Norwegian, British, or German men defending "our women" from Muslim men. This reflects traditional notions about gender divisions and women as the weaker sex, and is epitomized by depicting Western men being prevented from rescuing vulnerable women from the predations of Muslim men by the state. In a sense, men are the true victims in this perspective. On the other hand, equality frames are aligned with modern gender norms; this is evident in the inclusion of Muslim women and omitting the previously mentioned male victimhood perspective.

Having stressed that the two frames are used by all the anti-Islamic actors, the salience of EF and PF nonetheless varies between the three country cases. This is partly traceable to differences in national contexts and the impact of the specific organizations. As a consequence of the central role played by HRS alongside the broader influence of Norwegian state feminism, the Norwegian case is dominated by EF, whereas PF are more prominent in the British and German cases.

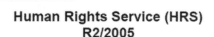

PICTURE 5.3 Propaganda material from HRS, the EDL, and PEGIDA which captures elements of protector and equality frames

Sources: a. Cover photo for a report by Human Rights Service, available at: www.rights.no/wp-content/uploads/2005/05/Norskf%C3%B8dte_jenter_-lemlestes052005.pdf. Downloaded November 2016; b. Caption from EDL's original Facebook page, no longer available. Downloaded November 2016; c. Picture uploaded to PEGIDA Deutschland's original Facebook page, no longer available. Downloaded November 2016.

Note: The picture of a young black girl is representative of the modern equality frame and has the text "Norwegian-born girls are gender mutilated" on it, whereas the latter two are in line with the traditional protector frames.

PICTURE 5.3 (Continued)

For instance, Norwegian anti-Islamic initiatives such as PEGIDA Norway[23] and HRS consistently make references to the oppression of Muslim women by other Muslims – especially female genital mutilation (FGM) and forced marriage. FGM has been a key issue for HRS, and was portrayed by the spokesperson as her gateway to understanding that Islam was a totalitarian ideology completely, unlike Christianity.[24] Gender equality seen in relation to the Islam and Muslim cultural praxis has also been salient over a longer time span in Norway, stretching back to the mid-1990s with reports about (Somali-Norwegian) Muslim girls being forced into marriage and subjected to FGM (Van Es, 2016). Public debate persisted over the years, and the importance of gender equality as a Norwegian value under threat from "Islamization" became increasingly salient following the Muhammed cartoon crisis in 2006, reinforcing the dichotomy between perceived Western values and Islam (ibid.). In contrast, gender and women's rights only became a high salience issue in the British and German cases after more recent sexual assault scandals. In Britain, the spark was the conviction of five men in a "grooming scandal", which became a major issue in 2010, where predominantly men with a Pakistani background were accused and in some cases convicted of luring underage girls into sexual relationships in return for such things as candy, alcohol, and drugs.[25] This also has a class dimension which is much less salient in Germany and Norway, both since the EDL began in the former industrial town of Luton and emphasize the working-class roots of their members, alongside the fact that most targeted girls are poor and white. In Germany, the sexual assaults on women on New Year's Eve in Cologne, 2015, became the main focal point. In their subsequent demonstrations, PEGIDA relied on the slogan "rapefugees not welcome", which quickly diffused among other anti-Islamic activist groups around Europe, including the EDL.[26] Both the case of FGM of Muslim girls and women, as well as sexual assaults and grooming, have been high-salience topics beyond the anti-Islamic "sphere". In Germany, for instance, the feminist magazine *EMMA* also linked it to the behaviour of Muslim men, and referred to "Tahrir-like scenes".[27]

It is plausible that the dominance of EF over PF is conditional on whether the antagonistic view of Islam or the inclusion of gender equality was the entry point. Was their initial concern women's rights or the notion of Islam as a destructive force in general? In the Norwegian case, gender equality and women's rights were the entry point to the broader anti-Islamic framework for HRS, whereas the temporal link was reversed for most other initiatives.[28] In other words, both pathways are possible. Regardless of this, the cases of sexual violence committed by people with a Muslim background have been catalysts for anti-Islamic initiatives in bridging the traditional PF and modern EF frames. Both frames are used by most anti-Islamic actors, sometimes appearing together within a single sentence or paragraph. In other words, the use of EF and the broader defence of modern gender norms does not exclude a male-centric perspective, but represents a novelty when compared with the older extreme and ethno-pluralist far right who have highlighted traditional gender roles and family values. It also creates a certain degree of overlap between the anti-Islamic collective action framework and feminist collective action framework(s).

Bridging a traditional and modern perspective on women's rights under the umbrella of the anti-Islamic collective action framing is an indirect or "nonrelational" channel of diffusion (Soule, 2004). Specifically, it allows the diffusion of the anti-Islamic collective action framework to actors who share a cultural understanding of gender equality and women's rights, yet have no direct political or organizational ties to each other (ibid., p. 312). The credibility of the frame bridging rests on how well the frames resonate with the culture of the actors they try include in their collective action framework; what Snow and Benford call "narrative fidelity" (1988, p. 1). This varies on an organizational level, as well as between the different country cases, and is probably most resonant in Norway.

Other scholars have noted the intermittent use of "traditional" and "modern" perspectives, particularly on populist radical right parties rallying against Muslims and Islam. Gender equality and women's rights has been defined as a transparently strategic vocabulary (Scrinzi, 2017), "instrumental" and "pseudo-feminist" (Larzillière & Sal, 2011), and that these actors exploit gender and LGBT arguments to vilify Muslim men (Mayer et al., 2014). However, the traditional gender perspectives and use of PFs have escaped being labelled "strategic", which implies that scholars use the concept of strategic to indicate that it is somehow false. This makes sense if we understand the use of, for instance, EF and PF as mutually exclusive, which rests on an unspoken assumption that the historical origins of the traditional and modern gender norms and the subsequent political divides are carved in stone. It also conflates incommensurability of ideologies – for instance, feminism and conservatism – with incommensurability (or illegitimacy) when specific actors' and movements draw on different normative and ideological strains. Within a framing theoretical perspective, varying between and incorporating messages from ideologies and traditions with an antagonistic history is not anomalous. Instead, framing ambiguity, i.e. vacillating between different frames can be used to forge alliances bridging political differences (Polletta & Lee, 2006). This back-and-forth between historically and sometimes logically opposed ideas is a consistent feature of the anti-Islamic collective action framework. This means that both frames are equally strategic, but for different audiences. The PF helps maintain their legitimacy with conservative factions, whereas the EF is key to their portrayal of feminists who do not mobilize against Islam as de facto anti-feminists conspiring with Wahabists and "woman haters":

> Because the International Women's Day march have taken sides. The wrong side. And if Norwegian "feminists" do not dare, cannot or will not demand that Islam's power over women is crushed in the free Norway (as they demanded that the power of Christian priests, churches and reactionaries be crushed), how can women standing in the midst of oppression dare to? If the International Women's Day march is not on the side of minority women – then who? Better to keep shut and accept ones fate. What an incomprehensible betrayal. The Wahabi hijab-brigade won. Again.[29]

The intermittent use of PF and EF to bridge the anti-Islamic collective action framework with the broader struggle for gender equality and women's rights enables them to level a multilayered critique of feminists who do not share their view. Thus, the anti-Islamic initiatives can claim to be the "true" feminists, while simultaneously employing traditional gender perspectives. On an overarching level, this strategic ambiguity stretches beyond framing women's rights and gender equality vis-à-vis Islam and Muslims. This also applies for the inclusion of "liberal values" and "progressive ideals" more broadly, such as LGBT and minority rights, portraying themselves as anti-racists and supporters of Jews. This is most apparent with initiatives which started out with a traditional perspective. For instance, some initiatives began by seeing Islam as a threat to their Christian identity, and the inclusion of gender equality and LGBT rights are a relatively new and partial realignment used in specific contexts. Furthermore, although Islam is likened to Nazism and they portray themselves as staunch defenders of Jews, the ambiguity is still evident in the specific manner Jews are portrayed. For instance, in the interview with the leader of SIAN, it was stressed that Jews never actually did anything to anybody, unlike Muslims. They were presented as the "model minority" – something which was not apparent without a Muslim presence. In other words, this back-and-forth between historically – and sometimes logically – opposed ideas are a consistent and core feature of the anti-Islamic collective action framework. Mirroring this strategic framing ambiguity, anti-Islamic initiatives claim to defend human rights, freedom of speech, and the political system, while simultaneously being explicitly hostile to human rights organizations, the media, and most established political parties (primarily on the left). It is always conditioned on their acceptance or rejection of Islam, Muslim culture, and immigration.

The master frame

To understand the transformative impact of anti-Islam, we must look at the ideologies that preceded it. Drawing on framing theory, Rydgren argues that the "extreme right" master frame of the 1920s became a prominent force in the 1930s and 1940s, carried by the fascist and Nazis, and basically became defunct following World War II (2005a, p. 413). He goes on to argue that the French FN and *nouvelle droite* of the 1970s became the ideological model for other radical right parties, who adopted their innovative master frame in place of the old extreme right master frame. Whereas the first extreme right master frame was characterized by an anti-democratic stance and biological racism, the second master frame's basic components were anti-establishment populism and xenophobic ethno-nationalism. The latter includes the notion of "separate but equal cultures" which should be confined to their own states, and which targets non-European nationalities such as Algerians and Moroccans. By contrast, the old extreme right emphasizes the biological superiority of the "white race". According to Rydgren, the doctrine of ethno-pluralism is a form of cultural racism which rejects hierarchical thinking, where superiority and inferiority of ethnicities and cultures does not come into the (official) equation (ibid., p. 427).

For simplicity's sake, the first master frame is hereafter defined as "fascist", whereas the second is defined as "ethno-pluralist". A third and vital component which Rydgren did not stress is their position on gender, family, and sexuality. This is perhaps because the fascist and ethno-pluralist master frame both rely on so-called traditional family values, which means that there was continuity in this regard. Jackson and Feldman (2014, p. 176), for instance, argue that the surge in anti-Islamic opposition (they use the term "Islamophobia") since the turn of the century is another expression of the cultural racism at the core of the ethno-pluralist master frame. Although there are similarities, I argue that the shift from targeting specific ethnicities to Muslims and Islam, particularly when coupled with progressive and liberal ideals and a defence of Jews, women, and LGBT is sufficiently different to constitute a third master frame for the far right.

Whereas there was continuation between the fascist and the ethno-pluralist master frames in their emphasis on traditional family values, the anti-Islamic master frame incorporates both traditional and modern perspectives. Anti-Islam also continues the ethno-pluralist master frame's anti-establishment line. The antagonism towards Islam and Muslims breaks with the ethno-pluralist line of "separate but equal" by explicitly defining Islam as inferior due to its inherent oppressive and violent character, yet both the anti-Islamic master frame and the ethno-pluralist master frame can be understood as "cultural racism" in its broadest sense. This thesis' argument that anti-Islam constitutes a third master frame therefore rests heavily on bringing the family/gender-dimension into the equation, which Rydgren excluded from his minimalist definition.[30] The political historian Vossen pointed out the likelihood of anti-Islam developing into a distinct master frame, highlighting Geert Wilders and his PVV party as innovators in this sense (2011, 2016). Moreover, he argues that anti-Islam may replace the previous, ethno-pluralist master frame identified by Rydgren among "nationalist populist parties and movements" (2011, p. 180).

Figure 5.2 presents the distinctions and overlaps between the three master frames are systematized along three dimensions: 1) how they view the system; 2) the basis for their understanding of the other; and 3) which values they otherwise uphold. This makes it clear that the anti-Islamic master frame is fundamentally different from the fascist master frame, whereas the ethno-pluralist master frame can be understood as a transitory phenomenon that bridges the fascist and anti-Islamic lines. Whereas the far-right parties that managed to succeed largely did so because they adopted the ethno-pluralist master frame (Rydgren, 2005a), the old extreme right master frame survived in the fauna of neo-Nazi, white power and fascist groups.

	Fascist master frame	**Ethno-pluralist master frame**	**Anti-Islamic master frame**
The system	Anti-democratic	Anti-elite	
The other	Biological racism (inferior races)	Ethno-pluralism (separate but equal ethnicities)	Anti-Islam (inferior religion and ideology)
Themselves	Traditional values (e.g. no to abortion, distinct gender roles, sanctity of heterosexual marriage)		Modern values (e.g. gender and LGBT rights)

FIGURE 5.2 The traits that unite and distinguish the three epoch-defining master frames for the far right: fascist, ethno-pluralist, and anti-Islamic

GA(LT)AN

The implications of a reorientation towards an anti-Islamic master frame becomes even more visible when seen in the light of the literature on political cleavages, which also captures the "gendered" dimension. Ideologically speaking, the anti-Islamic master frame transcends the so-called Green–Alternative–Libertarian (GAL) versus Traditional–Authoritarian–Nationalist (TAN) cleavage that much scholarly literature argues replaced the traditional left-right economic cleavage as the most salient the main dividing line in Western politics (e.g. Kriesi et al., 2008). The libertarian-traditional dimension has been considered the central component of this cleavage (e.g. Van der Brug & Van Spanje, 2009). Where libertarian is understood as being in favour of same-sex marriage, greater democratic participation, access to abortion, and so on (Bakker et al., 2015), traditional entails a rejection of these ideas and an emphasis on Christianity, the sanctity of heterosexual marriage and so forth. Bornschier identifies the populist radical right as challenging precisely the societal changes stemming from the "libertarian left" (2010, p. 5). According to this perspective, the electoral advances of populist right parties is driven by a reaction against the libertarian-universalistic issues' dominance over traditionalist-communitarian stances (Kriesi et al., 2008; Bornschier, 2010; Kriesi, 2010; Bornschier, 2011), meaning that these parties represent the TAN side of the cleavage. This is in line with Rydgren's definition of the radical right, ethno-pluralist master frame.

While I identify the website LGF as the genesis for the civilizational, anti-Islamic master frame outside party politics, its initial rise in party politics can largely be traced to the Dutch politician Pim Fortuyn and his party LPF (see Chapter 3). LPF have been described as ideological innovators in several studies (e.g. Akkerman, 2005; Kitschelt, 2007, 2012; de Lange & Mügge, 2015). Besides the LPF, some radical right parties have since undergone a partial ideological reorientation that breaks with the supposed GAL/TAN divide. For instance, in a comparative analysis of populist radical right party manifestos, de Lange and Mügge found that the relationship between gender and Islam became increasingly significant after 9/11 (2015, p. 74). Moreover, they argue that some of these parties, such as the Flemish LDD and the Dutch LPF, do not espouse traditional views on family and gender issues, and can therefore be defined as modern rather than traditional on this dimension (ibid., p. 71). Spierings, Lubbers, and Zaslove (2017) show that this has had an impact on the demand side, with voters in Norway, Sweden, and Switzerland in particular. They find that people who think LGBT rights are important but who are negative to immigration are actually more likely to vote for the populist radical right than those who are only negative to immigration.

Among radical right parties, however, the reorientation has not been total. The ethno-pluralist master frame has not become defunct. For whereas some initiatives seem to align with L rather than T on the libertarian-traditional dimension when it comes to gender equality and gay rights, others embody a limbo position. In the cases studied here, both traditional and libertarian/modern arguments and positions are used side by side – what I define as *strategic frame ambiguity*. In the case of the Dutch PVV, it seems to tilt clearly in the direction of the libertarian position, whereas the innovator of the previous master frame and one of the parties which have undergone at least a partial anti-Islamic reorientation, The French FN, under the auspices of Marine Le Pen, have engaged in protests against legalizing same-sex marriage and liberalizing adoption laws (Akkerman, 2015).

Coupling group and grid within a sectarian context

Grid-group analysis, initially developed by Mary Douglas (1982), enables us to further systematize the implications of the anti-Islamic, civilizational master frame. The terms grid and group refer to two separate dimensions of social order (1982, p. 191). Group refers to the general identity boundaries around a community, whereas grid indicates the amount of structural regulations and limitations. These two dimensions give rise to four separate fields or contexts that we can plot onto a matrix: first, an individualist, market-like context characterized by weak collective identities and few rules (low group/grid); second, an isolationist, and fatalistic context with weak collective identities and many rules (low group/high grid); third, a hierarchical and collectivist context (high group/high grid); and fourth, a sectarian context with strong collective identities and few rules (high group/low grid).

Originally meant to classify different societies, Kitschelt (2012) employed Douglas' framework to re-theorize the cultural libertarian-authoritarian dimension at the heart of the GAL/TAN divide to explain the rise of LPF. In this re-theorization,

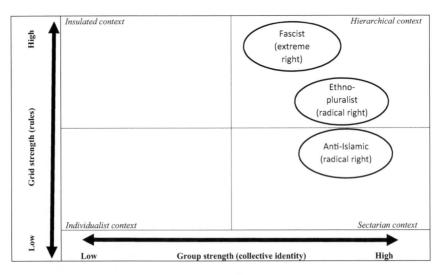

FIGURE 5.3 The three far right master frames placed within a grid/group matrix

Vertical axis indicates grid strength, which is the adherence to rules and hierarchies. The horizontal axis indicates group strength, which is the adherence to a collective identity. Fascist, extreme right and ethno-pluralist radical right are situated within the high grid/group quadrant, whereas the anti-Islamic radical right is situated within the low grid/high group quadrant.

we can split the libertarian-authoritarian dimension along group issues and grid issues. Whereas questions of immigration, integration, and ethnicity are group issues, questions of law and order, gender equality, and gay rights are grid-issues.[31]

Building on my findings and Kitschelt's re-theoretization, we can classify both the fascist extreme right and ethno-pluralist radical right as belonging to the upper right quadrant, which Douglas described as the hierarchical context, whereas the anti-Islamic radical right is situated in the bottom right quadrant. It is not a neat fit, however, as they espouse some clearly authoritarian positions vis-à-vis Muslims and Islam. For the radical right parties discussed by Kitschelt, the ideological changes they have undergone represent partial decoupling from authoritarianism through an adoption of liberal positions on many issues. As for the anti-Islamic initiatives which have arisen after 9/11, it is more apt to say that they have created a partial coupling between liberalism and authoritarianism, in large part from a liberal starting point. This coupling seems oxymoronic, but it is at least nominally driven by the anti-Islamic activists' view that Islam represents a totalitarian, intolerant force that must be met by intolerance itself to safeguard an otherwise tolerant society. For both the parties discussed by Kitschelt and the newer anti-Islamic initiatives studied in this book, the outcome is the same. Both transcend the GAL/TAN divide. We can therefore speak of an ideological convergence between pre-existing radical right parties and newer anti-Islamic initiatives.

Conclusion

This chapter shows that the anti-Islamic actors in Norway, Britain, and Germany share the same collective action framework. Their transnational coherence consolidates the understanding of anti-Islam as a potent, civilizational master frame. Narrowing down to the contentious issue of gender equality and women's rights vis-à-vis Islam and Muslims, it shows how they use both traditional protector frames with a male point of view and modern equality frames with a female point of view. Whereas the Norwegian opposition is strongly anchored in concern for all women's rights, the possessive notion of protecting "our women" is more predominant in the German and British cases. Nonetheless, all the anti-Islamic actors – often in quick succession – use both sets of frames. This framing ambiguity is a recurring phenomenon. Instead of understanding the inclusion of gender equality as a deceptive ploy, this chapter argues that both traditional and modern frames are equally strategic. The ambiguity evident in the simultaneous use of these frames makes it easier for anti-Islamic activists and parties to build alliances across previously untenable political differences, while sidelining those who disagree with their view of Islam and Muslims. Bridging frames also function as a channel for diffusion beyond establishing organizational or individual ties (Soule, 2004). This shift creates the potential for building negative coalitions between such varied actors' as Christian conservatives, nationalists, LGBT rights groups, women's rights groups, and Jewish groups.

As Kitschelt (2012) argued, the partial decoupling of group- and grid-related issues has opened up for a different set of radical right voters who do not stress authoritarian values across the board. Similarly, the voracious claims newer anti-Islamic initiatives make that they are standing up for an open, democratic, and tolerant society against the threat of a totalitarian force makes it possible for them to mobilize different activists than the "old" extreme and radical right.

Alongside the anti-Islamic and "liberal turn" of some radical right parties, the flourishing of new anti-Islamic initiatives and their drive to employ some clearly authoritarian solutions to safeguard an otherwise open, democratic, and tolerant society is – to my mind – the most pronounced development on the far right during the last two decades. It is, however, important to bear in mind that the carriers of this anti-Islamic, civilizational master frame which straddles the GAL/TAN cleavage do not constitute the entire far right, but a large subset.

Notes

1   The section on the anti-Islamic collective action framing builds and expands on parts of the article "The Collective Nature of Lone Wolf Terrorism: Anders Behring Breivik and the Anti-Islamic Social Movement" (2014), co-authored by Sveinung Sandberg. This is done with the explicit consent of Dr. Sandberg.
2   Previously covered in Chapter 2.
3   Quotes taken from the official EDL website, http://www.englishdefenceleague.org.uk/ (accessed 5 December 2016).
4   http://www.englishdefenceleague.org.uk/mission-statement/ (accessed 7 October 2016).
5   It is not uncommon that the leaders and spokespersons list many of these issues at once, as exemplified by a statement by Tatjana Festerling (PEGIDA) at a rally in Warsaw: "We have Sharia zones, patriarchy, polygamy, child marriage, FGM, hate preachers, religious slaughtering" (6 February 2016). Publicly available at: www.tatjanafesterling.de/down load/160206_Warsaw_TF_English.pdf (accessed 12 March 2016).
6   Quote from the blog Politically Incorrect, 3 March 2013. Publicly available at: www.pi-news.org/2013/03/islamic-sanctification-of-rape-and-the-horror-of-muslim-rape/ (accessed 5 December 2015).
7   Some of the most prominent historical events include the conquest and establishment of Al-Andalus in Spain beginning in 711, the conquest of Byzantium by the Ottomans in the 12th century, and the attack on Wien in 1683.
8   http://www.englishdefenceleague.org.uk/mission-statement/ (accessed 7 October 2016).
9   HRS stands out in this regard as the sole Norwegian initiative which doesn't explicitly single out the Labor Party.
10   www.independent.co.uk/news/world/europe/chancellor-angela-merkel-delivers-stinging-attack-on-germanys-growing-anti-islamic-protest-movement-9952274.html (accessed 10 January 2015).
11   Excerpt from Tatjana Festerling's speech made in Warsaw (6 February 2016).
12   www.theguardian.com/world/2010/oct/17/angela-merkel-german-multiculturalism-failed (accessed 10 January 2015).
13   HRS is the initiative most clearly advocating an emphasis on teaching about democracy in schools, which they have argued for in several articles, as well as in the interview conducted by Berntzen (4 October 2010).
14   Excerpt with interview of HRS spokesperson by journalist in *Frontepage Magazine*, available at: www.rights.no/2011/05/frontpage-intervjuer-hege-storhaug/ (accessed 31 May 2015).
15   In Norway, the fringe group SIAN is the one most fervently arguing for intervening in Muslim communities in such a manner. Intervention in Muslims communities was

generally something which the leader of SIAN advocated consistently in the interview (1 October 2010).

16 When talking about their internal opponents, they tend to identify them with the "radicals of '68". Radicals of '68 refers to the broad panoply of protest movements and cultural values pushed by the younger generations during the late 1960's, all of which were directed at and challenging the pre-existing cultural norms and institutions of Western societies in that era.

17 As such, HRS has published several reports on the rate of immigration and population growth based on datasets from the Norwegian Bureau of Statistics, Statistics Norway (SSB).

18 This excerpt is taken from the interview with the editor of the prominent webpage Document.no (29 September 2010).

19 My translation of statement by Michael Stürzenberger, the leader of the German Freedom Party, DF: "Schon bei den National-Sozialisten hat eine radikale Minderheit ausgereicht, um die Masse der Menschen ins Unheil zu stürzen. Genauso verhält es sich im Islam: Wenn der Dschihad ausgerufen ist, darf sich kein Moslem widersetzen, sonst gilt er als Apostat und muss gemäß Befehl von Mohammed getötet werden. Wie ähnlich sich die beiden Ideologien sind, beweist der enge Pakt, den sie beide damals schlossen. Auch heute ist „Mein Kampf" ein Verkaufsschlager in islamischen Ländern" (30 May 2015).

20 http://news.bbc.co.uk/2/hi/europe/2270642.stm

21 EDL mission statement (2016), http://www.englishdefenceleague.org.uk/mission-statement/ (accessed 7 October 2016).

22 Whether or not the elite is portrayed as willfully enabling Muslim men is a key distinction between "moderate" and "radical" anti-Islamic actors. The notion that the elite is willfully enabling Muslim men/Muslim patriarchy to the detriment of women is an extension of the Eurabia theory.

23 For instance, the leader of PEGIDA Norway stated that gender mutilation and forced marriage was because of Muslim immigration and the influence of Islam: www.dagbladet.no/2015/01/12/nyheter/innenriks/samfunn/politikk/pegida/37136855/

24 Interview with spokesperson from HRS.

25 www.channel4.com/news/rotherham-grooming-scandal-in-numbers (accessed 7 December 2016)

26 www.independent.co.uk/news/world/europe/cologne-attacks-what-happened-after-1000-women-were-sexually-assaulted-a6867071.html (accessed 7 December 2016)

27 *EMMA*, "Frauen berichten EMMA vom Terror", Emma Online, ticker, (accessed 5 December 2016), www.emma. de/artikel/koeln-frauen-berichten-emma-vom-terror-331129. Tahrir-like scene refers to the sexual molestation of women during the demonstrations taking place on Tahrir Square in Cairo, Egypt, during the Egyptian revolution of 2011.

28 In my interview with the HRS spokeswoman, she told me that they realized that Christianity was a positive force for society when they saw how it contrasted with Islam on the issue of women's rights.

29 My translation of the following text from Norwegian: "Fordi 8. mars-toget har valgt side. Feil side. Og hvis norske «feminister» ikke tør, kan eller vil kreve at islams makt over kvinner knuses i det frie Norge, (slik de før krevde at kristendommens presteskap, kirke og mørkemenn ble knust), hvordan skal kvinnene som står midt i undertrykkelsen våge da? Hvis ikke 8. mars-opptoget står på minoritetskvinnenes side – hvem gjør det da? Bedre å holde kjeft og finne seg i sin skjebne. For et ufattelig svik. Wahaabismens hijab-brigade vant. Igjen". Available from: www.document.no/2017/03/08/8-mars-et-opptog-av-hyklere/ (accessed 12 March 2017).

30 Rydgren does mention that the ethno-pluralist doctrine is embedded in "a general sociocultural authoritarianism, stressing themes like law and order and family values" (2005a, p. 433, n. 1).

31 McGann and Kitschelt introduced economic issues as a third dimension in addition to grid-group, which he labeled greed. The greed dimension is equivalent to the economic left-right, or socialist-capitalist dimension (e.g. McGann & Kitschelt, 1995, p. 15). While certainly relevant to model and explain the dimensions on which political parties (have to) compete, I contend that this third dimension provides little descriptive or explanatory power to the anti-Islamic turn itself.

Bibliography

Akkerman, T. (2005). Anti-immigration parties and the defence of liberal values: The exceptional case of the list Pim Fortuyn. *Journal of Political Ideologies, 10*(3), 337–354.

Akkerman, T. (2015). Gender and the radical right in Western Europe: A comparative analysis of policy agendas. *Patterns of Prejudice, 49*(1–2), 37–60.

Bakker, R., De Vries, C., Edwards, E., Hooghe, L., Jolly, S., Marks, G., & Vachudova, M. A. (2015). Measuring party positions in Europe: The Chapel Hill expert survey trend file, 1999–2010. *Party Politics, 21*(1), 143–152.

Bangstad, S. (2013). Eurabia comes to Norway. *Islam and Christian – Muslim Relations, 24*(3), 369–391.

Benford, R. D. (1997). An insider's critique of the social movement framing perspective. *Sociological Inquiry, 67*(4), 409–430.

Benford, R. D., & Snow, D. A. (2000). Framing processes and social movements: An overview and assessment. *Annual Review of Sociology, 26*(1), 611–639.

Berntzen, L. E., & Sandberg, S. (2014). The collective nature of lone wolf terrorism: Anders Behring Breivik and the anti-Islamic social movement. *Terrorism and Political Violence, 26*(5), 759–779.

Bornschier, S. (2010). *Cleavage politics and the populist right*. Philadelphia PA: Temple University Press.

Bornschier, S. (2011). National political conflict and identity formation: The diverse nature of the threat from the extreme left and extreme populist right. *Cultural Diversity, European Identity and the Legitimacy of the EU*, 171–200.

Cress, D. M., & Snow, D. A. (2000). The outcomes of homeless mobilization: The influence of organization, disruption, political mediation, and framing. *American Journal of Sociology, 105*(4), 1063–1104.

De Lange, S. L., & Mügge, L. M. (2015). Gender and right-wing populism in the low countries: Ideological variations across parties and time. *Patterns of Prejudice, 49*(1–2), 61–80.

Douglas, M. (1982). Introduction to grid/group analysis. *Essays in the Sociology of Perception*, 1–8.

Gamson, W. (1992). *Talking politics*. New York: Cambridge University Press.

Goffman, E. (1974). *Frame analysis: An essay on the organization of experience*. New York: Harper & Row.

Jackson, P., & Feldman, M. (2014). *Doublespeak: The framing of the far-right since 1945*. Stuttgart: Ibidem-Verlag.

Kitschelt, H. (2007). Growth and persistence of the radical right in postindustrial democracies: Advances and challenges in comparative research. *West European Politics, 30*(5), 1176–1206.

Kitschelt, H. (2012). Social class and the radical right: Conceptualizing political preference formation and partisan choice. In J. Rydgren (Ed.), *Class politics and the radical right* (pp. 224–251). London: Routledge.

Kriesi, H. (2010). Restructuration of partisan politics and the emergence of a new cleavage based on values. *West European Politics, 33*(3), 673–685.

Kriesi, H., Grande, E., Lachat, R., Dolezal, M., Bornschier, S., & Frey, T. (2008). *West European politics in the age of globalization* (pp. 154–182). Cambridge: Cambridge University Press.

Larzillière, C., & Sal, L. (2011). *Comprendre l'instrumentalisation du féminisme à des fins racistes pour résister*. Retrieved from www.contretemps.eu/interventions/comprendre-instrumen talisation-f%C3%A9minisme-fins-racistes-r%C3%A9sister

Lentin, A., & Titley, G. (2012). The crisis of "multiculturalism" in Europe: Mediated minarets, intolerable subjects. *European Journal of Cultural Studies, 15*(2), 123–138.

Mayer, S., Ajanovic, E., & Sauer, B. (2014). Intersections and inconsistencies: Framing gender in right wing populist discourses in Austria. *NORA-Nordic Journal of Feminist and Gender Research*, *22*(4), 250–266.

McGann, H. K. A., & Kitschelt, H. (1995). *The radical right in Western Europe: A comparative analysis.* Ann Arbor: University of Michigan Press.

Polletta, F., & Lee, J. (2006). Is telling stories good for democracy? Rhetoric in public deliberation after 9/11. *American Sociological Review*, *71*(5), 699–721.

Rydgren, J. (2005a). Is extreme right-wing populism contagious? Explaining the emergence of a new party family. *European Journal of Political Research*, *44*(3), 413–437.

Rydgren, J. (2005b). *Movements of exclusion: Radical right-wing populism in the Western world.* New York: Nova Publishers.

Scrinzi, F. (2017). A "new" national front? Gender, religion, secularism and the French populist radical right. In M. Köttig, R. Bitzan, & A. Petö (Eds.), *Gender and far right politics in Europe* (pp. 127–140). Springer International Publishing. DOI: 10.1007/978-3-319-43533-6

Snow, D. A., & Benford, R. D. (1988). Ideology, frame resonance, and participant mobilization. *International Social Movement Research*, *1*(1), 197–217.

Snow, D. A., & Benford, R. D. (1992). Master frames and cycles of protest. In A. D. Morris & C. M. Mueller (Eds.), *Frontiers in social movement theory* (pp. 133–155). New Haven: Yale University Press.

Snow, D. A, Benford, R. D, McCammon, H., Hewitt, L., & Fitzgerald, S. (2014). The emergence, development, and future of the framing perspective: 25+ years since "frame alignment". *Mobilization: An International Quarterly*, *19*(1), 23–46.

Snow, D. A., & Byrd, S. (2007). Ideology, framing processes, and Islamic terrorist movements. *Mobilization: An International Quarterly*, *12*(2), 119–136.

Snow, D. A., Rochford Jr, E. B., Worden, S. K., & Benford, R. D. (1986). Frame alignment processes, micromobilization, and movement participation. *American Sociological Review*, 464–481.

Soule, S. A. (2004). Diffusion processes within and across movements. In D. A. Snow, S. A. Soule, & H. Kriesi (Eds.), *The Blackwell companion to social movements* (pp. 294–310). Oxford: John Wiley & Sons.

Soule, S. A., & Olzak, S. (2004). When do movements matter? The politics of contingency and the equal rights amendment. *American Sociological Review*, *69*(4), 473–497.

Spierings, N., Lubbers, M., & Zaslove, A. (2017). "Sexually modern nativist voters": Do they exist and do they vote for the populist radical right? *Gender and Education*, *29*(2), 216–237.

van der Brug, W., & Van Spanje, J. (2009). Immigration, Europe and the "new" cultural dimension. *European Journal of Political Research*, *48*(3), 309–334.

Van Es, M. A. (2016). Norwegian Muslim women, diffused islamic feminism and the politics of belonging. *Nordic Journal of Religion and Society*, *29*(02), 117–133.

Vossen, K. (2011). Classifying wilders: The ideological development of Geert Wilders and his party for freedom. *Politics*, *31*(3), 179–189.

Vossen, K. (2016). *The power of populism: Geert Wilders and the party for freedom in the Netherlands.* Abingdon: Taylor & Francis.

6

NETWORKS

Broad and ideologically diverse

Introduction

Since the turn of the millennium, the far right in Western Europe and the United States has undergone two broad changes. First, much far-right activity has migrated online. Far-right groups were among the first to use online platforms in the United States (Burris, Smith, & Strahm, 2000), and their presence has not diminished since. Social media platforms have made far-right activists less dependent on taking to the streets to catch the attention of traditional mainstream media, giving them a larger degree of control over their image. Second, animosity towards Jews and targeting minorities based on ethnicity has declined, while we have seen a concomitant increase in hostility towards Islam and Muslims (Zúquete, 2008; Goodwin, 2013). Opposition to Islam and Muslims have, for instance, become dominant among the radical right parties (see e.g. Betz & Meret, 2009; Mudde, 2016). Outside party politics, we have seen a rise of activist groups and other initiatives that explicitly define themselves as counter-jihadists (Ekman, 2015), opponents of Islam and Muslims.

The proliferation of anti-Islamic activist groups such as the EDL (e.g. Allen, 2011; Jackson & Feldman, 2011; Kassimeris & Jackson, 2015) and PEGIDA (Daphi et al., 2015; Dostal, 2015; Berntzen & Weisskircher, 2016) indicate that the anti-Islamic far right has become a fixture in the broader political landscape. A small, but growing, body of research indicates that these actors are tending to amalgamate. For instance, in one of the first empirical studies of anti-Islamic actors in the United States, such as ACT! For America and Stop Islamization of America (SIOA), Ali et al. claim that "this core group of deeply intertwined [anti-Islamic, sic.] individuals and organizations manufacture and exaggerate threats of 'creeping Sharia', Islamic domination of the West, and purported obligatory calls to violence against all non-Muslims by the Quran" (2011, p. 2). Through detailed network analyses and the use of a plagiarism detection programme, Bail (2012, 2014) shows that the network of anti-Islamic organizations in the United States, such as Concerned Women for America, has grown in influence and become agenda-setters, at times dominating the news wave due to their emotionally charged language. Berntzen and Sandberg (2014) claim that these communities form a transnational social movement "sharing an anti-Islamic identity and rhetoric, and have overlapping and close ties" (ibid., p. 761). The transnational character of the anti-Islamic movement, with organizational and ideological roots across Europe and the United States, has been further outlined by several scholars. Meleagrou-Hitchens and Brun describe it as an "identifiable pan-European far-right movement" (2013, p. 1), and Goodwin defines it as "an amorphous network of think-tanks, bloggers and activists" (2013, p. 1), whereas Denes characterizes it as a "loose global fraternity" (2012, p. 295).

Yet the transnational scope of the anti-Islamic far right and their networks remains empirically underexplored (Macklin, 2013). Exceptions include Yang and Self (2015) and Lee (2015). Yang and Self conducted a network analysis starting from the anti-Islamic blog Atlas Shrugs, finding that it primarily had connections to other US right-wing sites. Beginning with five anti-Islamic websites, and tracing their hyperlinks, Lee made a partial mapping of what he defines as the "Counter-Jihadist Nebula", uncovering an online network of 46 websites (2015, p. 256). Apart from these studies, little is known about the full scope and configuration of this movement. Despite only having mapped parts of the anti-Islamic movement, these groups have consistently been defined as belonging to the far right (e.g. Zúquete, 2008; Jackson & Feldman, 2011; Archer, 2013; Lee, 2015). Meleagrou-Hitchens and Brun, as does Goodwin, distinguish them from the explicitly racist and anti-immigrant far right in their specific focus on Islam and Muslims.

In the previous chapter, I argued that their collective action framing builds on an ideological duality whereby they incorporate both traditional and modern values in their self-portrayal as defenders of Western civilization. Many of these views are usually associated with parties and movements on the left, not the far right. This includes presenting themselves as defenders of gender equality, LGBT, minorities, and even animal rights, against their main enemy – Islam. They combine this with rallying around Christianity and unwavering support for Israel, the latter being particularly inimical to the anti-Semitism of the traditional extreme right.

This chapter maps the size and configuration of the anti-Islamic movement as it manifests itself online, and grapples with the movement's specific composition and analyzes whether, and to what extent, it represents a break with the traditional extreme (fascist) and radical (ethno-pluralist) right as some of their ideological positions might entail.

Besides engaging in protest events, most anti-Islamic actors are primarily active on social media platforms such as Facebook and Twitter. Starting with 27 anti-Islamic organizations from North America and Western Europe, I conduct a one-mode network analysis, unravelling a network of 3,615 groups in March 2015 and 4,594 groups in March 2016. By historically tracing the anti-Islamic expansion of the far right, we saw how important major events such as 9/11 and the Muhammed cartoon crisis have been for their growth. Taking the importance of major events into account, data from before and after the refugee crisis that unfolded in the summer of 2015 allows us to discern some of the changes that occurred in its wake.

My analysis shows that, online, the anti-Islamic network is genuinely transnational, with groups in places such as India, Myanmar, and the United States, as well as in all Western European countries where they exist in a borderland between forming a movement and a subculture.[1]

Anti-Islamic groups in this online network also have ties to communities across the traditional left-right divide, such as Christian conservatives, Israeli and pro-Israeli groups, and groups focussing on animal rights, women's rights, and LGBT rights. Few extreme right groups fronting anti-Semitic and anti-systemic ideas connect with the anti-Islamic network.[2] However, actors can be part of a network without being a part of a coalition or movement. Ties to animal rights, women's rights and other groups do not mean that they themselves are part of an anti-Islamic movement or subculture. Nonetheless, it is clear that the anti-Islamic actors are distinct from the traditional extreme and ethno-pluralist right. Instead, some say it represents a form of "liberal nationalism" (Lægaard, 2007), where Muslims are the ones portrayed as threatening these rights and are therefore excluded.

In the competition between the traditional extreme right and the anti-Islamic far right, the latter seems to be dominant. The anti-Islamic turn and expansion can potentially contribute to a further marginalization of the homophobic, anti-Semitic extreme right. However, the refugee crisis may have sown the seeds for reversing their stance as defenders of liberal and progressive rights against the onslaught of Islamization. More Eastern European extreme right groups of the older variety have entered the online network in its wake. What this will entail is still unclear.

The chapter is structured as follows. I begin by detailing my use of social network analysis and the initial case selection, as well as the challenges of gathering data from online communities. I then give an overview of the anti-Islamic Facebook network in 2015 and 2016. I provide an in-depth analysis of the interrelations between the anti-Islamic communities and other communities present within the network, with a particular focus on "progressive" and extreme right forces.

Framing, ideology, and networks

Are these anti-Islamic groups as ideologically different from the traditional extreme and radical right as Chapters 4–5 and previous work would lead us to believe? Several studies have shown that networks are structured along ideological lines among non-government organizations (Murdie, 2014, p. 20), as well as on social media platforms such as Twitter (Yardi & Boyd, 2010; Himelboim, McCreery, & Smith, 2013, p. 41; Conover et al., 2011) and Facebook (Thorson & Wells, 2015). Furthermore, the degree of ideological segregation online is similar to that of offline communities (Gentzkow & Shapiro, 2011; Halberstam & Knight, 2016). In other words, homophily on the basis of ideology is predominant. If the ideological position of anti-Islamic groups has a relational impact, this should also be mirrored in who they seek information from and who they try to create alliances with on Facebook. This means that we should be able to uncover whether the anti-Islamic movement as a whole is distinct from the traditional extreme right based on the overall network structure. First, we would expect anti-Islamic groups to establish ties to other anti-Islamic groups. As noted, overviews and qualitative analyses of anti-Islamic groups' ideology show that they claim to defend freedom of speech, gay rights, women's rights and other minorities (Archer, 2013; Berntzen & Sandberg, 2014). If this is more than skin deep, and ideology truly is causally linked to network formations, then we can also expect that:

> H1: Anti-Islamic initiatives have ties to groups which the anti-Islamic initiatives themselves claim to defend against Islam and its adherents.

This includes Jewish groups and groups supporting LGBT rights, women's rights, and animal rights. We should stress that network ties are not the same as actual coalitions. Ties to, and even some reciprocation from, Jewish and "progressive" groups does not mean that they are actual coalition partners. Social movements are composed of overlapping networks encompassing a broad range of ideologies, social relations and issues (Diani, 1992; Mische, 2003) whereas coalitions are "interorganizational agreements formed for the purpose of collectively addressing a specific set of policy or political objectives" (Heaney & Rojas, 2008, p. 45). Networks transcend coalitional agreements (ibid.), but indicate which actors are desirable coalition partners (Heaney, 2004). In much the same way, the absence of connections indicates which actors are undesirable coalition partners. Since they represent themselves as anti-racist and equate Islam with Nazism, we should also find that:

> H2: Traditional extreme right groups are marginal in the anti-Islamic network.

Unlike the dominant strains of anti-Islamic ideology, traditional extreme right ideology includes reverence for violence and dictatorship at the expense of democracy. It also includes portraying Jews as the penultimate enemy, homosexuals as deviants, women as inferior, and other minorities as threats (Bjørgo, 1997). Whether or not the extreme right is marginal will be determined on the basis of three factors: the number of extreme right groups, the number of ties between these and anti-Islamic groups, and their structural position in the network as a whole. For instance, are they important in tying the network together and facilitating the flow of information? A confirmation of my hypotheses would support the argument that the anti-Islamic far right is a qualitatively distinct phenomenon from the traditional extreme right. On the other hand, the assumption that the anti-Islamic far right is distinct from the traditional extreme right on an organizational level is substantially weakened if they have no ties to progressive and liberal groups, while traditional extreme right groups constitute a strong component of the network in terms of the number of groups, ties, and their structural position.

Research design and data

In order to extract data from their Facebook groups, I relied primarily on the web-crawler Netvizz (Rieder, 2013) which is accessible as a Facebook application. It allowed me to scrape content from specific Facebook groups and connections between groups. This data was subsequently analyzed using UCINET.

To collect information on the anti-Islamic groups and their online network, I used what is known as a "saturation snowball" approach. This allows us to begin with a selection of key actors that clearly belong to the category under scrutiny. I began with 27 prior known cases of anti-Islamic actors from Norway, Britain, and Germany, in addition to offshoots across Europe and North America, as well as one group from India and one from Myanmar. Prominent groups include the EDL, SIOE, and PEGIDA.[3]

The snowball saturation consists of going two steps beyond the starting point, dividing the groups (nodes) into three subsets. The first step is to trace whom the 27 initial seed groups (subset 1) connect to (subset 2). In the second step, I identify all the ties subset 2 has back to both the original subset and out to new groups in subset 3. Finally, we see whether the groups in subset 3 connect back to subsets 1 or 2. This means that the network I analyze contains all the interrelations between all the groups in the three subsets for March 2015 and March 2016, respectively. On the one hand, the snowball approach and a vast amount of data allowed me to look at the size, scope, and geographic reach – both regionally and globally – of these anti-Islamic groups, capturing an operative reality completely different from that of traditional social surveys or regular qualitative analyses.[4] It allows a comprehensive identification and overview of the network, and is particularly helpful when the boundaries beyond a given core are difficult to predefine (Christopoulos & Aubke, 2014, p. 17). On the other hand, a snowball approach does make the study vulnerable in two ways. First, there is the risk of missing some of the most peripheral actors (isolates). The groups that will be missed are those that connect in to these 27 anti-Islamic groups but whose ties are not reciprocated by either the starting groups themselves or any other of the groups that the anti-Islamic groups in turn link to. Snowball selection may therefore lead to an overstatement of the connectedness of the actors within the network. Secondly, the identification is heavily influenced by where "we start the snowball rolling" (Hanneman & Riddle, 2005). The latter issue is not of particular concern for me, as my interest is naturally focussed on singling out anti-Islam and the additional fact that I was able to start with several major anti-Islamic actors, as well as some middling and small ones.

Each connection is a directional like on Facebook, meaning that somebody with administrative rights on one of the group pages has established a connection to another group by finding their site and clicking the like button. Connections are *not* established when individual members of a Facebook group like one another.

What does a group liking another group entail? Analytically, like-based connections share some similarities to hyperlinks between regular webpages. They allow

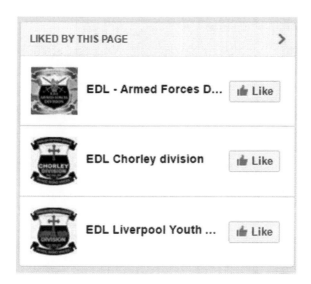

PICTURE 6.1   Screenshot of EDL's "like" roster on Facebook (November 2016)

users to jump to the other webpage instantaneously. However, Likes entail more than this. When an administrator of a Facebook group likes another group, this action shows up on their own group's wall for members and followers to see. Subsequently, all updates and posts from liked groups show up in the group administrator's feed. This makes it easy to re-share information such as written posts, videos, and photos. Information dissemination can be almost instantaneous. It also allows the administrators to like and comment individual posts of the other group, which is a good way to signal support. Even though the word "like" has positive connotations, it is not given that they have a positive view of the other group. On the contrary, it might also be used for monitoring purposes. Yet, this kind of neutral or hostile monitoring is easy to stop. As an administrator of a page, you can see which individuals and groups like your own page and simply delete their like. This severs the information flow, so that they no longer receive updates. It is also easy to reverse a like by going to a page and unselecting it. For purposes of journalistic or hostile monitoring, it is much harder to weed out individuals who like your page. Even though it is easy to detect organizations monitoring through the like function, removing them naturally depends on the administrator – their awareness, commitment, and possibly even paranoia.

In the following section, I begin with an overview of the anti-Islamic network captured in March 2015 before moving on to an in-depth comparison of the two time periods and the changes that have occurred. This is followed by a discussion of the specific hypotheses concerning the impact of the ideological inclusion of Jews, LGBT, women's rights, and the equation of Nazism with Islam on connections to both "progressive" and traditional extreme right groups.

The anti-Islamic networks

Starting with the 27 anti-Islamic groups, I uncovered a vast, transnational network. In 2015, the network was composed of 3,615 groups and 38,000 connections (likes) between them. The data is not symmetrized, which means that the original directionality of the connections remains intact. By 2016, the network has expanded by close to 1,000 groups, containing 4,594 groups and 43,733 connections. Some measures indicate a certain degree of stability, for instance the graph density scores. At 0.003 and 0.002, they are quite low, even for a large network. This indicates that the network is far from being a single tightly knit community. The average clustering coefficient is 0.3, which means that more than one in four possible triangles is complete at both points in time. This does not, however, tell us about the existence of larger communities. Newman's modularity metric is one way to delve into the specific clustering and pinpoint communities. Modularity reflects the concentration of edges (connections) within a given module, which is a subset of the entire network, compared with a random distribution of edges between all the given nodes, regardless of any clustering. The ability to locate local substructures like these is one of the most interesting features of social network analysis. Not only are we able to say something about the whole network and the individual groups, but we can also see the way in which the network divides into different cliques (Hanneman & Riddle, 2005). Applying Newman's modularity metric at the lowest resolution (1) produces a modularity score of 0.6, with 18 distinct communities at both points in time. The largest of these are dominated by explicitly anti-Islamic groups.[5]

The subsequent figures give the aggregated versions of the entire network, with each node (circle) representing all the groups in the separate communities. Node size is determined by the number of groups, and the ties between the nodes by the number of likes between the communities. The labels for the 18 communities reflect the main composition of each community.

The network can roughly be separated into five segments at both intervals: the anti-Islamic communities (dark grey); the extreme right (black); the broader far-right (dark grey with meshed web overlay); media organizations (white with vertical

TABLE 6.1 Key statistics for the anti-Islamic network in March 2015 and March 2016

Anti-Islamic network	March 2015	March 2016
Nodes	3,615	4,594 [+ 27%]
Edges	38,956	43,733 [+ 12%]
Average degree	10.7	9.5
Network diameter	24	29
Density	0.003	0.002
Communities	18	18
Modularity score	0.6	0.6
Average clustering coefficient	0.32	0.31
Average path length	5	6.4

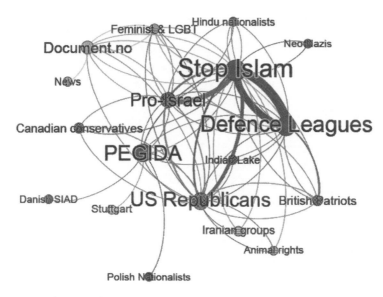

FIGURE 6.1   The anti-Islamic network in March 2015

Note: The 3,654 groups as part of their respective clusters in the anti-Islamic network, March 2015 (N = 18). Node size reflects number of groups in the given cluster. Dark grey marks the cluster dominated by explicitly anti-Islamic groups, black marks the extreme right clusters, dark grey with meshed web overlay marks other right-wing clusters, white with vertical stripes marks media clusters, and white with horizontal stripes marks "progressive".

stripes); and progressive groups (white with horizontal stripes) often labelled as part of the new social movements that began cropping up during the 1970s. In this study, it is the ties to the extreme right and the progressive groups that interest us. I begin by listing the networks and communities in 2015 (Figure 6.1), before moving on to the comparison with 2016 (Figure 6.2).

The anti-Islamic network 2015

In 2015, the anti-Islamic communities made up 54% of the network, with five communities and 1,953 groups. The largest community (766 groups) was characterized by groups whose name and descriptions included the words Stop Islamization of [England/Europe]. Although containing other groups, e.g. Gates of Vienna, labelling this community Stop Islam seems appropriate. I follow this strategy for all communities, and provide more in-depth exploration of each community in the following pages. The Stop Islam community is followed by the Defence Leagues (631 groups), PEGIDA (556 groups), the Hindu nationalists (25 groups), and the Stop Islamization of Denmark community (ten groups). The first three anti-Islamic communities are also the largest communities in the network. This is followed by five other far-right communities with 1,151 groups, or 32% of the network. In total, far-right groups including the anti-Islamic communities accounted for 86%

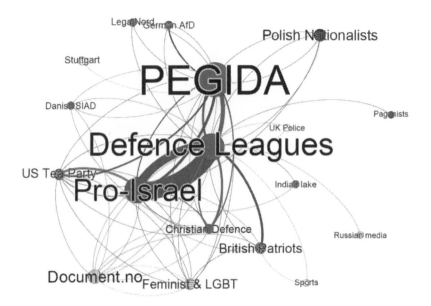

FIGURE 6.2 The anti-Islamic network in March 2016

Note: The 4,594 groups as part of their respective clusters in the anti-Islamic network, March 2016 (N = 18). Node size reflects number of groups in the given cluster. Dark grey marks the cluster dominated by explicitly anti-Islamic groups, black marks the extreme right clusters, dark grey with meshed web overlay marks other right-wing clusters, white with vertical stripes marks media clusters, and white with horizontal stripes marks "progressive".

of the network. The two media clusters (293 groups) and three progressive communities (152 groups) made up the rest.

With its 766 groups, the Stop Islam community constituted the largest cluster in the entire 2015 network. Besides the explicitly Stop Islamization groups, this community also included several support groups for the Dutch politician and leader of the anti-Islamic populist radical right PVV, Geert Wilders, and the famous critic of Islam and Somali refugee, Ayaan Hirsi Ali. We also find some animal rights groups within this community – although most are single issue and focus on halal butchering. We also have Christian fundamentalist groups with names such as the Warriors of Christ, and Women Against Socialism and Islam. The Stop Islam community also contained support groups for famous anti-Islamic and self-labelled counter-jihadists such as Bat Ye'or (the woman who invented the term "Eurabia") and the website GoV, both of which received massive coverage in 2011 because they were widely cited in the personal manifesto of the Norwegian terrorist Anders Behring Breivik.

The Defence League community is the second largest within the network (631 nodes), the most well known of which is the EDL. Besides the many Defence League groups, this community includes groups such as the Sikh Awareness Society (SAS), Hindus and Punjabis (Sikhs) are Friends and United, Stop lowering the armed forces pension, and groups with names such as Prophet Muhammed was a Paedophile. As with the slightly larger Stop Islam community, we also find a couple of animal rights groups such Stop Animal Cruelty and Animal Rights UK. To the left, we come across the third largest community within the anti-Islamic network, the PEGIDA community, which had only started five months before the data collection. In addition to a large number of groups across Europe carrying the PEGIDA label, this community also includes some AfD groups. This is the nascent populist right party in Germany which first picked up steam on their anti-Euro message, but later came to adopt an anti-immigrant stance, as well. You also have several far-right Identitaire groups in this community, which originated in France. It is interesting to note that the Swedish radical right SD also pop up in this cluster – although as a minor player with five in-links and no out-links.

Besides the explicitly anti-Islamic communities, I have classified most other communities as belonging to the broader far right; the US Republican and Tea Party community, a pro-Israeli community, and a cluster of Canadian conservatives, as well as British patriot groups, the largest of which were the Tea Party and the pro-Israeli communities. The Tea Party community consists of 509 groups such as the Tea Party Patriots, National Rifle Association and support groups promoting television personalities such as Bill O'Reilly from Fox News. The pro-Israeli community has 397 groups such as Christians United for Israel (CUFI), Freundschaft Deutschland-Israel, Friends of the IDF (FIDF), Hindus United for Israel, and The Truth About Israel's Defensive Actions Against The Flotilla. This community contains explicitly anti-Islamic groups such as We Stand With Israel – Siotw (Stop Islamization of The World), but the pro-Israeli community is also closely interlinked with the broader Stop Islam community. Due to the number of links to the Stop Islam and Defence League communities, as well as the presence of many explicitly anti-Islamic groups within the cluster itself, the pro-Israeli community straddles the border between anti-Islamic and the broader far right. The British patriot community is the third largest far-right cluster, with 102 groups. These are mainly groups such as Support Our Armed Forces in all they do for our Nation and Keep the Falklands British. In addition, there are fan pages for well-known political and military leaders such as Winston Churchill, and support groups for populist radical right figures such as Nigel Farage, former leader of UKIP. There was also a relatively large cluster consisting of Canadian conservative groups (95), with ties to the Defence League, Stop Islamization, and the Tea Party and Republican communities.

There are two clusters of media outlets in the network, with 280 and 37 groups, respectively. The key actor in bringing the biggest cluster of media organizations into the network is the Norwegian anti-Islamic news site Document.no. This is one of the most prominent anti-Islamic actors in Norway, with a large readership (Berntzen & Sandberg, 2014). Document.no was also one of the main groups the Norwegian terrorist Anders Behring Breivik tried to establish contact with before he decided to turn to violence. As a whole, this cluster has almost no links into/with other anti-Islamic groups, and as such are structurally peripheral. Document.no, however, has an important role as an information outlet for the anti-Islamic community.

Finally, there are the communities of progressive groups. The biggest of these is the community consisting of feminist and LGBT groups (73), with names such as Astraea Lesbian Foundation for Justice, STOP FGM NOW!, Girls Are Not for Sale, LGBT News, Muslim & Exmuslim Women for Secularism, Women Who Change The World, and Smashing the Patriarchy. There was also an Iranian anti-regime community (69 groups), and an animal rights community (ten groups).

I now turn from an overview of the communities and groups present in March 2015 to the reconfiguration of the network in March 2016.

Changes between 2015 and 2016

By 2016, there were 18 distinct communities in the anti-Islamic network on Facebook, and the network had undergone profound changes (Table 6.2). New communities emerged, and old ones disintegrated or disappeared. Three factors affect the new composition of the network. First, growth is caused by the addition of new groups via the like function. The network expanded a great deal by 2016, consisting of over 4,500 groups. Second, 38% of the groups present in 2015 were no longer in the network in 2016. Groups vanish from the network either because Facebook or group moderators have deleted them, or because they are no longer on the like

TABLE 6.2 A comparison of the communities present in the anti-Islamic network in 2015 and 2016

	2015	2016
▦ Anti-Islamic	2,347	3,171
▣ Other far right	757	475
■ Extreme right	17	255
▨ News media	293	331
▩ Progressive	83	184

Note: The communities present in the anti-Islamic network on Facebook in March 2015 and March 2016 shows a large growth in the anti-Islamic communities and a decline in other far-right groups.

list of other groups. Third, groups can move from one cluster to another as the configuration of ties changes; this occurred in 23% of the groups.

The anti-Islamic communities have expanded the most, accounting in 2016 for 69% of the network – growing from 1,953 to 3,171 groups. The biggest change comes from the PEGIDA community's growth, from 556 to 1,262 groups. The Defence League community also expanded, consisting of 922 groups. The explicitly anti-Islamic community also grew, with the addition of the Christian Defence League as a new community (118 groups). More significantly, the Stop Islam community evaporated as a distinct cluster, as did the Hindu nationalists, and the already tightly interlinked pro-Israeli community grew by including a large amount of anti-Islamic groups. Since the pro-Israeli community had a very strong component of anti-Islamic groups, this integration means that we can define this community as belonging within the sphere of the anti-Islamic movement.

The number of groups belonging to other far-right communities is nearly halved despite the inclusion and emergence of the German AfD (57 groups) and the Italian LN (53 groups). Looking back to 2015, the network included a community of Canadian conservative groups (95) with ties to the Defence League and Stop Islam, together with the US Republican and Tea Party communities. However, by 2016, this community had vanished. More surprisingly, the Republican and Tea Party community also declined significantly, from 509 to 186 groups. Of these, 374 groups fell out of the network altogether.

The extreme right presence in the anti-Islamic network transformed when the small community of neo-Nazi groups fell out and two new communities emerged: a small pagan community (seven groups), and a community of Polish nationalists (248 groups).

The news media communities have grown and consolidated, with the former Le Parisien community merging with the Document.no community. We also see the appearance of a small community of Facebook groups (four) for Sputnik, the Russian pro-Putin news organization. Turning to the community of progressive groups, the small animal rights community and the Iranian exile community disappeared, whereas the feminist and LGBT community more than doubled in size (184 groups).

Groups entering and falling out of the network are only part of the explanation for the changes. Internal restructuring and migration within the network is another pivotal factor. In fact, 24% of the existing groups from 2015 migrated from one community to another. As we can see in Figure 6.3, most of these went from one anti-Islamic community to another.

As noted earlier, the Stop Islam community has disintegrated. A large portion of the groups formerly in this cluster migrated to the Defence League community (320 groups), with the EDL at its core. This constitutes the single largest migration of groups in the period of time examined. Another large section broke off and migrated to the pro-Israeli community (237 groups). A take-home point from this is just how much the pro-Israeli community transformed and grew in importance.

FIGURE 6.3 The movement between communities in the anti-Islamic network between 2015 and 2016

Note: This shows the fracturing of the Stop Islam community and integration with the pro-Israeli community. Node size reflects number of groups in the given cluster. Red indicates the clusters dominated by explicitly anti-Islamic groups, black marks extreme right clusters, blue marks other right-wing clusters, yellow marks media outlets, and green marks "progressive".

It also points to the "attractiveness" of the pro-Israeli and Israeli groups on Facebook. In addition to the groups from the former Stop Islam community, the pro-Israeli community has also expanded with the addition of a large chunk of the Tea Party community (124 groups). Besides these internal rearrangements, there have been few shifts between other communities.

Progressive and extreme right presence in the anti-Islamic network

Moving on to the specific hypotheses about the anti-Islamic communities and the ties to other progressive and extreme right groups, we note that previous studies found that ideology is consistently correlated with the structure of online and offline alliances and information networks. We can use this knowledge to test whether the findings from qualitative analyses of anti-Islamic groups hold. Does the broader anti-Islamic movement incorporate progressive ideals at an organizational level and shy away from the traditional extreme right views? If so, we should find two things. First, progressive groups should be present. Second, traditional extreme right groups should be marginal.

To delve into this, I draw on the material presented earlier, as well as two other aspects: the specific ties between the communities (see the density matrices, Tables IV and V, Appendix II) and the possible power position of the progressive and extreme right, respectively. To say something about the power position of these communities, I turn to their brokerage positions, calculating their "honest broker-age" scores (see Table III, Appendix II). The goal is to pinpoint not only which community plays the role of a broker in a traditional sense, but also in a wider sense. Honest brokerage is much more sophisticated measure than regular ones such as betweenness centrality that pinpoints actors who provide unique connections or exclusive control of resources between other social actors (Christopoulos & Qua-glia, 2009). The honest brokerage measure distinguishes between pure brokerage, weak brokerage, and no brokerage. Pure brokerage means that there are no other ties between any pair of alters joined by a broker, whereas weak brokerage means that one directed tie is allowed between pairs of alters joined by a broker. Non-brokerage means that alters who have ties to a broker have two-way ties with each other, as well (Walther & Christopoulos, 2012, p. 13). In other words, pure brokerage means that you are the sole connector between different communities, whereas weak brokerage means that you are the predominant connector. Centrality and brokerage consistently equal power in political systems such as these. However, the role of brokerage comes with a price. This is because brokers are seen as "Janus faced", which by definition implies that they are under pressure "from conflict-ing norms of any groups they connect. The more extreme the difference between groups, the more likely that they are under strain" (Walther & Christopoulos, 2012, p. 19). This kind of norm conflict and ambiguity can also be a resource, allowing recipients to emphasize different aspects of collective action framing, as well as giving representatives the opportunity to tailor their message to differing contexts. Ambiguity of this kind can therefore forge agreement and identity across political differences (Polletta, Chen, Gardner, & Motes, 2011).

Ties to progressive forces

My first hypothesis was that the anti-Islamic groups have ties to groups they claim to defend from Muslims, particularly Jewish groups and LGBT rights, women's rights, and animal rights groups.

The cursory overview at a community level supports this. However, to verify, we need to delve more deeply into the relations between the communities and subsequently the specific groups. In 2015, 23 of the groups in the Stop Islam community and seven in the Defence League community had ties to the com-munity of 83 feminist and LGBT groups. None of the feminist or LGBT groups reciprocate the ties from the Defence League community, but have seven ties to the Stop Islam community. Strikingly, there pro-Israeli community has 25 links to the feminist and LGBT community, and these are reciprocated by 18 feminist and LGBT groups. The Stop Islam community also had 12 ties to the small animal rights community of ten groups, but there was no reciprocation. By 2016, these animal rights groups disappeared altogether from the network. By 2016, the number of groups in the feminist and LGBT community had more than doubled, to 182. The number of ties from the pro-Israeli community which absorbed so many of the anti-Islamic groups rose to 42, followed by 18 ties from the Defence Leagues and three from the PEGIDA community. Thirty groups from the feminist and LGBT community reciprocated the ties from the pro-Israeli community, followed by four to the Defence League and one reciprocation to PEGIDA. The feminist and LGBT community has also grown in importance, as indicated by their brokerage score in Table III in Appendix II. They have gone from zero to 0.167, meaning that they have become more pivotal in tying together the network as a whole and thereby function as more important channels for information dissemination. The pro-Israeli and other anti-Islamic communities form a triangular relationship with the feminist and LGBT community, although the latter is much smaller.

In a study of the Swedish far right, anti-Islamic website Flashback, Törnberg and Törnberg find that "gender equality seems to be used as a discursive strategy in order to criticize Islam" (2016, p. 2). They reach this conclusion through a combination of critical discourse analysis and topic modelling on a corpus of 90 million sentences. My findings indicate that the issue of gender equality has become deeper embedded than just as a discursive strategy. Not only does the anti-Islamic movement have ties to leftist and progressive groups, but their online impact on the movement has increased within the given time span, as indicated by their brokerage score. The feminist and LGBT community is clearly less central to the anti-Islamic movement than the pro-Israeli community, but it is more pivotal than, for instance, the American far right with the Tea Party and similar groups. So, what then of the extreme right?

Ties to extreme right forces

In 2015, there was an almost total absence of traditional extreme right groups. No white power or neo-Nazi groups showed up, with the exception of a small cluster consisting of five Norwegian and Swedish anti-immigrant and racist actors such as the racist "news site" Fyret.nu, and Realisten.se. These groups only had two ties out to the Stop Islam community, and were therefore very marginal players. By 2016, they had fallen out of the network. Instead, we saw the inclusion of an equal number of paganist groups, but these are not as clear-cut extremist. There was also a small, marginal community of seven Polish groups. Over the course of a year, the Polish and Eastern European extreme right community had grown by well over 200 groups. ONR Brygada Podlaska is an offshoot from the self-described "radical nationalists" in the National Rebirth of Poland, and dominates this community of groups. They take a strong position against LGBT rights and have been characterized as openly anti-Semitic by the Anti-Defamation League.[6] Many of these groups have several hundred thousand followers. This community also includes explicitly anti-Islamic groups, like the Polish group No to the Islamization of Europe (*Nie dla Ilamizacji Europy*), with 281,832 followers in 2015 and 307,043 in 2016. Some actors outside Poland also show up, such as the Hungarian radical right party Jobbik. However, this community has few ties to the anti-Islamic communities. Of the explicitly anti-Islamic communities, PEGIDA is the one with the most ties to the Eastern European extreme right, with 38 likes emanating from the PEGIDA community. This may be partly driven by geographical proximity between the German-speaking countries, Poland, and Hungary. This was followed by four ties from the Defence League community and two from the pro-Israeli community. Interestingly enough, these groups had fewer ties out than in. There are two ties out to the pro-Israeli camp, two to the newfangled AfD community, and one to the Defence League community. Unlike the brokerage position held by the feminist and LGBT community, the extreme right does not have a brokerage position. The marginal position for neo-Nazi and other traditional extreme right groups – combined with the strong presence of Jewish groups and pro-Israeli communities, as well as progressive groups – consolidates the fact that the anti-Islamic movement is a qualitatively very different entity than the traditional extreme right (those who ascribe to the fascist master frame).

Discussion

What are the main conclusions we can draw from the network analysis of anti-Islamic groups on Facebook? First, the transnational scope and large size of the network gives a picture of a phenomenon straddling the borders between a movement and a subculture. It has been claimed that "the 'counter-jihad' network seems to have dissolved, as many right-wing populists have branded themselves primarily anti-EU" (Fleischer, 2014, p. 69). The picture we get from their online presence on Facebook tells a completely different story, and that is a story of growth – not dissolution. Although the data only give us two static snapshots of the network, we know that a major branch has been added quite recently with the upsurge of PEGIDA in Germany and then across Europe.

Second, the picture provided by the online data is of a movement that is also internally unsettled and fluid. One-third of the existing Facebook network from 2015 had fallen out a year later, whereas over 2,000 groups joined. There were also major internal shifts, with close to one-third of the groups present in 2015 migrating from one community to another by 2016. When operating with more limited information, it is therefore easy to understand precisely why some could think that the so-called counter-jihad was dissolving. Beyond the actual demise of specific organizations, the large changes can be partly attributed to the nature of the media platform itself. Setting up a new group on Facebook is not resource demanding, although being noticed and accepted by pre-existing anti-Islamic groups does require some effort.

Third and most importantly, we see that birds of a feather really do flock together. The overview of clusters within the network in 2015 and 2016 give us an immediate picture that closely mirrors the findings in Chapters 4–5, as well as what other qualitative studies have uncovered regarding the rhetoric and world-view of anti-Islamic groups (e.g. Zúquete, 2008; Goodwin, 2013; Busher, 2013). For instance, they have strong ties to Israeli and pro-Israeli groups, which consists of everything from Christians for Israel to the official website of the Israeli Defence Forces. By 2016, there had been a further integration of the anti-Islamic movement and the pro-Israeli community, with a large section of the former Stop Islam community being absorbed by the former. This means that the anti-Islamic far right is clearly different from the traditional anti-Semitic extreme right on this dimension. We know that movements rely on bridging ties between narrow cliques. Social systems lacking weak ties will be fragmented and incoherent which translates into less political staying power (Granovetter, 1983). We also know that weak ties directly affect the diffusion of ideas and innovation, the structure of social systems and relations between individuals (Christopoulos & Quaglia, 2009, p. 192). Seen in this light, the role played by the women's rights and LGBT community as transmitters of ideas becomes even more important. Their presence emphasizes the fundamental shift that the focus on Muslims and Islam means for the far right, particularly in Western Europe and North America. If progressive and liberal initiatives and ideas continue to exert influence on the anti-Islamic movement and subculture, the far right as a whole seems to be set on a course which solidifies their difference from other far-right ideologies, movements, and groups.

Negative coalitions

The presence of LGBT groups and other "progressive" forces in the network does not mean that they are a part of an anti-Islamic movement or any coalitions. Managing coalitions is generally difficult, partly because they often unite the movement's moderate and radical strands, which are normally in conflict with one another (Rucht, 2004). Coalitions that go beyond the confines of a specific movement can be even more demanding, as they can challenge the identity of an organization or movement (Heaney, 2004; Hojnacki, 1997; Meyer & Corrigall-Brown, 2005). What kind of coalitions can we expect to find between anti-Islamic actors and "progressive" actors? Guenther's work on the feminist movement in Eastern Germany's weak coalitions (2010) provides some clues. Weak coalitions do not require full recognition and discussion of identities, ideologies, and goals, and they only allow limited challenges to group boundaries. The closer collaboration and tighter communication and understanding necessary for strong coalitions is likely to generate conflict and highlight differences. Low levels of integration allow coalitions to thrive in coalition environments where differences are rarely explicitly acknowledged or discussed (ibid., p. 135).

Eastward expansion

The inclusion of Eastern European right-wing extremists at the periphery of the anti-Islamic network represents a countervailing tendency to the presence of "progressive" actors and integration with Jewish, Israeli, and pro-Israeli groups. Why is their presence stronger? Major events can have a strong impact on political alliances (Leifeld, 2013). So-called critical events have also been found to have a strong impact on the structure of social media networks (Omodei, De Domenico, & Arenas, 2015, p. 1). The anti-Islamic movement has grown in fits and spurts over the last decade, and the growth seems to be event driven. As already outlined in Chapter 4, the anti-Islamic movement started growing in the wake of the terror attacks on 9/11, and first took to the streets in Europe not long after the Muhammed cartoon crisis. In 2015 and 2016 there have been several events that have played into their narrative of conflict with Islam and the Muslim world. The most significant events have been: the attacks on *Charlie Hebdo* in January 2015, the sexual assaults on women by refugees in Cologne on 1 January 2016, and the terror attacks in Paris on 13 November 2015, which killed 130 people. Yet, all of these merged into the backdrop of the larger refugee crisis that began to unfold in summer 2015. Whereas the previous events fuelling the movement had taken place in the United States or Western European countries, the refugee crisis was a truly trans-European crisis. It shook governments across Europe and the European Union, which is likely to have had a strong impact on the reconfiguration of political alliances. The inflow of migrants and refugees from Middle Eastern and North African countries met with very different responses from national governments. Angela Merkel and the German government was one of the most open, together with the Swedish government,[7] whereas the Visigrad countries broadly refused to receive refugees and argued for stricter border controls. The Hungarian Prime Minister, Viktor Orbán, stated that Islam was incompatible with European culture[8] and the Slovak Prime Minster, Robert Fico, that said they would only take in Christian refugees.[9] The Central and Eastern European countries are now widely perceived to have a more restrictive stance on immigration and Muslims, more in line with the anti-Islamic far right.[10] This expansion of the political debate on Islam and immigration to a trans-European scale may well have raised awareness of potential allies for the anti-Islamic groups to the East. An eastward expansion might have major consequences, because the far right in Eastern Europe is overall far less reformed and more openly racist (for overviews, see e.g. Mudde, 2005; Minkenberg, 2015; Pirro, 2015). Even though the Eastern European extreme right is still marginal within the network, their presence may herald a return to the traditional extreme right. Another prospect is that the extreme right in Eastern Europe align themselves with the anti-Islamic forces in Western Europe, and thereby moderate themselves and move away from scapegoating and aggression directed towards sexual minorities, Roma, and Jews.

Absent anti-Semitism

Fleischer argued that "anti-Semitism and anti-Muslim racism, just as anti-Roma racism, are perfectly compatible prejudices, which are present in every part of Europe's radical right" (2014, p. 70). Although empirically supported at the individual level and theoretically plausible at an organizational level, the constellations uncovered in the network analysis indicate that this is not predominant. More specifically, the argument about anti-Semitism does not hold water if we take into account the reciprocated ties between anti-Islamic groups on the one hand, and pro-Israeli and official Israeli groups on the other. However, further analysis of their framing activity is needed before coming to a decisive judgement. This is not to say that there are no xenophobic, extreme right communities and groups equally hostile to Jews, Muslims, and Roma, but that they are not closely linked to the specifically anti-Islamic far right on an organizational level online.

Limitations and alternative avenues

My claims regarding the presence of traditional extreme right groups in the online network is limited by two important factors. First, their presence may be underreported by the mere fact that I started the snowball sampling with anti-Islamic groups, which means the analysis may miss the fringe outliers that link to anti-Islamic groups without being reciprocated. If this is the case, it still goes to show how toxic and unpopular the traditional extreme right is – even for groups labelled and perceived as being part of the same phenomenon. As anti-Islamic groups have few ties to neo-Nazi and traditional extreme right groups this also means that there is very little information flowing from them to the anti-Islamic movement through Facebook. Second, it is important to bear in mind that the size and presence of traditional extreme right groups in the network would probably be higher, were it not for Facebook's own policing of hate speech. This has driven racist, neo-Nazi and white supremacist groups to establish themselves on the Russian alternative to Facebook, Vkontakte.[11]

My broader claims are also limited by the fact that I have only examined the online network configurations, leaning on previous qualitative studies that tell us something about their ideology. This analysis says nothing about the composition of progressive or extremist ideas discussed by the members and followers of these groups. For this, we need detailed studies of the anti-Islamic and broader far right discourse and framing. Only then can we untangle the possibly divergent impact of liberal and progressive forces on the one hand and the new inclusion of Eastern European right-wing extremists on the other. For a deeper understanding, we also need ethnographic fieldwork along the lines of Joel Busher's study of the EDL (2013) and David Art's interviews with far-right activists (2011), in addition to qualitative and quantitative content analyses of their publications and online writing. The trajectory of the far right and the anti-Islamic movement and subculture towards either moderation or extremism will be a key issue for social scientists in the coming decades, especially since the Muslim minority is likely to grow.

Notes

1 Following Diani's definition, a movement is understood as "networks of informal inter-actions between a plurality of individuals, groups, or associations, engaged in a political or cultural conflict on the basis of a shared collective identity" (Diani & Bison, 2004, p. 282), whereas a subculture is one in which actors experience a sense of commonality that cuts across the boundaries of specific groups, but there is no systematic exchange between organizations (ibid., p. 285).

2 The analysis does not include data on more traditional arenas of activism or collabora-tion. A group or constellation of groups within the network that is sizeable online may only have a small institutional footprint or presence on the streets.

3 The groups come from the three last waves of anti-Islamic activist groups, which are cited in Chapter 4.

4 The survey approach certainly is able to get at the broader support in the population, as well as the electoral support for these platforms, but completely neglects the reality of these groups' present existence. Let us not forget that it does not take a large amount of people to become engaged for this phenomenon to have staying power, certainly less than is within the margins of statistical error (normally calculated as in the 3% range). Similarly, a qualitative approach, while being able to provide much insight into specific phenomenae, suffers from a severe blind spot in not being able to rigorously trace net-works and movements because of their innately high demand on resources.

5 See Tables I and II in Appendix I for a full list of communities ranked by the number of groups.

6 http://archive.adl.org/international/polanddemocracyandextremism.pdf

7 Sweden received over 160,000 asylum applicants in 2015, second only to Germany in the entire EU. See Table 1 in the article "Overwhelmed by Refugee Flows, Scandi-navia Tempers its Warm Welcome" by the Migration Policy Institute (2016): https://www.migrationpolicy.org/article/overwhelmed-refugee-flows-scandinavia-tempers-its-warm-welcome (accessed 21 November 2016).

8 https://www.theguardian.com/world/2015/sep/03/migration-crisis-hungary-pm-vic tor-orban-europe-response-madness (accessed 21 November 2016).

9 https://www.washingtonpost.com/news/worldviews/wp/2015/08/19/slova kia-will-take-in-200-syrian-refugees-but-they-have-to-be-christian/ (accessed 21 November 2016); https://www.dw.com/en/slovakia-vows-to-refuse-entry-to-muslim-migrants/a-18966481 (accessed 21 November 2016).

10 In an interview with Vox, Cas Mudde is quoted saying that "2015 unleashed an orgy of Islamophobia": www.vox.com/2016/5/31/11722994/european-far-right-cas-mudde (accessed 21 November 2016).

11 www.theatlantic.com/technology/archive/2016/05/extremist-groups-vkontakte/ 483426/ (accessed 23 June 2016).

Bibliography

Ali, W., Clifton, E., Duss, M., Fang, L., Keyes, S., & Shakir, F. (2011). Fear, Inc. *The roots of the Islamophobia Network in America*. Washington, DC: Center for American Progress. http://www. americanprogress.org.

Allen, C. (2011). Opposing Islamification or promoting Islamophobia? Understanding the English Defence League. *Patterns of Prejudice*, 45(4), 279–294.

Archer, T. (2013). Breivik's mindset: The Counterjihad and the new transatlantic anti-Muslim right. *Extreme Right Wing Political Violence and Terrorism*, 169–185.

Art, D. (2011). *Inside the radical right: The development of anti-immigrant parties in Western Europe*. Cambridge: Cambridge University Press.

Bail, C. A. (2012). The fringe effect: Civil society organizations and the evolution of media discourse about Islam since the September 11th attacks. *American Sociological Review*, 77(6), 855–879.

Bail, C. A. (2014). *Terrified: How anti-Muslim Fringe organizations became mainstream*. Princeton, NJ: Princeton University Press.

Berntzen, L. E., & Sandberg, S. (2014). The collective nature of lone wolf terrorism: Anders Behring Breivik and the anti-Islamic social movement. *Terrorism and Political Violence*, 26(5), 759–779.

Berntzen, L. E., & Weisskircher, M. (2016). Anti-Islamic PEGIDA beyond Germany: Explaining differences in mobilisation. *Journal of Intercultural Studies*, 37(6), 556–573.

Betz, H-G., & Meret, S. (2009). Revisiting Lepanto: The political mobilization against Islam in contemporary Western Europe. *Patterns of Prejudice*, 43(3–4), 313–334.

Bjørgo, T. (1997). *Racist and right-wing violence in Scandinavia: Patterns, perpetrators and responses*. Oslo: Tano Aschehoug.

Burris, V., Smith, E., & Strahm, A. (2000). White supremacist networks on the Internet. *Sociological Focus*, 33(2), 215–235.

Busher, J. (2013). Grassroots activism in the English Defence League: Discourse and public (dis) order. In M. Taylor, P. M. Currie, & D. Holbrook (Eds.), *Extreme right wing political violence and terrorism* (pp. 65–84). London: Bloomsbury Publishing.

Christopoulos, D., & Aubke, F. (2014). Data collection for social network analysis in tourism research. In *Knowledge networks and tourism* (pp. 126–142). New York: Routledge.

Christopoulos, D., & Quaglia, L. (2009). Network constraints in EU banking regulation: The capital requirements directive. *Journal of Public Policy*, 29(2), 179–200.

Conover, M., Ratkiewicz, J., Francisco, M. R., Gonçalves, B., Menczer, F., & Flammini, A. (2011). Political polarization on twitter. *ICWSM*, 133, 89–96.

Daphi, P., et al. (2015). *Protestforschung am Limit. Eine soziologische Annäherung an PEGIDA*. Retreived from www.wzb.eu/sites/default/files/u6/pegida-report_berlin_2015.pdf

Denes, N. (2012). "Welcome to the Counterjihad": Uncivil networks and the narration of European public spheres. *Journal of Civil Society*, 8(3), 289–306.

Diani, M. (1992). The concept of social movement. *The Sociological Review*, 40(1), 1–25.

Diani, M., & Bison, I. (2004). Organizations, coalitions, and movements. *Theory and Society*, 33(3), 281–309.

Dostal, J. M. (2015). The PEGIDA movement and German political culture: Is right-wing populism here to stay? *The Political Quarterly*, 86(4), 523–531.

Ekman, M. (2015). Online Islamophobia and the politics of fear: Manufacturing the green scare. *Ethnic and Racial Studies*, 38(11), 1986–2002.

Fleischer, R. (2014). Two fascisms in contemporary Europe? Understanding the ideological split of the radical right. In M. Deland, M. Minkenberg, & C. Mays (Eds.), *In the tracks of Breivik: Far right networks in Northern and Eastern Europe* (pp. 53–70, 54). Vienna and Münster: LIT.

Gentzkow, M., & Shapiro, J. M. (2011). Ideological segregation online and offline. *The Quarterly Journal of Economics*, 126(4), 1799–1839.

Goodwin, M. J. (2013). *The roots of extremism: The English Defence League and the Counter-Jihad challenge*. London: Chatham House.

Goodwin, M. J., Cutts, D., & Janta-Lipinski, L. (2016). Economic losers, protestors, islamophobes or xenophobes? Predicting public support for a counter-Jihad movement. *Political Studies*, 64(1), 4–26.

Granovetter, M. (1983). The strength of weak ties: A network theory revisited. *Sociological Theory*, 201–233.

Guenther, K. (2010). *Making their place: Feminism after socialism in Eastern Germany*. Stanford, CA: Stanford University Press.

Halberstam, Y., & Knight, B. (2016). Homophily, group size, and the diffusion of political information in social networks: Evidence from Twitter. *Journal of Public Economics, 143*, 73–88.

Hanneman, R. A., & Riddle, M. (2005). *Introduction to social network methods*. Published online. Retrieved from http://faculty.ucr.edu/~hanneman/nettext/

Heaney, M. T. (2004). Issue networks, information, and interest group alliances: The case of Wisconsin welfare politics, 1993–99. *State Politics & Policy Quarterly, 4*(3), 237–270.

Heaney, M. T., & Rojas, F. (2008). Coalition dissolution, mobilization, and network dynamics in the US antiwar movement. In *Research in social movements, conflicts and change*. Bingley: Emerald Group Publishing Limited.

Himelboim, I., McCreery, S., & Smith, M. (2013). Birds of a feather tweet together: Integrating network and content analyses to examine cross-ideology exposure on Twitter. *Journal of Computer-Mediated Communication, 18*(2), 40–60.

Hojnacki, M. (1997). Interest groups' decisions to join alliances or work alone. *American Journal of Political Science*, 61–87.

Jackson, P., & Feldman, M. (2011). *The EDL: Britain's "new far right" social movement* (NECTAR, the Northampton Electronic Collection of Theses and Research). The University of Northampton, Northampton.

Kassimeris, G., & Jackson, L. (2015). The ideology and discourse of the English Defence League: "Not racist, not violent, just no longer silent". *The British Journal of Politics and International Relations, 17*(1), 171–188.

Lægaard, S. (2007). Liberal nationalism and the nationalisation of liberal values. *Nations and Nationalism, 13*(1), 37–55.

Lee, B. (2015). A day in the "swamp": Understanding discourse in the online counter-Jihad nebula. *Democracy and Security, 11*(3), 248–274.

Leifeld, P. (2013). Reconceptualizing major policy change in the advocacy coalition framework: A discourse network analysis of German pension politics. *Policy Studies Journal, 41*(1), 169–198.

Macklin, G. (2013). Transnational networking on the far right: The case of Britain and Germany. *West European Politics, 36*(1), 176–198.

Meleagrou-Hitchens, A., and Brun, H. (2013). *A neo-nationalist network: The English Defence League and Europe's counter-Jihad movement*. London: International Centre for the Study of Radicalisation and Political Violence.

Meyer, D., & Corrigall-Brown, C. (2005). Coalitions and political context: US movements against wars in Iraq. *Mobilization: An International Quarterly, 10*(3), 327–344.

Minkenberg, M. (2015). *Transforming the transformation?: The East European radical right in the political process*. London: Routledge.

Mische, A. (2003). Cross-talk in movements: Reconceiving the culture-network link. *Social Movements and Networks: Relational Approaches to Collective Action*, 258–280.

Mudde, C. (2005). *Racist extremism in Central & Eastern Europe*. London: Routledge.

Mudde, C. (2016). *The study of populist radical right parties: Towards a fourth wave*. C-REX Working Paper Series, 1.

Murdie, A. (2014). The ties that bind: A network analysis of human rights international non-governmental organizations. *British Journal of Political Science, 44*(1), 1–27.

Omodei, E., De Domenico, M. D., & Arenas, A. (2015). Characterizing interactions in online social networks during exceptional events. *Frontiers in Physics, 3*, 59.

Önnerfors, A. (2017). Between Breivik and PEGIDA: The absence of ideologues and leaders on the contemporary European far right. *Patterns of Prejudice, 51*(2), 159–175.

Pirro, A. L. (2015). *The populist radical right in Central and Eastern Europe: Ideology, impact, and electoral performance.* London: Routledge.

Polletta, F., Chen, P. C. B., Gardner, B. G., & Motes, A. (2011). The sociology of storytelling. *Annual Review of Sociology, 37,* 109–130.

Rieder, B. (2013, May). *Studying Facebook via data extraction: The Netvizz application.* Proceedings of the 5th annual ACM web science conference, pp. 346–355.

Rucht, D. (2004). Movement allies, adversaries, and third parties. In *The Blackwell companion to social movements* (pp. 197–216). Oxford: Oxford University Press.

Thorson, K., & Wells, C. (2015). Understanding media effects in an era of curated flows. In T. Vos & F. Heinderyckx (Eds.), *Gatekeeping in Transition* (pp. 25–44). London: Routledge.

Törnberg, A., & Törnberg, P. (2016). Combining CDA and topic modeling: Analyzing discursive connections between Islamophobia and anti-feminism on an online forum. *Discourse & Society, 27*(4), 401–422.

Walther, O., & Christopoulos, D. (2012). *A social network analysis of Islamic terrorism and the Malian rebellion.* CEPS/INSTEAD Working Papers, 38.

Walther, O. J., & Christopoulos, D. (2015). Islamic terrorism and the Malian rebellion. *Terrorism and Political Violence, 27*(3), 497–519.

Yang, A., & Self, C. (2015). Anti-Muslim prejudice in the virtual space: A case study of blog network structure and message features of the "ground zero mosque controversy". *Media, War & Conflict, 8*(1), 46–69.

Yardi, S., & Boyd, D. (2010). Tweeting from the town square: Measuring geographic local networks. *ICWSM,* 194–201.

Zúquete, J. P. (2008). The European extreme-right and Islam: New directions? *Journal of Political Ideologies, 13*(3), 321–344.

7

MOBILIZATION

Activist messages and emotions

> Islam is a philosophy of darkness, murder, rape and utter mind controlling insanity. Wherever Islam walks death follows. The Christian does not possess the power to fight this evil because they would have to fight this darkness with darkness and then it is they who become savages. I guess the modern man now understands why God told the Israelites to eliminate the evil around them. Left to their own devises Islam will eliminate all that is good on the earth. Even nature is at risk, the hatred towards all animals by those who practice Islam is yet another sign of its rancid effect on the human mind.
>
> (Post on anti-Islamic Facebook group Jihad Watch,
> August 2016)

Introduction

Leaders and representatives of the anti-Islamic movement argue that they are fighting to save Western civilization from the totalitarian and violent threat of Islam.[1] As demonstrated in the quotation opening this chapter, they frame Islam in truly apocalyptic terms. In this civilizational framework, they portray themselves as defenders of the West and everything that it stands for, and that Islam is not. This is built on an ideological duality, where they simultaneously rely on traditional, authoritarian perspectives and modern, liberal perspectives. They position themselves as defenders of Christianity, "family values", and law and order, as well as defenders of gender equality, LGBT rights, and anti-racism.[2] The (partial) adoption of progressive and liberal positions appears paradoxical coming from a movement that is understood, by its opposition and academics alike, as far right. The overarching question is how deep the entanglement with liberal and progressive values goes. Perhaps it is nothing but a thin veneer, window-dressing masking the anti-democratic and racist views of the extreme right.

In Chapter 6, we saw that the traditional-liberal duality was reflected in their online networks. Anti-Islamic groups have ties to women's rights and LGBT rights groups. They are also closely integrated with Israeli, pro-Israeli, and conservative groups. Finally, they have few ties to "traditional" extreme right groups such as white supremacists, fascists, and neo-Nazis.

This chapter goes further by studying their online mobilization. If the anti-Islamic movement and subculture as a whole truly represents a different beast from the white supremacist, fascist and neo-Nazi extreme right, as well as the ethno-pluralist radical right, this should not only be represented through statements by social movement organization leaders or be visible through their organizational networks. What the activists write and respond to matters.

Here I investigate which message the already mobilized convey, and whether the activists can thus be described as moderates aligned with the official ideological platform, or extremists who only share the animosity towards Islam and Muslims. I also look at which emotions and messages drive internal mobilization and message diffusion beyond their Facebook groups.

In order to explore these two dimensions, this chapter uses a wide range of tools to analyze 1.8 million posts, shares, likes, and comments from a membership base of close to 5 million in 298 anti-Islamic groups between 12–18 August 2016.[3] The groups are of varying size across the world, ranging from large initiatives such as EDL and PEGIDA to small, regional groups. These were identified and selected on the basis of the previous network analysis. I examine three core aspects previously identified in the collective action framing of anti-Islamic leaders and representatives to uncover the degree of alignment between the organizations and their members (see Chapter 5). The first aspect consists of views on Muslims and race to see whether they are more focussed on Islam and Muslims than racial categories in their problem identification. The second aspect is their conceptualization of themselves, and whether their messages convey support for Jews, women, and LGBT as part of the in-group under threat from Islam and Muslims. The third and most significant aspect – whether they uphold democracy and propose peaceful solutions or promote and glorify violence against their opponents – is crucial in determining whether we can speak of an anti-Islamic movement that is fundamentally distinct from the extreme right embodied by neo-fascists and neo-Nazis.

The emotions and arguments of the members reveal a struggle of competing views and ideas. On the one hand, the diagnosis of Islam and Muslims as an existential threat is dominant. Defence of democracy and supportive statements towards women, LGBT, Jews, and other religious minorities are prominent. Democracy is the term most strongly associated with positive sentiments. On the other hand, views and arguments mirroring the traditional extreme right (white power, neo-Nazi, fascist) are also present. Derogatory views of women and homosexuals show up alongside views of violence as a necessary tool to "deal with" Muslims. Third, although they are a less prevalent enemy than Muslims are, there is an even stronger association between the category "black" and negative sentiments, whereas "white" is associated with positive sentiments. In other words, there is an undercurrent of explicit racism. Taken together, this indicates that there is a contingent of extremists. These extremists are not just *more radical* than their leaders, but to some extent, they represent older strains of far-right ideology.

Finally, joyful messages and expressions of trust towards their own members or authority figures drive internal mobilization. Angry messages focussing on Muslims also seem to mobilize, but the results are not as clear as for joyful and trusting messages. Joyful messages often rely on Christian themes, sometimes fused with arguments in favour of their expansive in-group, such as homosexuals. This reinforces the merger of liberal and traditional positions, previously documented in the leaders' framing. Nonetheless, it is still an open question whether the moderates or extremists will dominate among the anti-Islamic initiatives in the long run.

The chapter proceeds as follows. I begin by defining the anti-Islamic collective action framework, before I move on to theory and hypotheses. I then describe the data and choice of dictionary-based sentiment analysis, word networks without stop words and qualitative analysis of a random sampling of keywords in context (KWIC). This is followed by an overview of the groups and their members broken down by country of origin and region. The main analysis consists of two sections. The first, and largest, part speaks directly to the issue of frame alignment. It investigates whether members write and accept the same ideas as their leaders on: 1) Islam and race; 2) women, Jews, and homosexuals; and 3) democracy and violence. The second part identifies which emotions and messages get the most traction among members, relying on multilevel regression analyses where emotions expressed in posts are the independent variables and comments and shares of these posts the dependent variables.

Theory and hypotheses

In Chapter 5, I analyzed the statements and arguments (frames) presented by leaders and representatives of anti-Islamic organizations in interviews, newspaper articles, and their own pamphlets and manifestos. The anti-Islamic diagnosis consists of two main elements. They argue that Islam and Muslim culture represent a totalitarian threat which is destroying Western civilization through Islamizing everything from food (halal) to taking over neighbourhoods. Second, it is the elite – in the shape of politicians, the press, and academia – which is enabling Islamization. This is either through sheer ideological blindness and stupidity, or wilful treason by withholding information about the Muslim takeover and colluding with Muslim elites. The enemy is therefore both Muslims and the elite, a poignant "injustice frame" (Gamson, 1992, p. 10). Muslims and Islam are framed as antithetical to their Western "us": gender equality, democracy, freedom of speech, the Christian heritage, and rights of LGBT persons. Their prognosis is within democratic confines and non-violent. They argue for a halt to immigration, the assimilation of Muslims, and extended emphasis on Christianity and liberal values. Their rejection of violence is linked to the diagnostic framing of Western civilization as rights-based and peaceful. Their motivational framing consists of rallying cries to defend freedom and democracy, emphasized by portraying passivity as acceptance of a Muslim takeover. They rein-force their calls to action with apocalyptic statements and war metaphors, such as "traitor" and "invasion", drawing parallels with the Nazi attempt to conquer Europe during World War II. Thus, while non-violent solutions find support in the diagnostic framing of "us" as the peaceful and democratic ones, the motivational framing draws on the portrayal of Islam as an existential threat. The vital question is whether their members are aligned with these positions, or whether they espouse views and arguments from the agenda of the extreme right.

Extremist hypothesis

Social movements play a significant role in the diffusion of ideas and values (Rochon, 2000; Klandermans & Mayer, 2006). Social movement organizations (SMOs) are carriers of meaning which seek to promote their definition of the situation to the public at large – what is known as collective action frames (Gamson, 1992; Klan-dermans, 1997). A strong assumption is that those who join a movement share some part of its frames before joining (Klandermans & Mayer, 2006). A central tenet of framing theory is that the ability of SMOs to mobilize for street activism hinges on shared frame alignment[4] of activists and organizations (Snow, Benford, McCam-mon, Hewitt, & Fitzgerald, 2014). Just what kind of frames the activists who join anti-Islamic groups align with can tell us more about this movement, and the extent to which it is a "new" phenomenon as distinct from older extreme and radical right movements. Finally, it can provide an indication of their potential to mobilize for street action.

At the individual level, we know that prejudices are group-specific but prejudice against one minority strongly correlates with prejudice against others (e.g. Snider-man & Hagendoorn, 2007). For instance, if you are prejudiced towards Muslims it is likely that you are prejudiced towards people with a different skin colour. Work by Goodwin, Cutts, and Janta-Lipinski (2016) on who sympathized with the EDL indicate that they fit with this description. Their analysis shows that sympathiz-ers are more (openly) prejudiced than the population at large (ibid., p. 4). Despite what the leaders may claim the anti-Islamic initiatives stand for, their growth could therefore imply an increased, vocal support for everything that we associate with the far and extreme right: anti-Semitism and racism, authoritarianism, and patriar-chy. This means that anti-Islamic initiatives should draw a large amount of what Art (2011) defines as extremists, and not moderates. In line with these accounts, one should also expect the following:

H1: Activists only align with the official diagnosis of Islam and Muslims as a threat and enemy.

In other words, the expectation is that activists share a strong opposition to Islam and Muslims, whereas there is no common ground between activists and organiza-tions when it comes to just who (the "us") and what is being threatened and what to do about it. Instead of embracing women's and LGBT rights, democratic ideals and the Jewish minority, and a rejection of other pejorative discourses about race, we should find a stronger continuity with "traditional" extreme right frames. Specifically, we should find a large share of negative frames explicitly targeting people of colour, Jews, women, and sexual minorities, as well as promoting violence and a stronger emphasis on white identity.

Mobilization hypotheses

The extent to which activists are aligned with the anti-Islamic collective action framework is not the only relevant issue. What kind of messages actually manage to mobilize and spread is of paramount importance. Here it is vital to stir up the emotions of the target audiences (Goodwin, Jasper, & Polletta, 2000; Van Stekelenburg, 2006; Van Zomeren, Spears, Fischer, & Leach, 2004). Theoretical inclusions of emotions have a long pedigree in the study of the extreme and far right (Blee, 2017). The older literature emphasized that support for racist and far-right agendas was driven by irrationality and troubled personalities (Gusfield, 1986), and was a product of collective fear, frustration, paranoia, and anger (Caiani, della Porta, & Wagemann, 2012; Chirumbolo, Mayer, & De Witte, 2005; Klandermans & Mayer, 2006). As a backlash to this understanding of mobilization as collective irrationality, emotions were absent from social movement literature for several decades (Klandermans, van der Toorn, & van Stekelenburg, 2008). This was particularly true of studies employing a framing perspective (Benford, 1997), despite the fact that frames are tailored to elicit specific emotional responses.

Emotions are now back in the spotlight (Jasper, 2011), and social movement literature indicates that they are powerful mobilizers (Jasper, 1998, p. 414). Recent social movement and social psychology research identifies anger as the prototypical protest emotion (Van Stekelenburg & Klandermans, 2017). It is an approach-oriented emotion which boosts protest participation (Van Zomeren et al., 2004; van Troost, Van Stekelenburg, & Klandermans, 2013), promoting action against the responsible agent (diagnosis) and promoting a corrective response (prognosis). Anger lowers the individual's perception of risk (Lerner & Keltner, 2001) and increases reliance on prior conviction, thereby counteracting deliberation. Moreover, anger fosters support for aggressive policies (Cassese & Weber, 2011; Gault & Sabini, 2000; Huddy, Feldman, & Weber, 2007; Lerner, Gonzalez, Small, & Fischhoff, 2003; Petersen, 2010),[5] and heightens superficial information processing (Huddy et al., 2007; MacKuen, Wolak, Keele, & Marcus, 2010).

Positive emotions, such as happiness, joy, hope, love, and trust, are another set of emotions the literature indicates as a strong mobilizer. For instance, hope is understood as a "fundamental ingredient in supporting goal-seeking action" (Castells, 2012, p. 14). When it comes to risk perception, angry people resemble happy people (Lerner & Keltner, 2001). In the social movement literature, happiness is associated with affirmative statements about the in-group and articulating moral principles (Jasper, 1998, p. 418).[6] Research indicates that far-right activists themselves emphasize the importance of positive aspects of belonging to a group and sharing a sense of community as primary, and hostility to minorities as secondary (Klandermans & Mayer, 2006, p. 271). Together, expressions of joy and trust directed towards the in-group combined with anger directed outwards maintains the enthusiasm of activists.[7] On the basis of this, we can expect that expressions associated with the positive emotions of trust and joy to be positively connected with online mobilization. In much the same way, the negative emotion of anger should also be positively connected with online mobilization. In line with this, the three hypotheses are:

H2a: The more joy-associated words a message contains, the higher the response to this message.

H2b: The more trust-associated words a message contains, the higher the response to this message.

H2c: The more anger-associated words a message contains, the higher the response to this message.

It matters which emotions and messages cause the largest amount of response and diffusion. In addition to mobilizing, information from partisan sources (such as anti-Islamic activist groups) can help fuel negative feelings towards those holding differing political (and religious) views (Brundidge, Garrett, Rojas, & Gil de Zúñiga, 2014; Lelkes, Iyengar, & Sood, 2013). In this case, the explicit concern is that it can contribute to the legitimization of hate crimes and political violence against Muslims and others who do not share the anti-Islamic initiatives view of Islam as a totalitarian threat.

Data and analytical tools

As with the previous chapter on the anti-Islamic movements' Facebook network, data from this chapter was collected using the application Netvizz (Rieder, 2013). The data consists of the writings (posts and comments) and activity (likes, shares, and other reactions) in 298 anti-Islamic Facebook groups. The selected cases are groups with activity during the summer of 2016. The total amount of posts, shares, likes, and comments amounts to 1,799,970 within the timespan of one week, from 12–18 August 2016.

Facebook is an increasingly prominent arena for social activism and dissemination of ideas and propaganda. In the United States, six out of every ten people aged 18–33 and five out of ten people aged 34–49 get their political news from Facebook (Duggan, 2015, p. 8). Approximately three out of ten follow issue-based groups – the flora which anti-Islamic groups are part. In total, Facebook had over 2 billion members as of June 2016, of which 200 million were from the United States. In comparison, the more studied platform Twitter had 313 million users (in June 2016), and is a less common source for political news (14% and 9% for the same age groups) (ibid., p. 12).

The data is analyzed using a combination of tools. First of these are dictionary-based automated sentiment analysis and word networks. The patterns identified with these tools are then investigated qualitatively with random samples of text surrounding specific search words, known as keywords in context (KWIC). The word networks identify the co-occurrence of one word alongside another in a sentence after filtering out stop words, such as "go" and "to", that tie sentences together. A subset of the posts and comments are written in a wide variety of languages besides English, such as Polish, German, French, Norwegian, and Portuguese. All posts and comments were translated into English using Google Translate prior to analysis. Previously known for producing nonsensical translations on a word-by-word basis, by November 2016, Google Translate switched to a neural machine translation engine which translates "whole sentences at a time, rather than just piece by piece. It uses this broader context to help it figure out the most relevant translation, which it then rearranges and adjusts to be more like a human speaking with proper grammar".[8] The translation accuracy is highest with European and major world languages, as the engine was trained on United Nations and European Parliament transcripts.

In order to triangulate and identify the way in which specific categories and groups are framed, I employ the NRC Word-Emotion Association Lexicon (Mohammad & Turney, 2010, 2013). The lexicon contains association connections between words and positive and negative sentiments, in addition to the eight emotions identified by Plutchik (1980). These emotions belong to four opposites: 1) joy–sadness; 2) trust–disgust; 3) fear–anger; and 4) surprise–anticipation. The lexicon has valence and emotion associations for about 25,000 words. The lexicon was built using Amazon Turk, whereby respondents rank words by association.[9] Words can be associated with more than one emotion, and the lexicon can capture hundreds of thousands of valence and emotion associations (Mohammad & Turney, 2013). The more words in a piece of text, the higher the validity for the various sentiments such as fear, anger, trust, joy, and so forth. An important caveat is that we are not able to say whether a category – such as women – is the *target* of negative sentiments or whether it is portrayed as the *victim* of negative actions and circumstances. The qualitative reading in combination with the word networks that show the co-occurrence of words is therefore pivotal.

Descriptive overview – the groups and the members

The anti-Islamic expansion of the far right began in Western Europe and North America. The main genesis point was the website LGF in the United States, before spreading to the United Kingdom and Scandinavia.[10] Since then, it has spread throughout Europe and beyond. The 298 groups included in the analysis have members from 182 countries.[11] This pattern mirrors the transnational character of the network between groups.

The groups included in the analysis contain close to 5 million members. On average, each group has members from 30 different countries. Figure 7.1 gives an overview of activists by region, alongside a list with the 15 countries with the

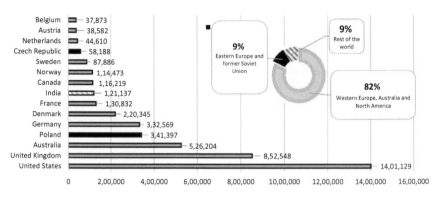

Belgium — 37,873
Austria — 38,582
Netherlands — 44,610
Czech Republic — 58,188
Sweden — 87,886
Norway — 1,14,473
Canada — 1,16,219
India — 1,21,137
France — 1,30,832
Denmark — 2,20,345
Germany — 3,32,569
Poland — 3,41,397
Australia — 5,26,204
United Kingdom — 8,52,548
United States — 14,01,129

0   2,00,000   4,00,000   6,00,000   8,00,000   10,00,000   12,00,000   14,00,000   16,00,000

9%
Eastern Europe and
former Soviet
Union

9%
Rest of the
world

82%
Western Europe, Australia and
North America

FIGURE 7.1   The 15 countries with the most members in the selection of anti-Islamic
groups on Facebook

largest shares of activists. Of these, 82% of the 5 million hail from Western Europe,
Australia, and North America, and 9% from countries previously on the other side
of the Iron Curtain which divided Europe. I make this analytical divide as the
"traditional" forms of right-wing extremism still flourish there. Finally, another 9%
come from other countries around the world.

As we can see, English-speaking countries are strongly represented, with the
United States, the United Kingdom, and Australia ranked in the top three, followed
by Poland, Germany, and Denmark. With 120,000 members, India is the only non-
European country present in the top 15 outside the Anglo-Saxon sphere. These ties
are also manifested ideologically. The conflict between Hindus and Muslims, often
erupting in violence, is frequently mentioned by anti-Islamic ideologues.[12]

In addition to Poland, the Czech Republic is the second "Visigrad" country
with a substantial share of members in these anti-Islamic groups. The Republic had
one of the first anti-Islamic rallies in the former Soviet satellites in 2015, organized
by a group calling itself Bloc Against Islam, and inspired by the rise of PEGIDA
in Dresden, Germany. The rally included anti-Islamic dignitaries such as Tommy
Robinson, the former leader of the EDL. However, this time they were also joined
by the Czech president Miloš Zeman.[13] The warm welcome extended to top politicians is something altogether different from what has been playing out so far in
most Western European countries.

The Defence League groups are by far the largest contingent, ranging from
national to local initiatives. The English divisions make up 73 of the 298 groups,
with 90 groups in total around the globe. This is followed by PEGIDA with 82
groups, Stop Islamization with 21, ACT! For America with 15 groups, Infidel (also
American) with 13 and Reclaim Australia with six. The remainder is a hodgepodge
of activist groups, the pages for anti-Islamic newssites and support groups for individual far-right politicians or polemicists. The latter are a small minority in the
network itself, but they are nonetheless key actors in the anti-Islamic fauna. The
number of cases is too large for an in-depth exploration, so this section is limited
to elaborating on the five groups with the most Facebook members and followers.

The group with most followers (386,735) is dedicated to the activist, author, and commentator Pamela Geller. She became famous for her opposition to an Islamic community centre being built near the former Twin Towers. She also sponsored a "Draw the Prophet" contest and, as the founder of SIOA, consistently warned against "creeping Sharia". She is also known for her staunch support for abortion rights and same-sex marriage.

American Infidel is the second largest Facebook group in my analysis (360,357 followers). It is a company established in 2011 selling propaganda material, stickers, mugs and patches for clothes warning against jihad and mocking Islam.[14] Besides selling merchandise, the group is a forum for discussing Islam, Muslim immigration, jihadist terrorism, and opposition to these.

With 307,043 members by 2016, the Polish No to the Islamization of Europe is the third largest Facebook group in the analysis. Set up in 2012, they define themselves as a grassroots citizens' initiative intended to stop Poland from "making the same mistakes as the West", and to stop "Islamization", which they argue is caused by "inept economic policy and European Union immigration, weakening the position of Christianity and cultural Marxism terror".[15]

The EDL is the fourth largest of the anti-Islamic Facebook groups, with just under 300,000 members. Active since 2009, they are the most studied anti-Islamic group to date. This is primarily due to their frequent and disruptive protest events around Britain between 2009 and 2011. In their own description and mission statement from January 2016, they stress their working-class roots and the need to combat "global Islamification". They claim the mantle of being a human rights organization fighting to save democracy, the rule of law, English traditions, and freedom of speech with a goal to "educate the British public about Islam".[16] Some of the issues they expressly mention are oppression of women, female gender mutilation, homophobia, anti-Semitism, and organized sexual abuse of children.

ACT! For America is the fifth largest group. Founded by the Lebanese-born Brigitte Gabriel in 2007, they claim to have over 1,000 chapters across the United States.[17] ACT! For America have pushed for the introduction of a so-called anti-Sharia bill in state legislatures and warn against the threat of Islam.[18] They define their platform as confronting terrorism, preserving the constitution, securing the border, energy independence, empowering women and protecting children, and support for Israel.

Extremists or moderates?

In this section, I try to identify the degree to which anti-Islamic initiatives have managed to recruit activists aligned with their official ideological platform by studying their messages. The following keywords are used as starting points for the sentiment analysis, network analysis and as text samples for qualitative analysis: *black, white, Muslim, Jew, woman, gay, homosexual, lesbian, LGBT, democracy*, and *violence*. These are found throughout the diagnostic, prognostic, and motivational framing of the anti-Islamic collective action framework.

The enemy

The main component of the anti-Islamic diagnosis is that Islam and Muslims constitute an existential threat. A word network analysis of the most frequently used words in sentences containing the word "Muslims" indicates that it is the case for regular online activists as well. For instance, Muslims are often mentioned in relation to words such as "rape", "death", "majority", "hate", "terrorism", and "invasion". The corpus of text containing the word "Muslim" shows that they are consistently framed as an ominous and deadly threat. A random sample of text using the KWIC method highlights this. Statements about molestation, decapitation, and other gratuitous acts of violence are recurring in activists' posts and comments that mention Muslims, exemplified by statements such as "Muslims want to impose shariah law and the radical [Muslim] wants to cut off your head". Although more explicit and focussed on the grotesque than what the leaders (Chapter 5) mention, the framing is more or less identical. The notion of impending war is also common, especially connected to Germany and the so-called refugee crisis of 2015: "Civil War is also immanent in Germany. Non [Muslims], you have to stand up for your rights!!".

The sentiment analysis indicates that the activists are aligned with the official framing of Muslims and Islam. The word Muslim is connected to more negative

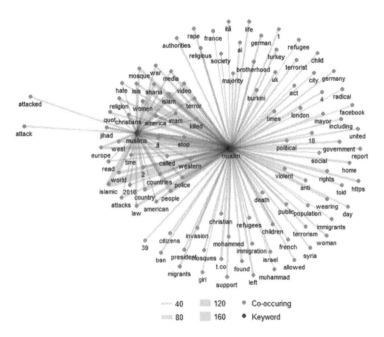

FIGURE 7.2 Words most frequently co-occurring together with Muslim in posts and comments by activists on anti-Islamic Facebook groups

PICTURE 7.1   Propaganda material from the EDL

Picture uploaded to EDL's original Facebook page, no longer available. Downloaded November 2016.

(14%) than positive (9%) sentiments, but a slightly larger amount of words related to fear (9%) than anger (7%).

A diagnosis also makes clear just what and who is being threatened. A slogan for the EDL, one of the most prominent anti-Islamic groups, is that they are "not racist, not violent, just no longer silent".[19] The EDL has gone furthest in establishing specific subdivisions for people from different backgrounds to certify their "anti-racism" and progressive stances, but the anti-racist proclamations are by no means unusual. Most anti-Islamic activist groups go out of their way to stress that they are not racist. Let us compare the emotions and sentiments associated with the words "Muslim", "black", and "white" in Figure 7.3 to see how this plays out among the online activists. Since the words "white" and "black" can be used to denote and describe a wide variety of topics, posts which use the words as anything else than ethno-racial terms have been manually excluded from the overview.

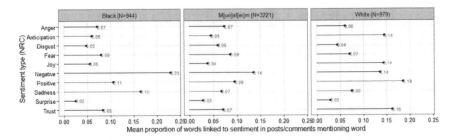

FIGURE 7.3 Comparative overview of mean proportion of words linked to sentiments in posts and comments mentioning the word black, Muslim and white

We see that the words black (N=944) and white (N=979) are used on an equal basis. These words are numerically eclipsed by the word Muslim, but another pattern appears if we compare the specific sentiments and emotions. First, although Muslims are talked about more frequently, we also find racial terms. There is also a stronger association between black and negative sentiments than for Muslims. On the other hand, white is associated with positive sentiments.[20] This indicates that many members of anti-Islamic groups define the in-group, namely those threatened by Muslims, in racial terms. The lower frequency of race terms but strong connection to negative (black) and positive (white) sentiments indicate that the framing is split between the official anti-racist position and racist positions in line with the traditional far right.

The word network and KWIC analysis supports this. For instance, statements such as "There is only one race, it's the human race, be it black, white, brown, yellow etc, etc. Fact." are juxtaposed with statements such as "Exterminate the black race because they are like weeds" – one denying the idea of race, and another explicitly racist view advocating the annihilation of black people. Another comment suggests that they have to abandon notions of race because their country has undergone irreversible demographic change. Statements about Muslims also stress this divide between those who use explicitly racist frames and those who do not. For example, some express misgivings about black people being "easy prey" for Muslim conversion, whereas others emphasize that Muslims will kill all infidels, and that non-Muslims have to stand up for their rights.

The victims

What about the other groups that anti-Islamic leaders explicitly frame as belonging to their in-group, which are often the target of slander and vilification by the "traditional" extreme right – jews, the LGBT community, and – to a certain extent – women? White supremacists, neo-Nazis, and fascists usually portray Jews as the ultimate and nefarious enemy, homosexuals as deviants corrupting the nation and its people, and finally women as the weaker sex and breeding machines for the survival of the race. A first indicator for the degree of alignment between the online

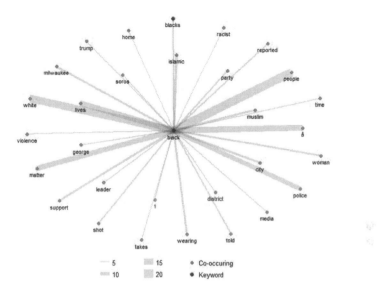

FIGURE 7.4   The words most frequently co-occurring together with "black" in posts and comments by activists on anti-Islamic Facebook groups

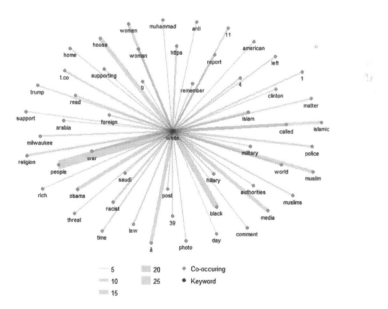

FIGURE 7.5   The words most frequently co-occurring together with "white" in posts and comments by activists on anti-Islamic Facebook groups

activists and the official platform can be teased out by seeing whether these groups are associated with less negative sentiments than Muslims.

Overall, the sentiment scores are similar among the four categories. Of the three categories belonging to the in-group in the anti-Islamic master frame, however,

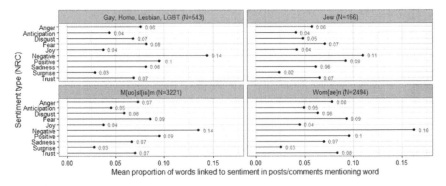

FIGURE 7.6 Comparative overview of mean proportion of words linked to sentiments in posts and comments mentioning the words "gay, homo, lesbian, LGBT", "Jew", "Muslim", and "women"

women stand out as most associated with negative sentiments, and Jews with the least. In fact, women and homosexuals are just as, or more, associated with negative sentiments than the main antagonists: Muslims. To understand what this means, we must scrutinize their posts and comments. Muslims are portrayed as the perpetrators of violence, but women and homosexuals are the victims, with statements such as "So which is it, Women's and Gay rights or Islam? They aren't mutually compatible" and "It is the doctrines of Islam, the subjugation of women, the hatred of anything and everything not Islam". This highlights why the automated sentiment lexicon is a very rough tool when it comes to making valid interpretations. The co-occurrence word network underlines the diagnostic frame alignment with seeing women as a target of Muslim violence and oppression, with words such as "killed" and "attacked".

The fixation on the sexual dimension is also clear – "sex", "naked", "rape", "body", "miniskirts", "control", "slave". The distinction between independent Western women and controlling, fearful Muslim men are seen in statements such as "very scared men in Iran, terrified a woman can think for themselves" and "We English women stand up for ourselves and we decide what to do". However, some comments also convey a sense of ownership and fear of loss, that "our" women might choose Muslim men as sexual partners. This argument mirrors the protector frames which the leaders employ side by side with equality frames (Chapter 5). This "traditional" orientation is also in line with the ideas of the white supremacists, fascists, and neo-Nazis who see women as vessels for the continuation of the race and nation.

Compared to women, LGBT are more consistently portrayed as vulnerable victims in need of protection, and not autonomous agents able to stand up for themselves. For instance, with references to the killing of 49 people in Orlando, Florida or the attacks on transgendered people in Turkey with statements such as "LGBT (lesbian gay bisexual and transgender) community in Turkey are raped and burnt to death in Istanbul". Several comments equate LGBT people giving support to Muslims with black people supporting slavery. When we turn to the word

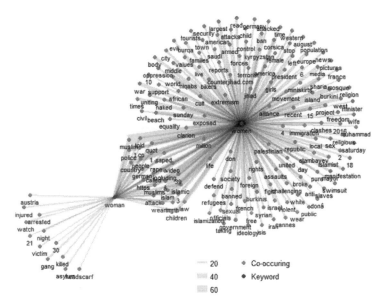

FIGURE 7.7   The words most frequently co-occurring together with "women" in posts and comments by activists on anti-Islamic Facebook groups

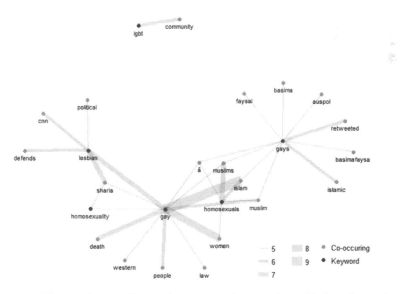

FIGURE 7.8   The words most frequently co-occurring together with "gay, homo, lesbian" or "LGBT" in posts and comments by activists on anti-Islamic Facebook groups

network "gay", "homosexual", "lesbian" and "LGBT" co-occur with the words "defend", "women", "Western", "law" as well as "Muslim", "Islam" and "Sharia". This cements the picture of frame alignment between activists and anti-Islamic

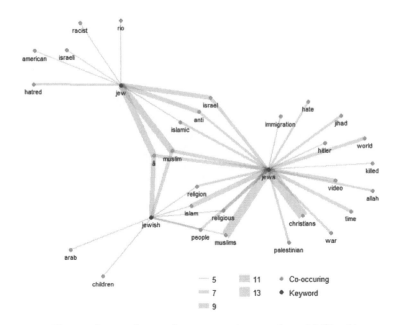

FIGURE 7.9 The words most frequently co-occurring together with "Jew" in posts and comments by activists on anti-Islamic Facebook groups

diagnosis and prognosis – with LGBT strongly identified as belonging to the in-group under attack and meriting protection.

Jews are also taken as belonging to the in-group under attack in many of the posts and comments. Moreover, they are put in direct connection to the other groups which anti-Islamic initiatives claim to defend, as demonstrated by statements such as: "The goal is to stop the truth from being told. This is a direct assault on free speech. Christians, Jews, and the LGBTQ communities need to flood these police departments with complaints and drown them". The overarching theme is that Islam and Muslims are out to destroy all non-Muslims. Yet, as in the other cases, there are also some statements that adhere to a traditional extreme right point of view, such as "Just feel that there is not enough information out there to expose the New Jew Order". In this competing narrative, Jews are portrayed as using Muslims as the unwitting foot soldiers to destroy the white race and European civilization. In other words, a majority of the statements regarding women, Jews, and LGBT people seem to align with the anti-Islamic collective action framework, but traditional extreme right arguments are also present.

The solutions – democracy and violence

I now come to the way they relate to democracy and violence. As with the other categories, these words can be found in all three categories of framing. If activists align with the anti-Islamic master frame, then democracy should define "us", what is under threat from Muslims, and what is worth fighting for. In Figure 7.10,

I compare the mean proportion of words linked to sentiments that mention democracy to the entire body of text (a-z).

Democracy is found alongside words classified as positive almost twice as often as negative ones. This is the highest score in my selection, superseding, for instance, "white". However, the KWIC samples also reveal the same underlying tension between pro-democratic views and anti-democratic ones as we have seen with views of race, women, and Jews. On the one hand, there are statements that define "we" in terms of democracy, freedom of thought and expression together with women's rights

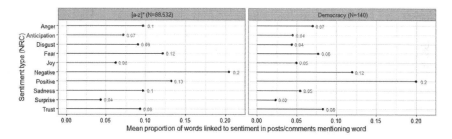

FIGURE 7.10   Comparative overview of mean proportion of words linked to sentiments in posts and comments mentioning the words "a-z" and "democracy"

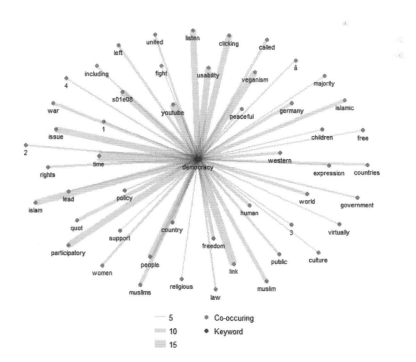

FIGURE 7.11   The words most frequently co-occurring together with "democracy" in posts and comments by activists on anti-Islamic Facebook groups

and gay rights – those threatened by Muslims and Islam. On the other hand, there are statements such as "[we will] not defeat Islamic demographic takeover through democracy. Forget it. Human rights must be tossed out the window".

But what about violence? Should it be included in prognostic frames, or only used to describe the actions of Muslims and the Islamic threat? If we look at the fascist tradition, violence is associated with glory and control – a necessary factor for rejuvenation and unity. This extreme tradition is not evident in the sentiment analysis.

The KWIC sample tells a similar story. Violence is occasionally portrayed as a permissible defensive act, whereas Islam is portrayed as inherently violent. The right to defence is reinforced with statements such as "enough is enough!" and giving

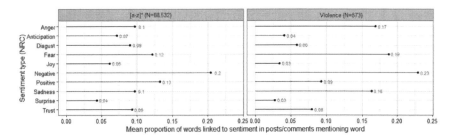

FIGURE 7.12 Comparative overview of mean proportion of words linked to sentiments in posts and comments mentioning the words "a-z" and "violence"

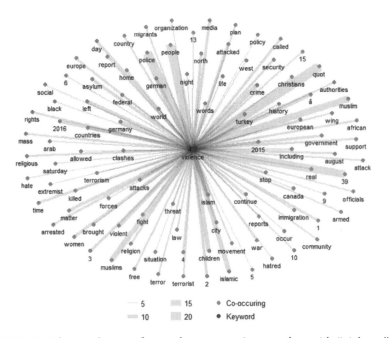

FIGURE 7.13 The words most frequently co-occurring together with "violence" in posts and comments by activists on anti-Islamic Facebook groups

them "a taste of their own medicine". In other words, there is an ambivalence when it comes to the use of violence as solution. It is not glorified (as in fascism), but it is occasionally justified by claiming that Muslims are the instigators and that Islam is a religion that is basically about violence. The word network consolidates this impression, with the most frequent co-occurrences being with the words "people", "Muslim", and "Islam".

Overall, the analysis of the coherence between activists and the anti-Islamic master frame reveals that there is substantial frame alignment on some issues. In the diagnostic, framing of Islam and Muslims as the ultimate threat is dominant. However, internal tension is evident. Racist, anti-Semitic, and other extreme right narratives are present in the posts and comments alongside the new, dominant anti-Islamic narrative which operates with the broad "us" of LGBT, women, Jews, and other minorities united in the struggle against Muslims and Islam. Speaking to the individual categories, LGBT people are consistently framed as part of the broader Western and civilized "us", and as victims of Muslim violence and oppression. They are not scorned or derided. This is a break with the traditional extreme and ethno-pluralist right. Women's rights are framed in positive terms as something which is inherent to "us" and alien to Muslims, but women are also written about in a possessive form. This mirrors the ideological duality evident in the leaders' positions and their use of male-centric protector frames, which is indistinguishable from the fascist extreme right and ethno-pluralist radical right. Comments about Jews indicate a larger divide. The conspiracy theory that Jews are using Muslims as their foot soldiers against the "West", understood in racial terms, is striking, especially since Israel and the plight of the Jewish minority are played up by anti-Islamic leaders, and the selfsame anti-Islamic groups and pro-Jewish organizations have become more integrated online. Hostility against Jews goes hand in hand with the use of denigrating rhetoric about black people. A competing set of solutions is also present. Some reject dealing with Muslims within democratic parameters on the pretext that it is simply too late, even though democracy is idealized as inherently Western.

Emotions and messages driving online mobilization and diffusion

We have seen that activists espouse many of the liberal and progressive positions that the anti-Islamic initiatives have incorporated in their platform. These are often wedded to Christian themes and expressions of devotion. However, racist and anti-democratic stances are also present. Relying on multilevel regression analyses, this section tries to tease out the emotions and messages that drive internal mobilization in anti-Islamic groups and that spread beyond those groups.

When somebody writes a post on the wall of a group, Facebook users can choose to add comments, like (a thumbs-up symbol), or react with other emoticons. They can also share posts directly with friends via personal chat, on their own walls and other groups' pages. I include comments and shares of these in my analysis. Whereas comments capture substantial responses that simple likes and reactions do not, shares are pivotal because they let us know whether (and which) messages get traction beyond the given anti-Islamic group.

The individual words associated with a specific emotion or sentiment in a post are treated as independent variables, with comments and shares as dependent variables. If the proportion of one emotion in a post is increased by 100%, then the number of comments and shares will increase or decrease accordingly when the others are held constant. There are 5,514 posts divided over 298 groups included in the analysis. Drawing on the literature on mobilization and emotions, I hypothesized that the negative emotion of anger and positive emotions of joy and trust increase the amount of comments and shares a post gets. The results are presented in Table 7.1 and Figure 7.14.

The overall consistency of the directional effect which the individual independent variables have on the amount of comments and shares is reassuring. Moreover, this empirical pattern roughly mirrors Plutchik's (1980) binary distinctions between joy and sadness, trust and disgust, fear and anger, and surprise and anticipation. The empirical gap between these theoretically assumed dichotomous emotions holds for both comments and shares.

We see that increases in joy-related and trust-related words have a statistically significant impact on the number of comments made by activists in response to a post. Both are significant at the level of 1%, and substantially significant with an average increase of 2.7 and 1.5 comments, respectively, for every proportionate increase of joy-related or trust-related words. The results are not as clear when it

TABLE 7.1 Main results of multilevel regression analysis, with emotions and sentiments as independent variables and comments and shares as dependent variables

	Comments	*Shares*
Fixed Effects		
Joy	2.738*** (0.947)	4.848 (3.151)
Trust	1.530*** (0.585)	3.828** (1.947)
Anger	1.413* (0.850)	5.523* (2.830)
Sadness	0.833 (0.857)	0.446 (2.854)
Anticipation	−0.697 (0.768)	1.362 (2.557)
Disgust	−0.796 (0.966)	−0.872 (3.214)
Negative	−0.434 (0.661)	−1.990 (2.199)
Fear	−0.226 (0.641)	−2.270 (2.133)
Positive	−1.543*** (0.505)	−3.188* (1.681)
Surprise	−2.796*** (0.930)	−7.693** (3.096)
Intercept	46.520*** (11.479)	72.513* (38.209)
Model summary		
N posts/group	5514/298	5514/298
Log Likelihood	−30,039.860	−36,670.710
AIC	60,699.72	73,961.42
BIC	62,750.39	76,012.09

***p < .01; **p < .05; *p < .1; two-tailed test.

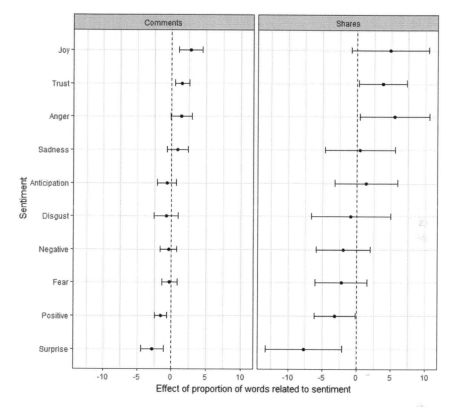

FIGURE 7.14   Main results of multilevel regression analysis – emotions and sentiments are independent variables, and comments and shares dependent variables; joyful and trusting messages are strongly associated with increases in comments to a post

comes to anger, which is only statistically significant at 10% – resulting in an average increase of 1.4 comments. Both statistically and substantially speaking, then, expressions of joy and trust are stronger drivers of internal mobilization than anger in the anti-Islamic groups.

There are indications of a similar pattern for diffusion; however, joy is not statistically significant, and trust is only statistically significant at the 5% level. Substantially, the average effect on the number of shares is stronger for both trust and anger than on the amount of comments, but the large standard deviations tell us that the effect is less consistent.

In sum, joy and trust have a clear effect and the directionality of that effect along the lines postulated in the hypotheses, which are in turn derived from previous studies. Although the directional impact of anger also seems to be in line with expectations, the results are not significant at an equally stringent level as joy and trust.

Neither sadness, anticipation, disgust, nor generalized expressions of negativity have a clear impact on the number of comments and shares. In contrast, positive sentiments and surprise actually drive down both the number of comments and shares obtained by a post. As with the mobilizing emotions and sentiments, the effect is clearer when it comes to comments than for shares. An increase in the proportion of positive sentiments in a post leads to an average decrease of 1.5 comments, whereas an increase in surprise-associated words leads to an average decrease of 2.8 comments, which is statistically significant at the 1% level. The effect of joy and surprise is exactly the reverse. Turning to their effect on the number of shares, we again see a negative covariation.

Delving further into what these findings actually mean we must look at what messages the specific emotions are connected with. I begin with the three mobilizing emotions, followed by the two demobilizing emotions and sentiments.

Mobilizing messages

Of the three mobilizing emotions, the literature indicates that the positive emotions are associated with affirmations of the in-group. The posts by anti-Islamic activists are no exception, and follow this pattern. Posts with a high share of joy-associated words contain combinations of Christian themes and expressions of faith with liberal and progressive positions. They clearly delineate the boundaries of precisely what they stand for, and which values they strive to embody. In the post containing the most joy-associated words, the activist writes:

> If you are homophobic, you are a hater! My God loves all he commands us to love one another! So does your god! You are disobeying the law of God! If you believe homosexuality is a sin don't partake! Judge not lest you be judged. It's not complicated. Jesus said, of Faith Hope and Charity the greatest is Charity – love![21]

The particular emphasis on Christianity is commonplace in the writings of anti-Islamic leaders and activists alike, either as a major component of Western cultural heritage and reason for "our" benevolence, or as profession of actual faith. Historically speaking, the combination of Christian themes with liberal and progressive positions bears more resemblance to the American civil rights movement than the fascist extreme right. Other posts stress gratitude to fellow activists for arranging offline events and otherwise partaking in the activities of the group. To illustrate this, in another post with a high score in joy-associated words, an activist stated that:

> We thank everyone who came to the meeting . . . we are happy to have finally met!!! We are happy for this first meeting. I feel a hope that something will finally materialize. All together without division can go very far. As you asked there will be a next meeting in October or November 2016. If you have applications or important recommendations for the next meeting that will be our great pleasure to discuss with you :) Thanks again to you who are traveling for this meeting THANK YOU !!!! !!!!

Posts containing a high number of trust-related words are often about concrete individuals and the efforts they have made or that activists believe they can make on behalf of their cause. In particular, trust-associated words are often used by anti-Islamic activists when talking about people with some authority who stand up to Muslims and describe Marxist cultural elites as politically correct, as in this expression of support for a police official:

> And Sheriff . . . also has my respect. What he says and what he has constantly said is true. He should be our police commissioner over here in England. He would not stand for none of this that the police and we are getting. It's time to get tough. He should run for president. Hats off to you. . . . Respect from England.

Some of these posts contain elements that can be described as prognostic – namely, they identify what has to be done, exemplified here by the statement, "time to get tough". Others denote the human bonds of affection which have been built up among the activists, stressing their sacrifice and their dedication to the cause.

The results indicate that anger plays a role as an emotional driver of online mobilization and diffusion, but that it is not necessarily the prime mover indicated in social movement literature. In line with the literature, however, posts containing a high number of anger-associated words are linked with problem identification and rallying cries; namely, what is defined as diagnostic and motivational framing. The post registered with the highest proportion of anger-associated words is a diatribe against Islam and Muslims, saying they have made enemies of all religions, homosexuals, and democracy itself, and that appeasers of Islam trick themselves into believing otherwise. A random sample of posts containing words associated with anger also show a similar pattern of tirades against Islam as a malevolent entity. The content in these angry messages reinforces the broad coalition of people with a varied background united against Islam and Muslims:

> ISLAMOPHOBIC HATE SPEECH. Islam is a Death Cult. I am an Atheist. I disagree with Islam I disagree with all religion. I have and always will. Hate speech does not exist. Hate speech and Racism will not be used to silence us. As the late great Hitchens said, freedom of speech means freedom to hate. Hate is just someone elses negative opinion. The number one target of criticism is truth.

Angry diatribes are far from unique to anti-Islamic initiatives. Strong emotional language is often used to express opinions online (Papacharissi & de Fatima Oliveira, 2012), and news organization websites are full of uncivil and emotional comments (Coe, Kenski, & Rains, 2014). However, anger used to mobilize for political action against a specific minority has some ominous connotations. Here, the previously mentioned similarities with the arguments and slogans of the American civil rights movement come to an abrupt end.

Demobilizing messages

The results also show that surprise and positive sentiments are demobilizing. In contrast to posts associated with joy and trust which affirm and strengthen in-group solidarity, posts which contain a lot of positive sentiments do not speak explicitly to the in-group as such. Instead, these posts come across as generic self-improvement and self-help messages that deal with common vices and issues such as alcohol abuse, marital problems or looking for a purpose in life. Many of these posts come under the rubrics of "Thought of the day" or "Meditation of the day":

> Make it a daily practice to review your character. Take your character in relation to your daily life to your dear ones, your friends, your acquaintances and your work. Each day try to see where God wants you to change. Plan how best each fault can be eradicated or each mistake be corrected. Never be satisfied with a comparison with those around you. Strive towards a better life.

Posts with a high number of surprise-associated words have a completely different character. Rather than containing generalized moral chastisement or self-help advice, they primarily appear in fact-oriented and number-heavy posts. They include electoral statistics, descriptions of events and so forth. For instance, the posts with the most surprise-associated words in the entire corpus deal with election results. Other posts with a large amount of surprise-associated words include reposts of stories from major news outlets covering jihadist terror attacks and plots, such as this:

> [3] "ISIS terror plot to bomb German festival is foiled after police seize explosives as Oktoberfest organisers announce they will ban rucksacks from the event. Swat team arrested a suspected terrorist in Eisenhuettenstadt. Officials believe the man was planning to bomb the City Festival. The arrest comes after a string of attacks in Germany last month. Read more: Follow us: @MailOnline on Twitter | DailyMail on Facebook"

It is striking that news which conforms to the anti-Islamic narrative can cause a drop in mobilization, and seems counter-intuitive from the perspective of cumulative extremism where the assumption is that jihadist terror fuels and drives increased mobilization and radicalization of anti-Islamic activists.

Where is the fear?

Another striking finding is that fear has no significant impact on mobilizating online responses or the diffusion of messages. The literature on emotions indicates that fear is demobilizing and associated with avoidance, deliberation, and desistance (see, for example, Bodenhausen, Sheppard, & Kramer, 1994; DeSteno, Petty, Wegener, & Rucker, 2000; Bushway & Paternoster, 2013), but much work on the far right and on opposition to Islam and Muslims actually describes fear as mobilizing. For instance, Ruth Wodak's central argument is that the populist radical right "continuously construct fear" to which only they "seem to offer simple and clear-cut answers to" (2015, p. 5). The fact that expressions of fear have no clear connection to mobilization among online activists in anti-Islamic groups contributes to nuance the prevalent description of the far right as, fundamentally speaking, a fear-constructing and fear-inducing phenomenon.

Conclusion

In this exploration of anti-Islamic activism online among 298 groups across 182 countries, two things stand out. First – and contrary to what we might assume on the basis of literature on prejudice and survey data of EDL sympathizers – my findings indicate that a sizeable number of activists embrace liberal and progressive positions included in the anti-Islamic initiative's official platform. This implies that the anti-Islamic, organizational expansion of the far right has also expanded the recruitment pool beyond individuals who are generally prejudiced against all minorities. These findings resonate with qualitative evidence from interviews with EDL activists (Busher, 2015), in which proclamations of being against racism were common. Busher argues that this genuinely reflected their self-identity, rather than being a strategic attempt to develop a "reputational shield" (ibid., p. 97).

Second, unlike fear, expressions of joy and trust drive online mobilization. These are messages that focus on the in-group and on building a common identity. There are indications that anger also plays a mobilizing role, but less so than these positive emotions. Their merger of Christian messages with rights-based claims for minorities has some striking similarities to the American civil rights movement. The inclusion of progressive and liberal stances such as support for gay rights in the messages which drive mobilization also demonstrates that it is more than a façade employed by the leadership. The overarching theme seems to be one of belonging.

As indicated in the first part of the analysis, however, there is still an undercurrent of openly anti-democratic and racist self-expression. This reveals an ideological tension between the official platform and the moderate activists on the one hand, and the extreme activists on the other. It is not given that the current leadership and moderates who now incorporate the liberal and progressive positions will dominate the anti-Islamic movement in the long run.

Notes

1 Awareness of this turn has been picked up by major newspapers and media outlets for some time. For instance, as noted an article on LGBT and racism in *The Guardian*: "The far-right movements on the march across the western world are consciously trying to co-opt the LGBT rights campaign for their own agenda. Muslims are portrayed as an existential threat to gay people, particularly after Orlando" (*The Guardian*, 24 November 2016, accessed 25 November 2016). Available from: www.theguardian.com/commentisfree/2016/nov/24/no-asians-no-blacks-gay-people-racism?CMP=fb_gu

2 For instance, when focusing on women vis-à-vis Muslims, they vacillate between traditional, male-centric "protector frames" and feminist "equality frames".

3 Members and followers are not self-reported, but official Facebook statistics. They can inflate the numbers by creating "fake" Facebook profiles and having them join, but that means setting up new email accounts and using a phone number registered in their name.

4 Frame alignment is defined as "linkage of individual and SMO interpretive orientations, such that some set of individual interests, values and beliefs and SMO activities, goals, and ideology are congruent and complementary" (Snow, Rochford, Worden & Benford, p. 464).

5 For instance, in a study on the use of emotional stimuli in presidential speeches Villalobos and Sirin (2017) found that anger leads to higher support for military interventions in civil conflict.

6 Joy and happiness are associated with collective activities such as singing and dancing during protests – what Durkheim described as "collective effervescence" (Jasper, 1998).

7 More specifically, hatred of outsiders (Scheff, 1994) and love of the group have been claimed to maintain activist enthusiasm (Berezin, 2001).

8 www.blog.google/products/translate/found-translation-more-accurate-fluent-senten ces-google-translate/ (accessed 4 December 2016).

9 Respondents were asked whether specific terms were strongly associated, moderately associated, weakly associated, or not associated with the target emotion.

10 The second, and parallel genesis point of import was the Dutch party LPF. See Chapter 4 for an overview of the anti-Islamic expansion, which is largely synonymous with the establishment of an anti-Islamic movement and subculture.

11 The share of various nationalities is naturally skewed by the network analysis starting with Western groups such as the EDL, PEGIDA, and SIOE. The network analysis was large enough to capture a majority of anti-Islamic groups that are present on Facebook, but misses isolated outliers.

12 It also made its way into the "manifesto" of the terrorist Anders Behring Breivik in his justification for seeing Islam as a totalitarian force that must be destroyed before it obliterates the West. For analysis of Breivik's manifesto, see Berntzen and Sandberg (2014).

13 www.breitbart.com/london/2015/11/17/eastern-europe-rising-czech-president-speaks-anti-islam-rally-pegida-leaders-tommy-robinson/ (accessed 8 October 2016).

14 http://americaninfidel.com/faq (accessed 4 October 2016)

15 www.facebook.com/niedlaislamizacjieuropy/about/?entry_point=page_nav_about_ item (accessed 7 October 2016).

16 www.englishdefenceleague.org.uk/mission-statement/ (acessed 7 October 2016).

17 www.actforamerica.org/chapters (accessed 7 October 2016)

18 www.nytimes.com/2011/07/31/us/31shariah.html?pagewanted=all&_r=0 (accessed 6 October 2016).

19 www.wlv.ac.uk/about-us/news-and-events/academic-blog/2014/january/edl-not-rac ist-not-violent-just-no-longer-silent/ (accessed 26 September 2016).

20 Of the words in my analysis, white is also the one most strongly associated with trust.

21 Taken as a whole, this specific post could be interpreted as containing both anger and joy.

Bibliography

Art, D. (2011). *Inside the radical right: The development of anti-immigrant parties in Western Europe.* Cambridge: Cambridge University Press.

Benford, R. D. (1997). An insider's critique of the social movement framing perspective. *Sociological Inquiry, 67*(4), 409–430.

Berezin, M. (2001). Emotions and political identity: Mobilizing affection for the polity. In J. Goodwin, J. M. Jasper, & F. Polletta (Eds.), *Passionate politics: Emotions and social movements* (pp. 83–98) Chicago: University of Chicago Press.

Berntzen, L. E., & Sandberg, S. (2014). The collective nature of lone wolf terrorism: Anders Behring Breivik and the anti-Islamic social movement. *Terrorism and Political Violence, 26*(5), 759–779.

Blee, K. M. (2017). How the study of white supremacism is helped and hindered by social movement research. *Mobilization, 22*(1), 1–15.

Bodenhausen, G.V., Sheppard, L. A., & Kramer, G. P. (1994). Negative affect and social judgement: The differential impact of anger and sadness. *European Journal of Social Psychology, 24*(1), 45–62.

Brundidge, J., Garrett, R. K., Rojas, H., & Gil de Zúñiga, H. (2014). Political participation and ideological news online: "Differential gains" and "differential losses" in a presidential election cycle. *Mass Communication and Society, 17*(4), 464–486.

Busher, J. (2015). *The Making of anti-Muslim Protest: Grassroots activism in the English Defence League*. London: Routledge.

Bushway, S. D., & Paternoster, R. (2013). Desistance from crime: A review and ideas for moving forward. In *Handbook of life-course criminology* (pp. 213–231). New York: Springer.

Caiani, M., Della Porta, D., & Wagemann, C. (2012). *Mobilizing on the extreme right: Germany, Italy, and the United States*. Oxford: Oxford University Press.

Cassese, E., & Weber, C. (2011). Emotion, attribution, and attitudes toward crime. *Journal of Integrated Social Sciences, 2*(1), 63–97.

Castells, M. (2012). *Networks of outrage and hope: Social movements in the Internet age*. Cambridge: Polity Press.

Chirumbolo, A., Mayer, N., & De Witte, H. (2005). Do right- and left-wing extremists have anything in common? In *Extreme right activists in Europe: Through the magnifying glass*. London and New York: Routledge.

Coe, K., Kenski, K., & Rains, S. A. (2014). Online and uncivil? Patterns and determinants of incivility in newspaper website comments. *Journal of Communication, 64*(4), 658–679.

DeSteno, D., Petty, R. E., Wegener, D. T., & Rucker, D. D. (2000). Beyond valence in the perception of likelihood: The role of emotion specificity. *Journal of Personality and Social Psychology, 78*(3), 397.

Duggan, M. (2015, August 19). *Mobile messaging and social media 2015*. Pew Research Center.

Gamson, W. (1992). *Talking politics*. New York: Cambridge University Press.

Gault, B. A., & Sabini, J. (2000). The roles of empathy, anger, and gender in predicting attitudes toward punitive, reparative, and preventative public policies. *Cognition & Emotion, 14*(4), 495–520.

Goodwin, M. J., Cutts, D., & Janta-Lipinski, L. (2016). Economic losers, protestors, islamophobes or xenophobes? Predicting public support for a counter-Jihad movement. *Political Studies, 64*(1), 4–26.

Goodwin, M. J., Jasper, J., & Polletta, F. (2000). The return of the repressed: The fall and rise of emotions in social movement theory. *Mobilization: An International Quarterly, 5*(1), 65–83.

Gusfield, J. R. (1986). *Symbolic Crusade: Status politics and the American Temperance movement*. Champaign: University of Illinois Press.

Huddy, L., Feldman, S., & Weber, C. (2007). The political consequences of perceived threat and felt insecurity. *The ANNALS of the American Academy of Political and Social Science, 614*(1), 131–153.

Jasper, J. M. (1998). The emotions of protest: Affective and reactive emotions in and around social movements. *Sociological Forum, 13*(3), 397–424. Springer Netherlands.

Jasper, J. M. (2011). Emotions and social movements: Twenty years of theory and research. *Annual Review of Sociology, 37*, 285–303.

Jost, J. T., Glaser, J., Kruglanski, A. W., & Sulloway, F. J. (2003). Political conservatism as motivated social cognition. *Psychological Bulletin, 129*(3), 339–375.

Klandermans, B. (1997). *The psychology of social protest.* Oxford: Blackwell.

Klandermans, B. (2003). Collective political action. *Oxford Handbook of Political Psychology,* 670–709.

Klandermans, B., & Mayer, N. (2006). *Through the magnifying glass: The world of extreme right activists.* London: Routledge.

Klandermans, B., Van der Toorn, J., & Van Stekelenburg, J. (2008). Embeddedness and identity: How immigrants turn grievances into action. *American Sociological Review, 73*(6), 992–1012.

Lelkes, Y., Iyengar, S., & Sood, G. (2013). *The hostile audience: Selective exposure to partisan sources and affective polarization.* Working Paper. Stanford, CA: Stanford University Press.

Lerner, J. S., Gonzalez, R. M., Small, D. A., & Fischhoff, B. (2003). Effects of fear and anger on perceived risks of terrorism: A national field experiment. *Psychological Science, 14*(2), 144–150.

Lerner, J. S., & Keltner, D. (2001). Fear, anger, and risk. *Journal of Personality and Social Psychology, 81*(1), 146.

MacKuen, M., Wolak, J., Keele, L., & Marcus, G. E. (2010). Civic engagements: Resolute partisanship or reflective deliberation. *American Journal of Political Science, 54*(2), 440–458.

Mohammad, S. M., & Turney, P. D. (2010, June). *Emotions evoked by common words and phrases: Using Mechanical Turk to create an emotion lexicon.* Proceedings of the NAACL HLT 2010 workshop on computational approaches to analysis and generation of emotion in text. Association for Computational Linguistics, pp. 26–34.

Mohammad, S. M., & Turney, P. D. (2013). *Nrc emotion lexicon.* NRC Technical Report.

Papacharissi, Z., & de Fatima Oliveira, M. (2012). Affective news and networked publics: The rhythms of news storytelling on# Egypt. *Journal of Communication, 62*(2), 266–282.

Petersen, M. B. (2010). Distinct emotions, distinct domains: Anger, anxiety and perceptions of intentionality. *The Journal of Politics, 72*(2), 357–365.

Plutchik, R. (1980). *Emotion: A psychoevolutionary synthesis.* New York: Harper & Row.

Rieder, B. (2013, May). *Studying Facebook via data extraction: The Netvizz application.* Proceedings of the 5th annual ACM web science conference, pp. 346–355.

Rochon, T. R. (2000). *Culture moves: Ideas, activism, and changing values.* Princeton, NJ: Princeton University Press.

Scheff, T. J. (1994). *Bloody revenge: Emotions, nationalism, and war.* Boulder, CO: Westview Press.

Sniderman, P. M., & Hagendoorn, A. (2007). *When ways of life collide: Multiculturalism and its discontents in the Netherlands.* Princeton, NJ: Princeton University Press.

Snow, D. A., Benford, R., McCammon, H., Hewitt, L., & Fitzgerald, S. (2014). The emergence, development, and future of the framing perspective: 25+ years since "frame alignment". *Mobilization: An International Quarterly, 19*(1), 23–46.

Snow, D. A., Rochford Jr, E. B., Worden, S. K., & Benford, R. D. (1986). Frame alignment processes, micromobilization, and movement participation. *American Sociological Review,* 464–481.

Van Stekelenburg, J. (2006). *Promoting or preventing social change: Instrumentality, identity, ideology and group-based anger as motives of protest participation* (PhD thesis). VU Amsterdam, Amsterdam.

Van Stekelenburg, J., & Klandermans, B. (2017). Individuals in movements: A social psychology of contention. In *Handbook of social movements across disciplines* (pp. 103–139). New York: Springer.

Van Troost, D., Van Stekelenburg, J., & Klandermans, B. (2013). *Emotions of protest* (pp. 186–203). New York, NY: Palgrave Macmillan.

Van Zomeren, M., Spears, R., Fischer, A. H., & Leach, C. W. (2004). Put your money where your mouth is! Explaining collective action tendencies through group-based anger and group efficacy. *Journal of Personality and Social Psychology, 87*, 649–664.

Villalobos, J. D., & Sirin, C. V. (2017). The relevance of emotions in presidential public appeals: Anger's conditional effect on perceived risk and support for military interventions. *Presidential Studies Quarterly, 47*(1), 146–168.

Wodak, R. (2015). *The politics of fear: What right-wing populist discourses mean.* Los Angeles, London and New Delhi: Sage.

8
TRANSNATIONAL AND SEMI-LIBERAL

Introduction

The aim of this book has been to provide an understanding of the anti-Islamic turn at a macro level, and to grasp the theoretical implications for understanding the current far right produced by this. It has not been to explain the success or failure of individual parties or activist groups. Empirically, it concerns what I have classified as the anti-Islamic expansion of the far right with new political initiatives, as opposed to the anti-Islamic reorientation of pre-existing radical right parties. The expansion includes electorally successful radical right parties, such as the Dutch LPF and PVV, but is predominantly an extra-parliamentary affair of electorally unsuccessful parties, an array of activist groups, online forums, alternative news sites, and think-tanks.

The radical right parties, including the Dutch cases, have received a large amount of scholarly attention (Mudde, 2016). A much smaller, but growing, body of literature examines the extra-parliamentary anti-Islamic far right. Laudable research has been conducted on individual activist groups such as the EDL (e.g. Busher, 2013, 2015) and PEGIDA. There have also been studies looking at the ties between anti-Islamic groups and websites, especially online (e.g. Lee, 2015). The scholarship on the anti-Islamic expansion and extra-parliamentary activism has been hampered, however, by the fact that most of these studies are empirically rather narrow. Christopher Bail's work on anti-Islamic activist influence in the United States (2012, 2014) is a prominent exception, but as with similar work, the transnational perspective is missing.

The most novel aspect of both the anti-Islamic reorientation of pre-existing radical right parties and the anti-Islamic expansion of the far right is their apparent incorporation of some liberal and progressive values. Even though existing literature points to the importance of ideology and uses it as the common denominator to understand the far right, the literature has been sceptical about these "new" elements. To this day, there is a shortage of studies that investigate this striking development. Those who do mention it predominantly look at pre-existing radical right parties that have undergone ideological reorientation – and the inclusion of, for instance, gender equality, LGBT rights, and freedom of speech has been characterized as strategic tools to circumvent political and normative sanctions.

This points to two large gaps in our understanding of the anti-Islamic turn and the expansion of the far right. One gap concerns the overall structure of the anti-Islamic far right, both outside institutionalized radical right party politics and beyond the scope of single countries. The other gap concerns the extent and impact of the inclusion of liberal and progressive values by anti-Islamic initiatives.

Aiming to fill some of these gaps, I initially posed the following questions. First, what characterizes the anti-Islamic movements' structure and composition? Second, how, and to what extent, does the anti-Islamic movement incorporate progressive and liberal values? To answer these questions, I draw on and summarize the empirical findings and theoretical arguments from Chapters 4 ("Expansion and Legacy"), 5 ("Worldviews"), 6 ("Networks"), and 7 ("Mobilization").

In response to the first research question, I argue that the initiatives which make up the anti-Islamic expansion of the far right are part of a transnational movement and subculture with a consistent worldview and prominent ideologues. The leaders and representatives of these anti-Islamic initiatives come from both the political left and right, most of them strongly attached to liberal values. In contrast, very few had any connections to pre-existing radical or extreme right groups and parties. The expansion itself can be divided into four waves from 2001 onwards, all of which have been propelled by critical events such as 9/11 and the Muhammed cartoon crisis.

In line with the background of their leaders and intellectuals, anti-Islamic initiatives continuously incorporate both traditional and progressive/liberal values under the rubric of their civilizational, supranational identity. I argue that their diagnostic, prognostic, and motivational framing constitutes a distinct anti-Islamic master frame, and conceptualizes the ideological duality as a strategic frame ambiguity.[1] The anti-Islamic organizational network mirrors the civilizational framework and ideological duality, with ties to liberal and progressive, as well as Christian conservative initiatives. Furthermore, online activists are aligned with the official platform, and messages of belonging which incorporate both traditional and modern values seem to be the main driver of both internal mobilization and message diffusion. In response to the second research question, I therefore argue that the anti-Islamic movement and subculture is characterized by a semi-liberal equilibrium.

As the anti-Islamic movements' roots and original set of ideas come from outside the far right, it represents a partial coupling between liberalism and authoritarianism from a liberal starting point. In other words, the anti-Islamic expansion is in fact liberalism that has drifted to the far right. This demonstrates that who the enemy is really matters. Based on existing literature and my own findings, we can now identify two distinct pathways into adopting the worldviews espoused in the anti-Islamic movement and subculture. In the first, opposition to Islam precedes an inclusion of some progressive and liberal positions driven by strategic calculation to avoid social and political sanctions. In the second pathway, progressive and liberal positions precede the understanding of Islam as a totalitarian ideology and existential threat, driven by an emotional response to jihadi terror attacks and other critical events. It is only after they start to perceive Islam as an existential threat that they begin to embrace authoritarian solutions to ensure the self-preservation of society.

My own work exposes the precariousness of this semi-liberal equilibrium. First, between 2015 and 2016, the online network expanded eastward to include radical and extreme right groups of the old ideological order. Second, the Western anti-Islamic groups also hold activists who espouse racist and anti-democratic ideas. Third, the anti-Islamic worldview contains an inherent potential for radicalization, since it stresses the immediate and apocalyptic threat of Islamic domination. These sources of tension mean that the future direction of the anti-Islamic far right is uncertain.

The remainder of this chapter is divided into three sections. The first two answer the initial research questions, as summarized previously. Each section is prefaced with a restatement of the related main argument. The final section discusses two issues: first, the timing and scope of the anti-Islamic far right; and second, the inherent challenges to the current semi-liberal equilibrium, which I argue currently characterizes this movement and subculture.

A transnational movement and cohesive ideology

The anti-Islamic expansion of the far right consists of a broad range of initiatives whose leaders and intellectuals come from a variety of political backgrounds, from far left to far right. The expansion has been propelled by society-wide critical events, such as 9/11 and local moral shocks. Anti-Islamic initiatives have created, and are embedded in, a transnational movement and subculture with a cohesive ideology. This ideology is manifest at the organizational level and among their online membership. Put more succinctly: the initiatives that make up the anti-Islamic expansion of the far right are part of a transnational movement and subculture with a consistent worldview and prominent ideologues.

I will examine each of these subclaims, beginning with the waves of expansion, political backgrounds, worldviews, and transnational collaborations, networks, and members before finally dealing with the subjects of movement and subculture.

Four waves of expansion

Having made the central distinction between the anti-Islamic expansion and the anti-Islamic reorientation, I argue that we can divide the diffusion of anti-Islamic activism since 2001 into four waves of expansion (Chapter 4). The United States, the Netherlands, Britain, Norway, Denmark, and Germany stand out as strongholds of anti-Islamic activism. These are countries where a wave either began or which was the home of prominent and durable initiatives which underlie these waves.

The first wave began at the same time in the United States and the Netherlands. In the United States, it was the website LGF, run by a self-styled liberal, which was the initial platform for those who came to define themselves as "counter-jihadists". LGF was followed by now more prominent sites such as GoV and Jihad Watch. The Netherlands became the first country with an electorally successful anti-Islamic party, LPF. Each subsequent wave is defined by an upsurge in organizational activity, epitomized by the creation of a new activist group which managed to establish offshoots in several countries. The second wave was defined by the "counter-jihad" moving off the web and onto the streets and the formation of Stop Islamization, which was subsequently set up in countries across Europe. Furthermore, several pre-existing alternative news sites joined the anti-Islamic cause. The anti-Islamic movement and subculture was reinvigorated with the formation of EDL in 2009, which marks the advent of a third wave. Defence League affiliates were quickly set up around Europe, much in the same manner as the Stop Islamization initiatives before them. The EDL thus added another layer to the expanding landscape of anti-Islamic activism. Finally, the fourth wave is marked by the rapid establishment and diffusion of PEGIDA across Europe and North America.

Critical events and moral shocks – necessary but not sufficient

Every wave was propelled by critical events and moral shocks. The first and largest of these was 9/11, which provided an opportunity for the already staunchly anti-Islamic Pim Fortuyn to become an important figure in Dutch public debate. It was also a personal turning point for the founder of the LGF website, who became a convert to the cause of battling so-called Islamo-fascism. The counter-jihadi community's turn to the streets and transformation of websites such as Politically Incorrect, Document.no, and Snaphanen was driven by the unfolding Muhammed cartoon crisis which enveloped Denmark in 2005–2006. The visibility and reach of the pre-established anti-Islamic community from the first wave also grew massively, as their websites became some of the world's most read during that period. The third and fourth waves, in contrast, have been propelled by events of a more local nature. The EDL, whose creation in 2009 marks the onset of the third wave, was formed in response to Islamists picketing the funerals of fallen soldiers, while PEGIDA was created (online) by Lutz Bachmann in response to a PKK demonstration in Dresden. These "moral shocks" were the starting points, but did not necessarily play a significant role in the subsequent diffusion of these activist groups in Europe and beyond.

Finally, it is important to remark that most jihadi terror attacks, demonstrations or other events which *could* facilitate an expansion of the anti-Islamic movement and subculture have in fact *not* done so. There are therefore no grounds to say that these events as such cause anti-Islamic mobilization. In other words, critical events and moral shocks are necessary, but not sufficient, for sparking a wave of anti-Islamic expansion.

Broad composition of political legacies among anti-Islamic figureheads

The leaders and representatives of the prominent anti-Islamic initiatives during these four waves of expansion come from varied political and professional backgrounds. Of the 30 figureheads from the six national strongholds included in the overview, a majority had been politically active in one form or another prior to engaging in anti-Islamic activism. An equal number of figureheads have a history of left-wing activism as those who have a history of right-wing activism, whereas only a minority have any prior connections to radical or extreme right parties and groups. In other words, there is no clear organizational continuity between the parties, groups, and other organizations which have come to define the anti-Islamic expansion and the older, more traditional radical or extreme right at the top level.

When it comes to gender, men are in the clear majority. While a minority, women (most of whom are self-professed feminists) also play a prominent role, alongside people who incorporate their LGBT identity into their public persona. Half include their religious identity, be it Christian or atheist, and mobilization activity into their public persona. Religious affiliation intersects with political background, as atheists and agnostics primarily have left-wing backgrounds whereas Christians (of various denominations) mainly come from a right-wing background. Most of the figureheads have middle-class backgrounds and professional careers in journalism, publishing, or programming. Leaders of the street-oriented activist groups such as PEGIDA, the EDL, and others stand out with a larger share of working-class backgrounds.

Consistent worldviews – prominent ideologues

The cursory look at the positions taken by these figureheads and others, such as Bat Ye'or, and the scholarly work they draw on – most prominently Huntington's "clash of civilizations" thesis (1993), indicate that their views regarding Islam as an existential threat is consistent, and the label anti-Islam is thereby clearly merited. Moreover, when examining the collective action framing by anti-Islamic initiatives in Britain, Germany, and Norway in depth, I found that they were largely coherent and consistent in their diagnostic, prognostic and motivational framing across organizational – as well as country-specific – contexts. The salience of specific frames varied, for instance, with what I defined as "modern equality frames", with a female point of view, being more prominent in the Norwegian context, as opposed to "traditional protector frames" with a male point of view. Both frames, however, were used intermittently by all the anti-Islamic initiatives in question. Lee argues that these initiatives hold a myriad of different ideas and therefore cannot be treated as a monolithic phenomenon (2015, p. 251). Önnerfors takes it further, describing the "European Counter-Jihad Movement" as a right-wing discourse without a consistent worldview, dominant leaders, and prolific ideologues (2017, p. 159). My findings in Chapters 4–5 points in the opposite direction. In fact, the worldview is consistent (Chapter 5), and they have dominant leaders as well as prolific ideologues (Chapter 4). Not only that, but my findings indicate that these views are widely shared by online activists who take part in anti-Islamic groups (Chapter 7), and not just at the top level. This goes for the entire worldview, and not only the perception of Islam as a totalitarian ideology and existential threat.

Transnational coalitions, communicative networks and member-base

In addition to the reorientation of alternative news sites, and the establishment of offshoot and sister organizations to activist groups such as Stop Islamization of Denmark, the EDL, and PEGIDA across Western Europe and North America, the waves of anti-Islamic expansion have also been hotbeds of transnational cooperation and coalition-building. Since the start, it has been a transatlantic affair, with a lot of interaction and collaboration between US and European initiatives. Seen in its totality, each wave of expansion has resulted in an overall deepening of ties and mutual recognition across country and regional divides. The most prominent umbrella organizations have been the International Civil Liberties Alliance, SIOE, SION, IFPS, and Fortress Europa.

In addition to the establishment of transnational umbrella organizations and other forms of collaboration,[2] anti-Islamic initiatives have solidified their presence online via Facebook. There, my analyses uncovered a global network (Chapter 6), anchored in Western Europe and North America, which expanded by close to 30% between March 2015 and March 2016. The clusters of Facebook groups dominated by explicitly anti-Islamic initiatives ballooned from just under 3,200 to 4,200 within the same period. The anti-Islamic Facebook groups originate from 182 countries around the world, and on average, each anti-Islamic Facebook group had members from 30 countries. Besides serving as channels for the rapid dissemination of information, these networks can also facilitate mobilization. This was most clearly seen with the rapid establishment of PEGIDA across Europe, whose physical manifestations were preceded by activists setting up Facebook groups (Berntzen & Weisskircher, 2016).

Between a movement and subculture

Some earlier research has defined the anti-Islamic far right as constituting a transnational social movement (Berntzen & Sandberg, 2014; Meleagrou-Hitchens & Brun, 2013), others as a loose global fraternity (Denes, 2012), an amorphous network (Goodwin, 2013), and as a nebula in its online variety (e.g. Lee, 2015). Regardless of whether this is a movement, it is at least implicitly challenged by the chosen terminology of Goodwin and Lee, as amorphous is synonymous with formless and nebula refers to a cloud of gas – in other words, without substance.

I have operated with the synthesis definition of a movement as "networks of informal interactions between a plurality of individuals, groups, or associations, engaged in a political or cultural conflict on the basis of a shared collective identity" (Diani & Bison, 2004, p. 282). In comparison, a subculture is one in which actors experience a sense of commonality that cuts across the boundaries of specific groups, but where there is no systematic exchange between organizations (ibid., p. 285). The broad empirical scope of my own research does not fully resolve this "dispute". For example, online networks are not movements per se, although some argue that they indicate both ideological affinity, common objectives and shared interests (Burris, Smith, & Strahm, 2000; Tateo, 2005; Caiani, Della Porta, & Wagemann, 2012). Furthermore, all social movements are made up of coalitions, but not all coalitions produce social movements (Tarrow, 2005, p. 164).

Online networks can facilitate systematic exchanges, but whether they are consistently used in this manner is uncertain. The most apt description would be to say that at its core, there is a transnational anti-Islamic movement surrounded by a subcultural periphery. Just which initiatives form part of the movement can, and have, varied

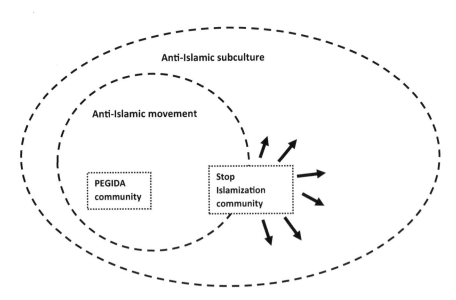

FIGURE 8.1 Illustration of the transnational anti-Islamic social movement as a core embedded in a broader anti-Islamic subculture (periphery)

Note: As specific initiatives or communities of initiatives begin to dissolve and only continue through low-intensity activity online, they move from the core movement to the subcultural periphery. This process is exemplified with the Stop Islamization community, which was important in the second and third wave of expansion, but which has since dissolved as a distinct community. Unlike organizations, neither movements nor subcultures have well-defined boundaries or a central unit dictating the criteria for inclusion or exclusion.

over time. Some initiatives, such as the Stop Islamization groups, have either dissolved completely or fallen into a period of what Billig (1978) described as abeyance.

Many activists nonetheless linger on, and their online groups gradually form part of the growing subculture. Within the "core" transnational movement, they have been replaced by initiatives such as PEGIDA. Outside the sui generis case of PEGIDA in Dresden, their "success" also reinvigorated some older activists, inspiring them to rejoin the cause. This was most prominent in Britain, with the former leader of the EDL co-founding PEGIDA UK.

Speaking of the extra-parliamentary, anti-Islamic far right, Goodwin (2013, p. 4), Busher (2013), and Lee (2015, p. 250) call it an "embryonic" phenomenon, whose future direction and possible influence remains to be seen. Based on my findings and the aggregate body of research, I argue that the anti-Islamic movement and broader subculture is not embryonic. In organizational and relational terms, it has been building and spreading for close to two decades (Chapter 4). There have been several attempts at building political parties (most notably various Freedom parties), and their ideological platforms appear to have been quite consistent, at least since the Muhammed cartoon crisis. The degree to which these initiatives have influenced the broader population is an open question, and we can probably expect some degree of variation between the countries where they are active. However, if we look at the American context Bail (2012, 2014) documents how anti-Islamic groups have become dominant players in the political debate. The network analysis also points to a high degree of cohesiveness and affinity between the various anti-Islamic initiatives when seen at the macro level. The fact that pre-existing radical right parties also have adopted anti-Islamic stances, and thereby undergone an ideological reorientation, certainly speaks to the viability of these views. The initiatives which are part of the anti-Islamic expansion of the far right, however, have not been very successful in institutionalizing their transnational collaborations. A lack of transnational institutionalization should not be taken to indicate that networks between anti-Islamic initiatives are fading away. In the next section, I turn to the second research question and substantive issues of ideology.

A semi-liberal equilibrium

Beginning at the organizational level (front stage), anti-Islamic initiatives continuously incorporate both traditional and progressive/liberal values under the rubric of their civilizational, supranational identity. I define this duality as strategic frame ambiguity. Furthermore, I argue that the anti-Islamic collective action framing is best understood as a distinct, (relatively) static master frame which constrains the activities and orientations of social movement organizations both within and between waves of activism. At an ideological level, the anti-Islamic master frame transcends the so-called Green–Alternative–Libertarian/Traditional–Authoritarian–Nationalist (GAL/TAN) divide. The anti-Islamic network mirrors the civilizational framework and ideological duality. Anti-Islamic groups across North America, Europe, Australia, and beyond have reciprocal ties. Moreover, these anti-Islamic groups also reach out to animal rights, LGBT rights, and women's rights groups, and to Christian conservative, Jewish, and pro-Israeli initiatives. Some, but not all, of these reciprocate. Turning to their online activists, my findings indicate that a majority are aligned with the official platform. Islam is viewed as a totalitarian ideology threatening Western civilization, hereunder Christianity, democracy, gender equality, and the rights of other minorities. Among online activists, messages which stress this supranational civilizational identity, which incorporates both traditional and modern values, seems to be the main driver of both internal mobilization and message diffusion. In sum, I therefore argue that: the anti-Islamic movement and subculture is characterized by a semi-liberal equilibrium.

This reflects their understanding of Islam and Muslims as the ultimate embodiment of authoritarianism, narrowmindedness, patriarchy and misogyny. It demonstrates that is matters who the enemy is, but not in the straightforward manner that some suggest. As documented, few of the figureheads have radical right backgrounds prior to becoming involved in the anti-Islamic cause, whereas many have left-wing backgrounds. A clear majority come from political factions that adhere to the key tenets of liberalism. The fervent espousal of women's and LGBT rights among some of the online activists resonates with this finding, indicative of an expansion in personnel and potential recruitment, and not just new organizations. This points to two pathways into the anti-Islamic movement and subculture: one pathway whereby opposition to Islam generates an inclusion of some progressive and liberal positions; and another where the embrace of certain progressive and liberal positions generates an acceptance of the notion that Islam is a totalitarian ideology and existential threat. Whereas the literature suggests that far-right nativists adopt the anti-Islamic, civilizational master frame based on strategic calculation in order to escape sanctions, my findings alongside studies of terror attacks suggest that people with a liberal outset do so based on emotional reactions to jihadist terror attacks and other critical events that make them see the world in a new light.

The anti-Islamic master frame – a civilizational identity

The 11 anti-Islamic initiatives I studied in Britain, Germany, and Norway were in unison in their portrayal of Islam as a political, totalitarian ideology. In official documents, they are careful to nuance and distinguish between Islam as an ideology and individual Muslims, although that distinction often vanishes in other texts and statements, thereby leading into explicitly anti-Muslim territory. Beyond this, they were also unified in their incorporation of both traditional values and progressive/liberal ones in their supranational, civilizational identity. Mirroring their portrayal of themselves and Western civilization as peaceful and democratic, they propose non-violent solutions within the confines of the democratic system. Whereas the ethno-pluralist radical right which shot to prominence in the 1980s also embraced democracy, the anti-Islamic far right is distinct in that it constructs a supranational identity by drawing on liberalism. I have argued that this is best understood as an anti-Islamic, civilizational master frame. This has been suggested by Vossen, based on his study of Geert Wilders' PVV (2011, 2016). However, unlike Vossen, I believe it is incorrect to view Wilders as the innovator, and prefer to stress the gradual establishment and diffusion of this anti-Islamic, civilizational master frame by individuals and political initiatives which were able to draw on the intellectual work of Huntington and others from the 1990s. Within the broader political landscape, the Dutch politician Pim Fortuyn and the counter-jihadi online community stand out as the most crucial early innovators and disseminators.

Placing anti-Islam in the far-right taxonomy

I now return to the far-right taxonomy in Chapter 2 (p. 35), extricated from some of the most commonly held definitions of the far right and its various permutations. We can place anti-Islam within the taxonomy of the far right at the intermediary level of abstraction, adjacent to ethno-pluralism (Figure 8.2).

In this figure, two aspects clearly distinguish the anti-Islamic master frame from the ethno-pluralist master frame. First, whereas the ethno-pluralist form of nativism

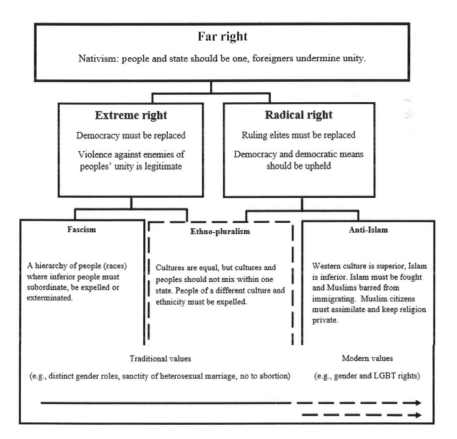

FIGURE 8.2 The far-right taxonomy revisited

built on the idea of separate but equal cultures and ethnicities, which leaves no room for cohabitation within a state, the anti-Islamic nativism is explicitly built on a value-based hierarchy whereby Islam (and, by consequence, practicing Muslims) are viewed as inferior. Second, the anti-Islamic master frame builds on a greatly expanded conception of the in-group, incorporating liberal values as part of their Western civilizational identity. It can be understood as a form of liberal nativism (Spierings & Zaslove, 2015) – that is, liberalism for the natives only (Pappas, 2016, p. 27), but just who makes up the natives is also fundamentally different from the older fascist and ethno-pluralist conceptions. It is, in essence, a liberalism for all those who are not Muslim.

The importance of the civilizational dimension actually challenges the use of the term nativist to describe the anti-Islamic far right.[3] At an ideological level, this also means that the anti-Islamic worldview transcends the so-called Green–Alternative–Libertarian/Traditional–Authoritarian–Nationalist (GAL/TAN) divide. By implication, the anti-Islamic variation of radical right ideology as espoused by these initiatives is, in fact, not a purely far-right phenomenon.

Liberal sectarianism

Relying on Douglas' grid/group scheme (1982) and Kitschelt's re-theoretization of the GAL/TAN cleavage (2012), I described this as a partial coupling of group issues with grid issues. This is the opposite relationship that Kitschelt described for radical right parties. The outcome is an ideological convergence around a semi-liberal worldview alongside some authoritarian solutions to combat the supposed Islamization of society. Rather than being singularly authoritarian, like the fascist extreme right and ethno-pluralist radical right, the anti-Islamic far right embodies a form of liberal sectarianism (see Figure 5.3, The three far right master frames placed within a grid/group matrix, p. 106). This approach lets us delineate further differences in the conception of belonging compared to the fascist extreme right and the ethno-pluralist radical right. For instance, in the ethno-pluralist master frame, the culturally or ethnically different outsider plays a less vital role than in the anti-Islamic master frame. In the latter case, everything revolves around what Islam is and is not, and by consequence what the West is and is not. Thereby, the in-group/out-group demarcation is more important in a functional sense, meaning that anti-Islamic "nativism" is a more salient issue.

Permeation of the semi-liberal identity

The civilizational, semi-liberal identity permeates the current anti-Islamic movement and subculture. This was demonstrated in my network analyses of their online organizational Facebook ties, as well as in my analysis of the messages espoused by their online members. Existing below the level of ideology, master frames, and collective action frames frequently includes elements from one or more ideologies. These function as both facilitators and constraints (Benford & Snow, 2000). The absence of Western European and North American traditional extreme right groups and structurally peripheral role of extreme right groups from Eastern Europe speaks to the restraining nature of their positioning as defenders of Western civilization. Similarly, the way in which their framing has facilitated potential for new alliances is evident in the presence of Israeli, Jewish, women's rights, and LGBT rights organizations in the overall network. For instance, Israeli and pro-Israeli groups were at the core of the network in 2015, and by 2016 had become structurally intertwined to such an extent that they had merged with an anti-Islamic cluster. Furthermore, the progressive elements, while only forming a small contingent within the network, had an important structural role as indicated by their degree and brokerage scores (see Chapter 6 and Table III, Appendix II). This suggests that ideas and claims pushed by the progressive elements have the *potential* for wide and rapid diffusion among anti-Islamic initiatives present on Facebook.

The enemy matters in more ways than one

Studies that have described the concomitant hostility to Islam and espousal of liberal and progressive values have quite consistently described it as strategy, front stage, and so forth (e.g. Larzillière & Sal, 2011; Mayer, Ajanovic, & Sauer, 2014; Deland, Minkenberg, & Mays, 2014, p. 12; Scrinzi, 2017). The implication is that they are attempting to deceive others by covering up their true beliefs and intentions. Moreover, it is frequently claimed that the adoption of liberal and progressive ideals has come after their animosity towards Islam and Muslims (e.g. Zúquete, 2008, p. 224; Brubaker, 2017, p. 1193). It is therefore a *function* of their anti-Islamic position. This bolsters the claims that the liberal and progressive elements are, in any case, included as a strategic façade to circumvent the stigma and sanctions open racism has been met with since the defeat of the Axis powers in World War II (Lentin & Titley, 2012, p. 20; Jackson & Feldman, 2014, p. 7). This is part of the story, but it is certainly not all of the story.

The sizeable amount of prominent anti-Islamic figureheads with left-wing backgrounds (Chapter 4), and the degree to which liberal and progressive claims are included in statements made by online activists in my sample (Chapter 7), point to an altogether different pathway. In this pathway, people start out identifying strongly with some liberal values or specific groups such as LGBT people, and through this vantage point come to see Islam as a totalitarian and existential threat. This is the reverse pattern from those who start out with what we can characterize as an exclusionary, nativist orientation. While it may be true for some, Islam and Muslims are therefore not easily interchangeable with Jews for a sizeable subset of those who engage in the anti-Islamic movement and subculture.

As I argued in the preceding section, critical events such as terror attacks and other moral shocks are a necessary, but insufficient, factor when it comes to triggering a transnational wave of anti-Islamic activism. Moving to the individual level, existing literature indicates that jihadist terror attacks have a differentiated impact on people depending on their political orientations. More specifically, nonauthoritarians and liberals become more prone to endorsing authoritarian policies, policies they would normally oppose in response to terror attacks and other threats (Hetherington & Suhay, 2011; Hetherington & Weiler, 2009; Jost, Glaser, Kruglanski, & Sulloway, 2003; Nail, McGregor, Drinkwater, Steele, & Thompson, 2009). This implies that moral shocks of this nature may work as a vital causal mechanism which leads people with otherwise at least some liberal and progressive inclinations to embrace the anti-Islamic, civilizational master frame.

Strategic calculation versus emotional response

In the light of this, we can now sketch out two fundamentally different pathways for individuals adopting the anti-Islamic master frame. In the first pathway, individuals with a far-right, nativist outlook attempt to circumvent social sanctions against xenophobia by strategically focussing on Islam rather than on Muslims, and who make claims of supporting those liberal and progressive positions Islam is thought to threaten, such as LGBT rights and free speech. I call this the strategic calculation (SC) pathway. In the other pathway, individuals have a conservative

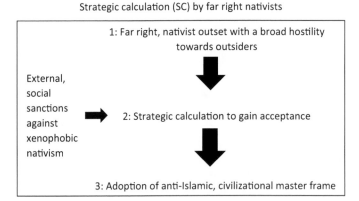

FIGURE 8.3   The two causal pathways for adopting the anti-Islamic, civilizational master frame

to progressive liberal outlook and are broadly inclusive towards outsiders. Jihadi terror attacks or other critical events perceived as a threat to rights and safety, however, trigger a fear-based and emotional response that pushes them toward the anti-Islamic, civilizational master frame. I call this the emotional response (ER) pathway.

Compared with the "liberal" ER pathway, we can logically conceive that terror attacks have little direct impact for the far-right nativist's choice of adopting the anti-Islamic, civilizational master frame, as it does not fundamentally alter their political and normative positions on Islam and Muslims. In addition to speaking of the importance of social sanctions against the far right and discrimination in post-World War II Western Europe and North America, the SC pathway more broadly indicates "liberalism's transformation from ideology to a supposedly neutral meta-ideology, capable of providing the ground rules for all legitimate ideological disputes" (Bellamy, 1999, p. 23).

These pathways to adopting the anti-Islamic, civilizational master frame are not exhaustive. Other pathways besides the SC provided by the broader far-right literature and the alternative ER pathway are also plausible. Yet these two different pathways – and thereby the coexistence of otherwise tolerant liberals who have turned toward intolerant solutions to combat Islam alongside broadly intolerant nativists – make it clear that what we classify as the anti-Islamic far right is, in some respects, internally diverse.

Far right and liberal, or illiberal?

One could argue that it does not make sense to talk of this phenomenon in terms of liberalism. Anchored in the notions of freedom, equality, and fraternity, liberalism asserts the existence of basic rights on the grounds of a common humanity (Griffin, 1995, p. 156). Clearly, categorically excluding a religion or the people who practice it cannot, per definition, be liberal in the Rawlsian sense. By systematically excluding adherents of a world religion, they are a priori basically illiberal and authoritarian. This is the case regardless of whether their starting point was as a self-professed liberal or progressive, or if their "liberal" claims were driven a calculated attempt to circumvent social norms and sanctions against prejudice. Historically and empirically speaking, however, liberalism has been deeply linked with exclusionary thinking (Bellamy, 1999, p. 28): first, through excluding citizens by establishing educational and economic preconditions necessary for making independent decisions (Bellamy, 1999, p. 28); second, even though liberalism includes universalistic ideals, it has been interlocked with nationalism (Griffin, 1995, p. 156); and third, as liberalism was formed against the backdrop of the wars of religion and the rise of modern science, liberal parties have long been associated with secularism (Lipset & Rokkan, 1967; Margulies, 2014) – a secularism which has in some cases veered off into a militant repression of religion. Seen through this historical lens, instead of a clearly delimited normative-theoretical lens, the anti-Islamic movement and subcultures is not anomalous in their exclusivist backing of liberal values.

In this sense, the anti-Islamic far right is not only qualitatively different from the old far right. It may also represent an *even more* liberal force than many of those groups and parties from previous eras which we describe as liberal. Similarly, anti-Islamic actors may be more liberal than many liberal political actors around the world that exist in contexts *outside* of liberal democratic systems. A counter-contention is that it is incorrect to make any of these three comparisons the main litmus test. We should rather judge them by "current" standards within today's liberal democracies where they threaten the rights of Muslims *as* Muslim. Therefore, *if* we take the expansion of civil rights as a constitutive part of current democracy, *then* the anti-Islamic far right is also anti-democratic.

In slightly different terms: if it is illiberal in the absolute sense, then it is also undemocratic. Democracy becomes reduced to the set of liberal democracies, and democratic political actors are reduced to those which at any point in time support the maximum extent of social and political rights built into the political system. A definitive answer to this dilemma does not exist. Without entering a normative debate, however, going down this road increases the conceptual contestedness of democracy itself (Capoccia, 2005, pp. 235–236).

Timing, scope, and challenges

Shock and structure – explaining timing and scope

In the previous section, I discussed the nature and composition of the anti-Islamic far right. Two related questions arise from my analysis of the anti-Islamic turn and expansion witnessed in the aftermath of 9/11. One pertains to the *timing* of the anti-Islamic turn and expansion, and the other pertains to the *scope* of the anti-Islamic far right. First, why did it not start before 9/11? Second, why has the anti-Islamic far right not successfully diffused across all countries in Western Europe?

Three dimensions allow us to provide a proximate answer to the question of timing. First is the political opportunity structure provided by the political-institutional setting, such as the space available to emerging political actors (see e.g. McAdam, 1996; Tarrow, 1994; Kriesi, 1995). Second is the cultural opportunity structure provided by the cultural context outside the immediate influence of the political actors (see Koopmans, 1999; Koopmans & Statham, 1999).[4] Finally is a large exogenous shock which undermines the existing system and creates new discursive opportunities from the existing cultural structure (Abbot, 1997; Soule & Olzak, 2004). These exogenous shocks can thereby produce a critical juncture in time where historical developments move onto a new path (Collier & Collier, 1991).[5]

My material indicates that the cultural opportunity structure conducive to anti-Islamic, liberal sectarianism is one whereby liberal and progressive values are salient, whereas authoritarian values are less so. Second, older cleavages such as the economic left-right conflict must be sufficiently unsettled for the post-material, cultural cleavage to rise in prominence in the first place.

The most relevant aspect of the political opportunity structure is the composition of the pre-existing right-wing milieu, both inside and outside party politics. If the political space is occupied by an authoritarian, ethno-pluralist or fascist right, then the potential for establishing new far right initiatives is constrained.

Besides leading to the war on terror and reorientation of NATO, the 9/11 terror attacks that struck the United States was the juncture point that opened for the anti-Islamic turn and expansion of the far right. Prior to these attacks, the democratic West had undergone a period of liberal and progressive consolidation, whereby not only did democratic institutions themselves become further entrenched, but issues of gender equality, LGBT rights, and minority rights became salient while the old economic cleavage lost prominence. The threat of militant Islamists and the increased awareness of the incompatibility between fundamentalist interpretations of Islam and liberal values created a discursive opportunity for initiatives intent on mobilizing against Islam and Muslim immigration.

To summarize, the first condition for an *initial* establishment of an anti-Islamic far right building on liberal sectarianism was the occurrence of an Islamist terror attack that received broad coverage as such and had international ramifications. The additional conditions which likely contributed was a cultural context of liberalism and progressivism, an absence of a dominant economic cleavage and finally an opening in the political space due to the lack of a strong fascist or ethno-pluralist right.

Up until that point in time, the 9/11 terror attacks were the only ones that fulfilled the first condition, and the United States and the Netherlands are two of a handful countries which fulfil the structural conditions. The French case meet none of these conditions, which otherwise seems like a possible starting point for the anti-Islamic far right *before* 9/11.

For instance, although France experienced a spate of Islamist terror attacks during the 1990s, they were of an insufficiently large scale to have international ramifications. *al-Jama'ah al-Islamiyah al-Musallaha* (Algerian Islamic Group, AIG), the organization behind these attacks, originated in the Algerian struggle for independence and the subsequent aftermath of civil war. The dominant narrative was therefore one of anti-colonial struggle and not Islam or Muslim culture per se. Furthermore, although France certainly has a vibrant tradition of liberalism and progressivism, many of these values are not close to the near valence position they have in countries with a Protestant legacy. Tellingly, one of the most marked cleavages in France have centred on the issue of Catholicism versus secularism.[6] The combination of full-blown authoritarianism and pro-Catholicism has been a hallmark for the radical right FN, as well as for the extra-parliamentary scene (Froio, 2018).

Even though the anti-Islamic movement and subculture is transnational in scope, the diffusion across Western Europe has been uneven. To this day, the adoption of the anti-Islamic master frame has been particularly limited in Southern Europe.

After the critical juncture and successful establishment of an anti-Islamic far right that mobilize on the grounds of liberal sectarianism, we should not assume that the conditions for the successful diffusion of the anti-Islamic master frame are identical to before 9/11.[7] As mentioned in the case of France, the first factor setting north apart from south is the divergence in cultural opportunity structures, traceable to the Catholic-Protestant divide. Due to the persistent combination of authoritarianism and Catholicism and the extent this is represented by the right, these countries are less conducive to liberal sectarianism. A second factor is the continued influence that economic left-right cleavages exert on political conflict. In combination, these limited political and cultural opportunity structures provide a plausible explanation for the divergent levels of anti-Islamic diffusion between the two regions after 9/11.

I have focussed on "successful" cases and then traced organizational networks from there. Systematic research which investigate the negative cases, as well, are therefore needed to provide compelling answers to these questions. Methodologically, a stringent use of set-theoretical thinking that deals with sufficient and necessary factors in the form of qualitative case analysis (QCA) provides an avenue to explore both questions of timing and uneven diffusion across Europe further. See Ravndal (2017) for a particularly fruitful use of this methodology to understand and explain the related issue of variation in extreme right violence.

Challenges to the semi-liberal equilibrium

While having argued that the anti-Islamic movement and subculture is characterized by a semi-liberal equilibrium, my investigations have also uncovered several factors which point to the possibility that this is just a temporary phase – a liberal moment. It is not given that the hostility toward Islam and Muslims should be tied to liberal sectarianism instead of the older symbiosis between traditional values and authoritarianism.

First, my network analysis uncovered an eastward expansion in the wake of the refugee crisis in the summer of 2015. Varieties of radical and extreme right groups (particularly Polish) that do not share the anti-Islamic inclusion of progressive and liberal ideals became a part of the network. The Facebook network is primarily a channel for spreading information in the form of posts, images, and pictures between these groups. Whether the Western European groups contribute to an ideological moderation of Eastern European groups, or vice versa, is an open question. At the level of specific groups, we can probably find both.

Second, the data shows that the online groups also serve as spaces for what Art (2011) defines as extreme activists, namely those who hold racist, anti-Semitic, and anti-democratic sentiments, which in these cases are openly at odds with the majority position and the stated positions of the leaders. Research by Goodwin, Cutts, and Janta-Lipinski (2016) on who sympathized and joined the EDL gives a clue as to why this is the case. Overall, self-identified EDL supporters hold more classic racial prejudice than the population at large (ibid., p. 4). Aside from the core issue of fighting Islam and Muslims, it may be the case that many online activists and followers only become aware of the given anti-Islamic initiative's other stances after joining. The question is then what the extreme activists choose to do. In the language of Albert O. Hirschman (1970), do they opt for exit when they realize this? Do they continue to voice their internal opposition, or do they downplay their general xenophobia and remain loyal? From the point of view of the leadership maintaining strict boundaries by excluding people who are, for instance, anti-Semitic remains a challenge if high levels of general xenophobia remain the major predictor for joining. Interviews with EDL leaders by Elisabeth Morrow starting in 2016 show how they handled this by accepting the presence of neo-Nazis on the condition that they kept a relatively low profile. Once again, in a macro perspective, what matters is not the fate of single initiatives, but what direction the movement and subculture take.

Third, there is also another, darker ambiguity than the one between traditional and libertarian positions on gender (Chapter 5). On the one hand, they frame Muslims and Islam as an apocalyptic threat. On the other hand, they define themselves as democratic, law-abiding, and peaceful, and propose non-violent solutions. The tension between the apocalyptic scenario of Muslim conquest and the democratic solutions is clear. It creates a logical opening for replacing the anti-Islamic movements' non-violent solutions with violent ones by drawing on the motivational framing, where they already use warlike metaphors to rally supporters. If Western civilization and all that goes with it faces imminent destruction, it makes sense to reject the democratic solutions in favour of violent ones. This makes the explicit antagonism towards political elites, human rights groups, and media organizations that do not share their view of Islam and Muslims all the more ominous. This is regardless of the intensity with which they themselves presently extoll the virtues of gender equality, democracy, freedom of speech, and so forth. This scenario is not a hypothetical one, as is evident in the manifesto of the Norwegian terrorist Anders Behring Breivik and his subsequent targeting of the government and Labour Youth camp (Berntzen & Sandberg, 2014).[8] Nonetheless, these attacks have been an outlier. Even though their collective action framing contains the seeds for violent solutions, there have been relatively few acts of anti-Islamic political violence to date. There is also some evidence of anti-Islamic initiatives actively downplaying their antagonism to Muslims during periods of conflict, such as the EDL abstaining from demonstrating after the killing of the soldier Lee Rigby by two jihadists in London (Busher & Macklin, 2015). Further indicating the "binding" nature of their democratically oriented solutions, PEGIDA never went against police or state bans of their demonstrations, even though this occurred so regularly that they were generally not able to demonstrate in specific countries (Berntzen & Weisskircher, 2016).

Finally, the prospect of cumulative extremism where one form of extremism feeds off and magnifies another (Eatwell, 2006) is said to represent a growing threat to liberal democracies (Eatwell & Goodwin, 2010, p. 243). This concern has been particularly linked to anti-Islamic versus extreme Islamist groups (Busher & Macklin, 2015, p. 899). From this perspective, anti-Islamic initiatives such as the EDL and PEGIDA threaten the wellbeing of society not because they *are* violent at present, but because their acts and views *may* cause the situation to spiral out of hand in the future.

Notions of civil war lurk in the shadows. In Chapter 4, I argued that jihadist terror attacks and the actions of extreme Islamists triggered the four waves of anti-Islamic mobilization stretching back to the creation of the online "counter-jihad", the breakthrough in Dutch party politics, and the first protests in London (2005), all the way up until the rise of PEGIDA. However, it is unclear whether Islamist extremism has had any further impact on the duration of anti-Islamic street activity, online activity, or their repertoires of contention. In other words, dynamics between anti-Islamic initiatives and extreme Islamists remain empirically underexplored and an important avenue of future research (see Busher & Macklin, 2015). The aspects I analyze are only part of the equation. Instead of the macro-level and ideologically oriented perspective taken in this book, a growing body of literature points to the relevance of relational mechanisms at a micro and meso levels for explaining the occurrence (or non-occurrence) of political violence (e.g. Della Porta, 2013).

Conclusion

Studies of the far right and anti-Islamic initiatives have written off or paid insufficient attention to the inclusion of progressive and liberal ideals. This has reduced our ability to grasp the nature of today's far right. Based on my findings, I made the case that the anti-Islamic movement and subculture has largely liberal roots. Anti-Islamic leaders and intellectuals portray themselves champions of Western civilization – both its Christian heritage and traditions, as well as gender equality, LGBT rights, and the rights of other non-Muslim minorities. This combined defence of both liberal positions and traditions sets them clearly apart from the older far right. The civilizational identity is mirrored in their online organizational networks and prevails among many of their adherents. Demonstrating that it matters who the enemy is, over time, the anti-Islamic movement has drifted in an authoritarian direction to combat what they see as the ultimate embodiment of intolerance: Islam. As such, the anti-Islamic movement represents a partial coupling between liberalism and authoritarianism from a liberal starting point – a semi-liberal equilibrium. This is the opposite trajectory of many radical right parties, which have undergone an anti-Islamic turn and subsequently come to embrace many liberal positions.

My work has uncovered some clear challenges to the current semi-liberal equilibrium characterizing the anti-Islamic movement and subculture. First, the expansion to the East carries the risk of the increased influence of traditional forms of right-wing extremist ideology. This is reinforced by the existence of a vocal racist and anti-democratic minority within Western European and North American anti-Islamic initiatives. Moreover, the entire anti-Islamic worldview rests on a precarious balance where Islam and Muslims are framed as an impending existential threat, but nevertheless should be dealt with using democratic means. This opens up for further ideological radicalization, regardless of the influence which "old" extreme right forces may have.

Semi-liberal or not, the anti-Islamic movement and subculture appears poised to remain an important political and cultural force for the indefinite future. The movements' overall trajectory towards moderation or radicalization, continued mainstreaming or relegation to the fringes, will therefore be of importance to us all.

Notes

1 By strategic, I do not attempt to indicate deception.
2 For instance, on its website the IFPS linked to a website for donating to Dutch PVV party leader Geert Wilders' trial defense fund: www.geertwilders.nl
3 As nativism explicitly refers the idea that the nation-state should only consist of members from the native group.
4 Related work by Koopmans, Statham, Giugni, and Passy (2005) indicate that political and cultural opportunity structures combined can account for much of the differences in extreme right framing between Western European countries.
5 Junctures are generally traced to economic crises, military conflicts, and other large-scale disasters (Hall, 1996).
6 To this day, the far-right initiative Soral considers French republicanism and secularism their primary target and solidarize with immigrant communities (Froio, 2018).
7 See e.g. Mark Beissinger's (2007) work on revolutions in the former Soviet Union. He introduces the concept of modularity to explain the interdependent spread of revolutions from one country to another.
8 It is important to stress that the motivation and causes for Breivik's radicalization and acts of political violence are many, and that it was the "anti-Islamic story" that he wanted to tell at the time. His actions and self-portrayal also share similarities with school shooters (Sandberg, Oksanen, Berntzen, & Kiilakasko, 2014).

Bibliography

Abbott, A. (1997). On the concept of turning point. *Comparative Social Research, 16*, 85–106.

Art, D. (2011). *Inside the radical right: The development of anti-immigrant parties in Western Europe.* Cambridge: Cambridge University Press.

Bail, C. A. (2012). The fringe effect: Civil society organizations and the evolution of media discourse about Islam since the September 11th attacks. *American Sociological Review, 77*(6), 855–879.

Bail, C. A. (2014). *Terrified: How anti-Muslim Fringe organizations became mainstream.* Princeton, NJ: Princeton University Press.

Beissinger, M. R. (2007). Structure and example in modular political phenomena: The diffusion of bulldozer/rose/orange/tulip revolutions. *Perspectives on politics, 5*(2), 259-276.

Bellamy, R. P. (1999). *Liberalism and pluralism: Towards a politics of compromise.* London: Psychology Press, Routledge.

Benford, R. D., & Snow, D. A. (2000). Framing processes and social movements: An overview and assessment. *Annual Review of Sociology, 26*(1), 611–639.

Berntzen, L. E., & Sandberg, S. (2014). The collective nature of lone wolf terrorism: Anders Behring Breivik and the anti-Islamic social movement. *Terrorism and Political Violence, 26*(5), 759–779.

Berntzen, L. E., & Weisskircher, M. (2016). Anti-Islamic PEGIDA beyond Germany: Explaining differences in mobilisation. *Journal of Intercultural Studies, 37*(6), 556–573.

Billig, M. (1978). *Fascists: A social psychological view of the National Front*. London: Academic Press.

Billig, M. (2001). Humour and hatred: The racist jokes of the Ku Klux Klan. *Discourse & Society, 12*(3), 267–289.

Brubaker, R. (2017). Between nationalism and civilizationism: The European populist moment in comparative perspective. *Ethnic and Racial Studies, 40*(8), 1191–1226.

Burris, V., Smith, E., & Strahm, A. (2000). White supremacist networks on the Internet. *Sociological Focus, 33*(2), 215–235.

Busher, J. (2013). Grassroots activism in the English Defence League: Discourse and public (dis) order. In M. Taylor, P. M. Currie, & D. Holbrook (Eds.), *Extreme right wing political violence and terrorism* (pp. 65–84). London: Bloomsbury Publishing.

Busher, J. (2015). *The making of anti-Muslim protest: Grassroots activism in the English Defence League*. London: Routledge.

Busher, J., & Macklin, G. (2015). Interpreting "cumulative extremism": Six proposals for enhancing conceptual clarity. *Terrorism and Political Violence, 27*(5), 884–905.

Caiani, M., Della Porta, D., & Wagemann, C. (2012). *Mobilizing on the extreme right: Germany, Italy, and the United States*. Oxford: Oxford University Press.

Capoccia, G. (2005). *Defending democracy: Reactions to extremism in interwar Europe*. Baltimore, MA: JHU Press.

Collier, R. B., & Collier, D. (1991). *Shaping the political arena: Critical junctures, the labor movement, and regime dynamics in Latin America*. Notre Dame: University of Notre Dame Press.

Deland, M., Minkenberg, M., & Mays, C. (Eds.). (2014). *In the tracks of Breivik: Far right networks in Northern and Eastern Europe* (Vol. 37). Münster: LIT Verlag.

Della Porta, D. (2013). *Clandestine political violence*. Cambridge: Cambridge University Press.

Denes, N. (2012). "Welcome to the Counterjihad": Uncivil networks and the narration of European public spheres. *Journal of Civil Society, 8*(3), 289–306.

Diani, M., & Bison, I. (2004). Organizations, coalitions, and movements. *Theory and Society, 33*(3), 281–309.

Douglas, M. (1982). Introduction to grid/group analysis. *Essays in the Sociology of Perception*, 1–8.

Eatwell, R. (2006). Community cohesion and cumulative extremism in contemporary Britain. *The Political Quarterly, 77*(2), 204–216.

Eatwell, R., & Goodwin, M. (Eds.). (2010). *The new extremism in 21st century Britain* (Vol. 5). London and New York: Routledge.

Froio, C. (2018). Race, religion, or culture? Framing Islam between racism and neo-racism in the online network of the French far right. *Perspectives on Politics, 16*(3), 696–709.

Goodwin, M. J. (2013). *The roots of extremism: The English Defence League and the Counter-Jihad challenge*. London: Chatham House.

Goodwin, M. J., Cutts, D., & Janta-Lipinski, L. (2016). Economic losers, protestors, islamophobes or xenophobes? Predicting public support for a counter-Jihad movement. *Political Studies, 64*(1), 4–26.

Griffin, R. (1995). *Fascism: A reader*. Oxford: Oxford University Press on Demand.

Hall, S. (1996). Cultural studies and its theoretical legacies. In K. H. Chen, & D. Morley (Eds.), *Stuart Hall: Critical dialogues in cultural studies* (pp. 262–275). London: Routledge.

Hetherington, M. J., & Suhay, E. (2011). Authoritarianism, threat, and Americans' support for the war on terror. *American Journal of Political Science, 55*(3), 546–560.

Hetherington, M. J., & Weiler, J. D. (2009). *Authoritarianism and polarization in American politics*. Cambridge: Cambridge University Press.

Hirschman, A. O. (1970). *Exit, voice, and loyalty: Responses to decline in firms, organizations, and states*. Cambridge, MA: Harvard University Press.

Huntington, S. P. (1993). The clash of civilizations? *Foreign Affairs*, 22–49.

Jackson, P., & Feldman, M. (2014). *Doublespeak: The framing of the far-right since 1945*. Stuttgart: Ibidem-Verlag.

Jost, J. T., Glaser, J., Kruglanski, A. W., & Sulloway, F. J. (2003). Political conservatism as motivated social cognition. *Psychological Bulletin, 129*(3), 339–375.

Kitschelt, H. (2012). Social class and the radical right: Conceptualizing political preference formation and partisan choice. In J. Rydgren (Ed.), *Class politics and the radical right* (pp. 224–251). London: Routledge.

Koopmans, R. (1996). Explaining the rise of racist and extreme right violence in Western Europe: Grievances or opportunities? *European Journal of Political Research, 30*(2), 185–216.

Koopmans, R. (1999). Political. Opportunity. Structure. Some splitting to balance the lumping. *Sociological Forum, 14*(1), 93–105.

Koopmans, R. (2004). Movements and media: Selection processes and evolutionary dynamics in the public sphere. *Theory and Society, 33*(3–4), 367–391.

Koopmans, R., & Statham, P. (1999). Political claims analysis: Integrating protest event and political discourse approaches. *Mobilization: An International Quarterly, 4*(2), 203–221.

Koopmans, R., Statham, P., Giugni, M., & Passy, F. (2005). *Contested citizenship: Political contention over migration and ethnic relations in Western Europe*. Minneapolis: University of Minnesota.

Kriesi, H. (1995). The political opportunity structure of new social movements: Its impact on their mobilization. In J. C. Jenkins & B. Klandermans (Eds.), *The politics of social protest: Comparative perspectives on states and social movements* (pp. 167–198). Minneapolis: University of Minnesota Press.

Larzillière, C., & Sal, L. (2011). *Comprendre l'instrumentalisation du féminisme à des fins racistes pour résister*. Retrieved from www.contretemps.eu/interventions/comprendre-instrumental isation-f%C3%A9minisme-fins-racistes-r%C3%A9sister

Lee, B. (2015). A day in the "swamp": Understanding discourse in the online counter-Jihad nebula. *Democracy and Security, 11*(3), 248–274.

Lentin, A., & Titley, G. (2012). The crisis of "multiculturalism" in Europe: Mediated minarets, intolerable subjects. *European Journal of Cultural Studies, 15*(2), 123–138.

Lipset, S. M., & Rokkan, S. (1967). *Party systems and voter alignments: Cross-national perspectives*. New York and London: Routledge.

Margulies, W. B. (2014). *Liberal parties and party systems* (Doctoral dissertation). University of Essex, Colchester.

Mayer, S., Ajanovic, E., & Sauer, B. (2014). Intersections and inconsistencies: Framing gender in right wing populist discourses in Austria. *NORA-Nordic Journal of Feminist and Gender Research, 22*(4), 250–266.

McAdam, D. (1996). Conceptual origins, current problems, future directions. In D. McAdam, J. D. McCarthy, & M. N. Zald (Eds.), *Comparative perspectives on social movements: Political opportunities, mobilizing structures, and cultural framings* (pp. 23–40). Cambridge: Cambridge University Press.

Meleagrou-Hitchens, A., & Brun, H. (2013). *A neo-nationalist network: The English Defence League and Europe's counter-Jihad movement*. London: International Centre for the Study of Radicalisation and Political Violence.

Mudde, C. (2016). *The study of populist radical right parties: Towards a fourth wave*. C-REX Working Paper Series, 1.

Nail, P. R., McGregor, I., Drinkwater, A. E., Steele, G. M., & Thompson, A. W. (2009). Threat causes liberals to think like conservatives. *Journal of Experimental Social Psychology, 45*(4), 901–907.

Önnerfors, A. (2017). Between Breivik and PEGIDA: The absence of ideologues and leaders on the contemporary European far right. *Patterns of Prejudice, 51*(2), 159–175.

Pappas, T. S. (2016). Distinguishing liberal democracy's challengers. *Journal of Democracy, 27*(4), 22–36.

Ravndal, J. A (2017). *Right-wing terrorism and violence in Western Europe: A comparative analysis* (PhD dissertation). University of Oslo.

Sandberg, S., Oksanen, A., Berntzen, L. E., & Kiilakoski, T. (2014). Stories in action: The cultural influences of school shootings on the terrorist attacks in Norway. *Critical Studies on Terrorism, 7*(2), 277–296.

Scrinzi, F. (2017). A "new" national front? Gender, religion, secularism and the French populist radical right. In M. Köttig, R. Bitzan, & A. Petö (Eds.), *Gender and far right politics in Europe* (pp. 127–140). Springer International Publishing. DOI: 10.1007/978-3-319-43533-6

Sedgwick, M. (2013). Something varied in the state of Denmark: Neo-nationalism, anti-Islamic activism, and street-level thuggery. *Politics, Religion & Ideology, 14*(2), 208–233.

Soule, S. A., & Olzak, S. (2004). When do movements matter? The politics of contingency and the equal rights amendment. *American Sociological Review, 69*(4), 473–497.

Spierings, N., & Zaslove, A. (2015). Conclusion: Dividing the populist radical right between "liberal nativism" and traditional conceptions of gender. *Patterns of Prejudice, 49*(1–2), 163–173.

Tarrow, S. (1994). *Power in movement: Social movements, collective action and mass politics.* Cambridge: Cambridge University Press.

Tarrow, S. (2005). *The new transnational activism.* Cambridge: Cambridge University Press.

Tateo, L. (2005). The Italian extreme right on-line network: An exploratory study using an integrated social network analysis and content analysis approach. *Journal of Computer-Mediated Communication, 10*(2).

Vossen, K. (2011). Classifying Wilders: The ideological development of Geert Wilders and his party for freedom. *Politics, 31*(3), 179–189.

Vossen, K. (2016). *The power of populism: Geert Wilders and the party for freedom in the Netherlands.* Abingdon: Taylor & Francis.

Zúquete, J. P. (2008). The European extreme-right and Islam: New directions? *Journal of Political Ideologies, 13*(3), 321–344.

ADDENDUM

The toll of intolerance

In this book, I have argued that the transnational, anti-Islamic movement which began to take shape in the aftermath of the 9/11 terror attacks straddles the boundaries between liberalism and authoritarianism. As their roots and ideas primarily come from left-wing and right-wing strains of liberalism, it is distinctively different from the old far right. The liberal aspects suffuses the movement from the leadership level and down to the online activists. Their emphasis on free speech, LGBT rights, gender equality, and so forth anchored in a form of civic nationalism is more than some thin veneer. Yet, this semi-liberal equilibrium is fragile, and the pendulum might swing in a decidedly authoritarian direction.

The developments between 2018 and 2019 shows the paradox of tolerance is taking its toll.[1] Seeing themselves as champions of Western civilization, anti-Islamic activists have argued that intolerant measures are necessary to preserve their otherwise tolerant, democratic, and free societies from the menace of Islamization. The intolerant measures they push include banning mosques and the Quran, completely halting Muslim immigration, and, in some cases, repatriating Muslims. This is pulling them into the orbit of authoritarian figures such as Viktor Orbán, leaders who also claim to be on a mission to save Western civilization from Islam. Anti-Islamic activists show admiration for such strongmen despite the fact that they not only clamp down on Muslim immigration, but also vilify other minorities and dismantle civil rights that anti-Islamic activists claim to defend.

In line with this embrace of unvarnished authoritarian figures in Central and Eastern Europe, some prominent anti-Islamic actors have begun to intermix civic nationalist arguments and a defence of liberal society with arguments from the ethno-pluralist handbook. This includes extolling the virtues of ethnic belonging and the birthrates of ethnic Norwegians, Germans, and so on. Remember the distinction between fascism, ethno-pluralism, and anti-Islam outlined in Chapter 8. These are the three major strains of far-right ideology. On the ground, the distinction between the anti-Islamic worldview rooted in liberalism and the ethno-pluralist worldview are blurring.

Besides these twin tendencies to advocate for increasingly authoritarian solutions and partial embrace of ethno-nationalism, a difference is also evident in their response to terror committed by right-wing extremists. Anti-Islamic activists resoundingly rejected Anders Behring Breivik after the attacks he committed on 22 July 2011.[2] In contrast, the New Zealand terror attacks in which Australian Brenton Tarrant killed 50 members of a Muslim congregation on 15 March 2019 saw these same figures saying that the blood was on the hands of the multicultural elites, and that the murders were an inevitable outcome of their "multicultural experiment".[3]

Nevertheless, the movement remains a non-militant phenomenon. No single anti-Islamic group has called for violence or committed themselves to violent tactics. The Australian terrorist drew on ethno-pluralist and anti-Islamic ideas, but espoused explicitly racist views and defined himself as a fascist. While some of the claims pushed by anti-Islamic and ethno-pluralist activists may have inspired him, at the time of writing this, we have no indication that they supported him.

Therefore, while there are some signs that the movement is becoming more authoritarian, the pendulum has not decidedly swung in this direction. They continue to define themselves as champions of Western civilization in its multifaceted nature; both the Christian and traditional elements as well as many of the newer, liberal elements. Their embrace of authoritarian solutions and talk of ethnic identity has not led to a wholesale abandonment of their liberal roots.

Notes

1 "If we extend unlimited tolerance even to those who are intolerant, if we are not prepared to defend a tolerant society against the onslaught of the intolerant, then the tolerant will be destroyed, and tolerance with them" (Popper, 2012, p. 226)
2 Whereas some rejected Breivik wholesale and decided to stop using polemical words such as "traitors" to describe their political opponents, others said they agreed with what he wrote about Islam but rejected his actions. See e.g.: www.telegraph.co.uk/news/worldnews/europe/norway/8670685/Norway-attacks-Is-the-man-who-inspired-Breivik-a-Briton.html (accessed 1 March 2019); www.rights.no/2011/08/han-massakrerte-ogsa-ordene/ (accessed 1 March 2019); www.document.no/2011/07/25/har-vi-laert-noe/ (accessed 1 March 2019); www.adressa.no/nyheter/terrorangrepet/rettssaken/article1808174.ece (accessed 1 March 2019).
3 See e.g: www.document.no/2019/03/15/vesten-har-fatt-sin-egen-hebron-massakre/ (accessed 1 March 2019); https://resett.no/2019/03/19/var-tids-storste-terrortrussel-kommer-fortsatt-fra-fanatisk-islam/ (accessed 1 March 2019); www.rights.no/2019/03/sivilisasjonenes-sammenstot-i-all-sin-groteskhet/ (accessed 1 March 2019).

Bibliography

Popper, K. (1945). *The open society and its enemies*. London: Routledge.

APPENDIX I

Key figures from strongholds of anti-Islamic activism

This Appendix provides a biographical overview of 30 key figures – leaders, ideologues and representatives – from six countries in the transnational, anti-Islamic movement that has expanded throughout liberal democracies since 2001. The countries are the United States, Britain, Germany, the Netherlands, Denmark, and Norway.

United States

Starting with the United States, the key individuals are: Charles Johnson, founder of Little Green Footballs; Pamela Geller and Robert Spencer of SIOA; Birgitte Gabriel, leader of Act! For America; and Edward S. May, founder of Gates of Vienna.

Charles Johnson

As the founder of LGF, programmer Johnson (born 1953), was the most prominent figure within the counter-jihadi scene for several years.[1] Johnson described himself as a centre-left agnostic with a keen interest in history, who experienced 9/11 as a tremendous shock. After the Belgian Vlams Belang were allowed to co-host a counter-jihad conference in 2007, Johnson began distancing himself from the community, and he is now an ardent critic of the other counter-jihadi and anti-Islamic activists.[2]

Brigitte Gabriel

Gabriel (born 1964), the founder of Act! For America and American Congress for Truth, has been described as "America's most prominent anti-Muslim activist".[3] She was born in Marjayoun, Lebanon, and fled to the United States with her parents during the Lebanese civil war, which she recounts as a harrowing experience which shaped her view of Islam as an existential threat, and Israel as a great force for good. Of a Christian Maronite background, Gabriel has established close ties with the Christian conservative, Republican right wing in the United States. She saw the 9/11 terror attacks as part of the same jihadi struggle that in her eyes had destroyed Lebanon – saying that she "I do not want to lose my adopted country America" as well. In 2008 she published the book *Because They Hate: A Survivor of Islamic Terror Warns America* (2008), in which she argues that radical Islam wants to conquer all non-Muslim countries, and has repeatedly expressed that the United States military and intelligence services is infiltrated by Islamists working to achieve this in secret.[4] In March 2017, she met President Trump at the White House, to which she claims to have a direct line.[5]

Pamela Geller

As the creator of the counter-jihadi blog Atlas Shrugs, and co-founder of SIOA, SION, and the American Freedom Initiative, Geller (born 1958) is one of the most prominent anti-Islamic activists worldwide. She worked at the *New York Daily News* during the 1980s, before becoming an associate publisher at the *New York Observer*. She defines herself as a Zionist and theist who is socially liberal on the issues of abortion and same-sex marriage, but economically right wing.[6] Having no previous political affiliations, Geller became active after 9/11, which she says was a turning point for her.

Robert Spencer

Spencer (born 1962) is, alongside Geller, one of the self-described counter-jihad's most prominent figures internationally. Besides running the website Jihad Watch, Spencer is the co-founder of AFDI and SIOA. Spencer is an active member of the Melkite Catholic Church and earned a Master's degree in religious studies in 1986, with a thesis on Catholic history. He has highlighted the plight of his grandparents, who fled Turkey partly because they were Christian.[7] In his youth, Spencer worked at the Maoist bookstore Revolutions Books in New York, but has since become a prominent conservative figure in the United States, making frequent appearances on Fox News.[8] He has written several best-selling books on Islam and the threat of jihad. For several years, he was also used as a seminar leader for the US military, the FBI and the Joint Terrorism Task Force (JTTF). Condemned by many, Spencer has received praise by figures such as Stephen Bannon from the Trump administration, who described him as "one of the top two or three experts in the world on this great war we are fighting against fundamental Islam".[9]

Edward S. May

May is the principal editor of Gates of Vienna under the pseudonym of Baron Bodissey, director of the Center for Vigilant Freedom (CVF), and a key figure in the

International Free Press Society. May has said that he was never politically engaged prior to joining the counter-jihad and setting up Gates of Vienna in 2004. May is an Episcopalian Christian, and has described himself as a right-wing anti-jihadist, arguing that they share common cause with anti-jihadist leftists and moderate Muslims, both groups which are – "vilified, ostracized, and threatened because of their heresy. A heretical leftist may get to keep his head, but he will likely find his property destroyed and his career ruined because of his apostasy".[10]

Britain

In Britain, the key individuals included from this time period are Alan Ayling of 4freedoms.com, Stephen Gash of Stop Islamization of Europe, Paul Weston of the British Freedom Party and Liberty GB, Stephen Christopher Yaxley-Lennon of the EDL, the British Freedom Party and PEGIDA UK, Kevin Carroll of the EDL and the British Freedom Party, and Anne Marie Waters of Sharia Watch UK and PEGIDA UK.

Alan Ayling

Ayling (born 1965), computer engineer and founder of the website 4freedoms. com, became known as a wealthy financier of the EDL between 2009 and 2010. Initially supporting the EDL anonymously, Ayling lost his lucrative job at a development bank in the City of London after he was outed. Prior to becoming active in the anti-Islamic scene, Ayling was involved with the Free Tibet Movement before joining the Pentecostal Church. According to Ayling, it was stories from African Christians he met in church which turned him against Islam, which he says is "against freedom of speech, democracy, equality before the law and cultural tolerance".[11]

Stephen Gash

Gash (born 1953), is a businessman and self-styled writer from Carlisle who led SIOE from 2007–2010. Prior to becoming a prominent anti-Islamic activist, Gash was engaged in the struggle for greater English autonomy.[12] He was a member of the National Council of the Campaign for an English Parliament until 2005, and later stood in the Sedgefield by-election in 2007 for the English Democrats Party, winning 0.6% of the vote. Gash has been outspoken in his opposition to the BNP, which he has denounced as racists.[13]

Paul Weston

Weston (born 1965), leader of the British Freedom Party (2011–2012) and its successor party Liberty GB (since 2013), identifies himself as a "classical liberal" and runs a property development and investment company in London. Weston became engaged with the anti-Islamic (counter-jihad) online community in 2006, and first entered party politics as a candidate for UKIP, which he subsequently left for being too soft on Islam.[14] The Liberty GB website states that they promote:

> Western civilisation, Christian values (but you don't have to be Christian), traditional morality, marriage and the family, Britain's beautiful countryside, the monarchy, patriotism and national pride, honesty and free speech, capitalism (to benefit Britain and the British), rationalism, animal welfare, meaningful lives over slavish materialism, national sovereignty, modernity (science and technology for the public good), history and tradition, national identity . . . and putting British people first![15]

Tommy Robinson

Stephen Yaxley-Lennon, alias Tommy Robinson (born 1982), founder of the EDL, comes from a working-class family in Luton, where he went on to run a sunbed shop.[16] Robinson describes himself as a Zionist,[17] and the most prominent anti-Islamic activist in Britain. He is also the youngest of the anti-Islamic leaders and ideologues. In 2004, he joined the British National Party at the age of 20. He remained a member for a year, stating that he "was looking for a way out, I was looking for somebody to be addressing this Islamic extremist problem",[18] saying he was unaware that the BNP was exclusively for white people. Robinson was also active in football hooliganism. After forming the EDL, he also became vice-chairman of the British Freedom Party in 2012. He left the EDL in 2013 to join the counter-radicalization think-tank Quillam Foundation, but reentered the anti-Islamic activist scene in 2015 when he co-founded PEGIDA UK.

As PEGIDA UK never managed to mobilize a substantial amount of people, Robinson began to style himself as a "citizen journalist" via various social media platforms, as well as acting as a correspondent for the Canadian *The Rebel Media*. In 2017, Robinson received a suspended sentence for contempt of court after livestreaming outside an ongoing rape trial,[19] and in May 2018, he was arrested and sentenced to prison for a similar offence. News of Robinson's arrest quickly spread via the transnational anti-Islamic network on Facebook, Twitter, and other platforms under the hashtag #freetommy. Support demonstrations in favour of Robinson were held in several countries, and prominent figures such as Geert Wilders and Donald Trump Jr. spoke out in his defence.[20] The arrest cemented Robinson's status as an anti-Islamic hero and martyr embodying the common man's resistance to the multicultural elite and Islamization of the West. An online petition for his release garnered over 500,000 signatures, traffic to Robinson's website surged, and he received substantial financial support.[21] That same year, Robinson was appointed as UKIP's advisor on grooming gangs. In 2019, he announced that he would run as a candidate for the European elections.[22]

Kevin Carroll

Carroll (born 1970) is a carpenter and the son of Irish immigrants, and the cousin of the EDL's founder, Tommy Robinson. He served as the deputy leader of the EDL from 2009 until becoming its caretaker leader in 2012 while Robinson served a prison sentence. He was also vice-chairman of the British Freedom Party alongside Robinson in 2012. Carroll left the EDL in 2013. Prior to joining the EDL, Carroll was not politically active.

Anne Marie Waters

Waters (born 1977) is leader of the minor party For Britain and the organization Sharia Watch UK, and co-founder of the activist group PEGIDA UK. She is a self-identified feminist, has engaged in LGBT activism since her youth, and is outspoken about her lesbian identity. She spent several years as a member of the Labour Party, and stood as a candidate twice. Waters was a spokesperson for an organization called One Law for All, and a council member of the National Secular Society. She set up Sharia Watch UK in 2014 to bring attention to the dangers which Sharia law poses "in relation to women's rights", and has argued that "There's a problem today and that problem is that gay rights campaigners, even prominent ones, are sanitising and ignoring religious homophobia, particularly from Muslim communities".[23] Waters subsequently joined UKIP in May 2014, and came second in the 2017 leadership elections. It was after her defeat that she went on to form the minor party For Britain in October 2017, whose main issues include leaving the European Union and ending "the Islamisation of the UK".[24]

Germany

In Germany, the key figures included are Stefan Herre of Politically Incorrect, René Stadtkewitz of Die Freiheit and Citizens' Movement Pax Europa, Lutz Bachmann of PEGIDA, and Tatjana Festerling of PEGIDA and Fortress Europa.

Stefan Herre

Herre (born 1965) is a primary school teacher from Cologne and founder of the website Politically Incorrect. Before he became active on the anti-Islamic scene, Herre primarily expressed pro-American positions, support for George W. Bush, and free speech.[25]

René Stadtkewitz

Stadtkewitz (born 1965) is co-founder of the German Freedom Party (2010–2013) and chairman of Citizens' Movement Pax Europa. He is a small businessman and self-identified "bourgeois-liberal" with a long history of right-wing activism. He became a member of the Christian Democratic Union (CDU) in 1995 and served as a local representative in Berlin between 2001 and 2011, when he was expelled for inviting Geert Wilders to speak. Shortly before he stepped down as leader of the Freedom Party, Stadtkewitz called on its supporters to vote for the newly founded Alternative for Germany (AfD).

Lutz Bachmann

Bachmann (born 1973), founder of PEGIDA in 2015, is a graphic designer, publicist, and former professional football player from Dresden with a long criminal record from the 1990s.[26] After being sentenced to several years in prison, Bachmann fled in 1998 to South Africa, where he claims to have opened a night club in Cape Town catering to black people.[27] Bachman was not politically active before founding PEGIDA.

Tatjana Festerling

Festerling (born 1964), prominent figure in PEGIDA between 2015 and 2016, and later in the PEGIDA-derived Fortress Europe, has an undergraduate degree in philosphy from the University of Hamburg and a professional background as an advertisement agent and publishing editor. She worked as an editor for Heinrich Bauer Verlag and Deutsche Spar and was press secretary for the Metronome railway company until 2010.[28] She became involved in party politics in 2014, when she co-founded an AfD subdivision in Hamburg. Festerling argues that the left suffer from a Stockholm syndrome, and that "'political correctness' [is] putting women and gay men at risk of assault".[29] She lost her job as a public relations manager and was later forced out of AfD for taking part in a demonstration organized by Hooligans against Salafists.

Netherlands

The key anti-Islamic figures in the Netherlands include Pim Fortuyn, founder of List Pim Fortuyn (LPF); Geert Wilders, founder of the Party for Freedom (PVV); politician, author and public speaker Ayaan Hirsi Ali; and Edwin Wagensweld of PEGIDA Netherlands. Fortuyn and Wilders have been subjects of considerable academic scrutiny already, and Hirsi Ali is a prominent public figure. In contrast, the head of PEGIDA is an undescribed character with far less clout.

Pim Fortuyn

Fortuyn (1948–2002) was a sociologist, professor, and founder and leader of anti-Islamic List Pim Fortuyn. In his youth, he was a communist and Marxist. He later joined the Dutch social-democratic Labour Party in 1974, before leaving in 1989. Before he founded his own party, Fortuyn was elected top candidate for the party Livable Netherlands. In the period before he was murdered, he made several appearances together with a Catholic priest, stressing his Catholic identity.[30] Fortuyn was openly gay, something which he held up as a big part of his public persona. He campaigned on his opposition to Islam, arguing in favour of a "cold war" against a "hostile religion" which he said threatened the liberal values of the Netherlands, women's rights, and sexual minorities (Rydgren & Van Holsteyn,

2005, p. 59). According to Klandermans and Mayer, "Pim Forutyn and his move-ment were uncorrupted by any connections with Nazism or other extreme right" (2006, p. 23).

Ayaan Hirsi Ali

Somali-born Hirsi Ali (born 1969) is a self-professed liberal, feminist, and atheist fighting against honour violence, child marriage, and female genital mutilation, and is currently a Fellow with the Hoover Institution at Stanford University.[31] Contrary to the other anti-Islamic activists included in this synopsis, Hirsi Ali has a Muslim background herself. She has been one of the most influential figures mobilizing against Islam and Muslim immigration within the framework of civilizational con-flict, first in the Netherlands and then internationally. She wrote the script for Theo van Gogh's movie *Submission* and was also a parliamentary member for the Dutch Liberal Party (VVD) between 2003 and 2006, at which point she was forced to resign after it was revealed that she lied in her asylum application. She was allowed to keep her Dutch citizenship, but moved to the United States, where she became a naturalized US citizen. In 2005, she was named as one of the 100 most influen-tial people in the world by *Time Magazine*. That same year she was awarded the Bellwether Prize by the Norwegian HRS, which described Hirsi Ali as "the lead-ing European politician in the field of integration". In 2007, she described Islam as comparable to Nazism, and that Islam was at war with liberal democracy and therefore represented an enemy that had to be crushed. By 2015, she had moder-ated her views, arguing that it is possible to reform Islam by defeating the Islamists and supporting reformist Muslims.[32]

Geert Wilders

Wilders (born 1963), founder and leader of the Dutch Freedom Party (PVV), started his political career as a speechwriter and assistant for the Liberal Party (VVD) in 1900. He went on to become a member of their parliamentary group in 1998. Wil-ders identifies as a Catholic, and has expressed a strong affinity with Israel, which he claims dates to his one-year stay at a Kibbutz in his teenage years (Wilders, 2005, pp. 13–17). By 1999, Wilders was already an outspoken critic of Islam, and his posi-tion hardened over the years. Alongside his then fellow party member Hirsi Ali, he called for a "liberal jihad" against Islam, which he portrayed as a totalitarian ideol-ogy akin to Nazism (Vossen, 2011; 2016). Previously identified as a potential leader of the Liberal Party, Wilders left in 2005 and founded the Freedom Party in 2006.

Edwin Wagensveld

Wagensveld (born 1969) has been the head of PEGIDA Netherlands since Novem-ber 2014. He owns a small business based in Germany selling air guns and other non-lethal weapons. Prior to becoming a PEGIDA leader, he participated in a

Hooligans against Salafists march in 2014. He lives in Germany on the border with the Netherlands and commutes across the border to stage demonstrations. He is a staunch supporter of Wilders and the PVV.[33]

Denmark

In Denmark, the key figures are Kim Møller of Uriasposten, Steen Raaschou of Snaphanen.dk, Lars Hedegaard and Jesper Langballe of the Free Press Society, and Anders Gravers Pedersen of SIAD and SIOE.

Kim Møller

Møller (born 1971) is the founder and editor of the anti-Islamic website Uriasposten, and a historian. He comes from a working-class background and was a leftist and member of the Danish Green Party in his youth. By 2003, he no longer identified himself as a leftist, and later described himself as a national-conservative.[34]

Steen Raaschou

Raaschou is a photographer, and founder and editor of the anti-Islamic website Snaphanen.dk. He remained anonymous until the assassination attempt on Lars Hedegaard, when he revealed his full support for Hedegaard.

Lars Hedegaard

Hedegaard (born 1942), co-founder and director of the Danish and International Free Press Society, is a self-professed Marxist and convert to Judaism. He was an active member of the Danish Socialist Workers Party until 1982.[35] A historian by education, he worked as a high-school teacher before becoming a journalist – most prominently for the newspaper *Berlingske Tidende*.

Jesper Langballe

Langballe (1939–2014), the second most prominent member and co-founder of the Danish Free Press Society, was a priest in the Danish Church and parliamentary member for the Danish Peoples Party (DF) between 2001 and 2011. Langballe also worked as a journalist in several newspapers and publications during his career, such as *Jyllands-Posten* (1964–1972).

Anders Gravers Pedersen

Pedersen (born 1960), co-founder of Stop Islamization of Denmark and Stop Islamization of Europe, is a butcher and self-sufficient farmer. Before he became an anti-Islamic activist and leader, Pedersen was a member in The Danish Union (*Den*

Danske Forening),[36] a nationalist organization formed by veteran resistance fighters from the struggle against the occupying Nazi forces during World War II. They fight against immigration, which they see as a continuation of the struggle against foreign invaders.[37]

Norway

In Norway, the main figures included from this time period are Hans Rustad of Document.no; Hege Storhaug of HRS; Arne Tumyr, founder and former leader of SIAN; Ronny Alte, former leader of ND; and Max Hermansen of PEGIDA Norway, as well as Fjordman, blogger and author associated with Gates of Vienna.

Hans Rustad

Rustad (born 1950) of Document.no has no former history of being a member of any extreme right or far right organization. On the contrary, he was an active member of the Socialist Youth Organization during his younger days.[38] He has written extensively about anti-Semitism,[39] and before founding Document.no he worked as a journalist for the newspaper *Morgenbladet*, which primarily caters to academics and people with a higher education. Since he founded Document.no, Rustad has become increasingly open and adamant about his Christian faith.

Hege Storhaug

Storhaug (born 1962), spokesperson for HRS, is a self-described atheist, leftist, and feminist motivated by humanism and protection of vulnerable children and women.[40] She began as a journalist, and the fight for women's rights has been prominent in her journalistic work. Initially getting recognition for covering the issue of anorexia, during the 1990s, she was among the first to cover the issue of forced marriage among immigrant girls in Norway. During that period, she lived in Pakistan for two years, which she said were formative years in her understanding of Islam and women's position in Muslim countries. She was adamant in her opposition to Christianity in her youth, but has since come to see it as a force for good when compared to Islam.[41]

Arne Tumyr

Tumyr (born 1933), leader of SIAN between 2007 and 2014, is a former journalist and senior figure in the Norwegian Humanist Association. In 1999, he published an article calling for a halt of the "Islamization of Norway", whereupon he left the Humanist Association following criticism of him for using hate rhetoric. Tumyr has remained an outspoken atheist and critic of religion, publishing a scathing book about Judaism, Christianity and Islam titled *Beacon Burning!* (*Varden brenner!*) in 2006. He was active member in the Norwegian social-democratic Labour Party

(*Arbeiderpartiet*, AP) for several years, but switched to the populist right Progress Party (*Fremskrittspartiet*, FrP), where he led a local chapter in the city of Kristiansand for some years. No formal cooperation exists, but Tumyr has consistently expressed support for the nationalist anti-immigration organization Peoples' Movement against Immigration (*Folkebevegelsen mot innvandring*, FMI) whose former leader, Arne Johannes Myrdal, was sentenced to one year's imprisonment for planning to blow up a refugee centre on the island of Tromøy in 1990.

Ronny Alte

Alte (born 1974), former leader of Norwegian Defence League (NDL) and a prominent figure in PEGIDA Norway, is a teacher from the town of Tønsberg. Alte calls himself a "liberal critic of Islam". During his youth he was part of a neo-Nazi gang, and said that he was a "racist", but later came to believe that Islam was the problem and that not all immigrants were bad. During 2015 he became the spokesperson for Sons of Odin in Norway, an organization founded by neo-Nazis in Finland which quickly spread across Europe during the refugee crisis in 2015. Alte, however, insists that the Norwegian version is not a vigilante group like the others.[42]

Max Jarl Hermansen

Hermansen (born 1960) founded PEGIDA Norway in 2015, staging 19 marches across the country between January and June that year. Prior to becoming a prominent anti-Islamic activist, Hermansen was engaged in the anti-monarchist, republican organization Norway as Republic (*Norge som Republikk!*). Hermansen was formerly an officer in the Norwegian navy. Later, he became a publicist for the Norwegian Sea Military Society in 2008, but was forced to resign because of his vocal opposition to the monarchy. In 2009, he began working as a high school teacher in Oslo, but agreed to resign in 2016 as a result of his anti-Islamic activism.

Peder Are Nøstvold Jensen

Jensen (born 1975), alias Fjordman, has been a prominent contributor to counter-jihadi blogs and websites since 2005, in particular Gates of Vienna. As with Rustad of Document.no and Tumyr of SIAN, he had been politically active on the left (briefly). He was a member of the Socialist Youth organization, and he claims to have voted once for the Norwegian Labour Party and subsequently the Progress Party. Jensen studied Arabic at the University of Bergen and American University in Cairo, where he was at the time of the 9/11 terror attacks. According to Jensen, his Cairene neighbours celebrated the attacks with a cake, which marked a personal turning point in his view of Islam and Muslims.[43] Between 2002 and 2003, he worked for the Norwegian Ministry of Foreign Affairs as an observer in Hebron on the West Bank. After this, he returned to Norway, finishing a master's degree in culture and technology at the University of Oslo. Jensen later became notorious after the terror attacks in Norway on 22 July 2011 because the terrorist (Anders Behring Breivik) included several of Jensen's texts in his "Manifesto".

Notes

1 https://web.archive.org/web/20110604220456/www.israelnationalnews.com/News/News.aspx/62000 (accessed 12 June 2015)
2 www.webcitation.org/5ne7OyVtM?url=www.nytimes.com/2010/01/24/magazine/24Footballs-t.html?hpw=&pagewanted=all (accessed 12 June 2015)
3 www.theatlantic.com/politics/archive/2017/03/americas-most-anti-muslim-activist-is-welcome-at-the-white-house/520323/ (accessed 5 March 2017)
4 www.nytimes.com/2011/03/08/us/08gabriel.html?_r=1&ref=global-home&pagewanted=all (accessed 23 May 2015)
5 www.theguardian.com/us-news/2017/mar/21/act-for-america-brigitte-gabriel-muslim-white-house-meeting (accessed 24 March 2017)
6 www.bbc.com/news/world-us-canada-32580059 (accessed 24 March 2017)
7 www.c-span.org/video/?193778-1/qa-robert-spencer (accessed 24 March 2017)
8 www.mediamatters.org/blog/2015/01/13/meet-the-extremists-who-lead-foxs-conversation/202119 (accessed 24 December 2015)
9 www.motherjones.com/politics/2016/09/stephen-bannon-donald-trump-muslims-fear-loathing/ (accessed 3 March 2017)
10 https://counterjihadreport.com/tag/baron-bodissey/ (accessed 3 March 2017); http://emmanuelchatham.typepad.com/emmanuel_episcopal_church/files/bishop_john_c_buchanan.pdf (accessed 4 March 2017)
11 www.haaretz.com/israel-news/what-are-israeli-flags-and-jewish-activists-doing-at-demonstrations-sponsored-by-the-english-defence-league-1.307803 (accessed 18 August 2015); https://socialistworker.co.uk/art/28820/Exclusive%3A+EDLs+Alan+Lake+loses+his+job+at+development+bank (accessed 18 August 2015)
12 http://tellmamauk.blogspot.no/2012/11/stephen-gash-man-for-all-seasons.html#!/2012/11/stephen-gash-man-for-all-seasons.html (accessed 18 August 2015)
13 www.frontpagemag.com/fpm/42792/collaborators-england-war-against-jews-jamie-jamie-glazov (accessed 23 November 2016); www.varsity.co.uk/news/2778 (accessed 23 November 2016)
14 www.newenglishreview.org/Jerry_Gordon/A_Future_for_Britain_Free_from_Islamization:_An_Interview_with_British_Freedom_Party_Chairman,_Paul_Weston/ (accessed 14 September 2015)
15 https://libertygb.org.uk/q-a (accessed 4 March 2016).
16 http://news.bbc.co.uk/2/hi/programmes/newsnight/9385009.stm (accessed 23 November 2016)
17 www.thejc.com/lifestyle/features/what-makes-the-edl-s-former-leader-who-says-he-is-a-friend-of-the-jews-tick-1.65493 (accessed 23 November 2016)
18 www.huffingtonpost.co.uk/2013/06/16/tommy-robinson-bnp-edl-andrew-neil_n_3449252.html (accessed 25 August 2015)
19 https://apnews.com/3731bef1c5bf4ee9a1c07ed2847fffb0 (accessed 3 March 2019)
20 www.washingtonpost.com/news/worldviews/wp/2018/05/29/conservative-outrage-after-anti-muslim-campaigner-tommy-robinson-secretly-jailed-in-britain/?utm_term=.0119abd50035 (accessed 1 April 2019)
21 www.theguardian.com/uk-news/2018/dec/07/tommy-robinson-global-support-brexit-march (accessed 3 April 2019). According to *Guardian* journalist Josh Halliday, the largest amount of traffic to Robinson's webpage came from the United States, the United Kingdom, and Norway (personal correspondence).
22 www.independent.co.uk/news/uk/politics/tommy-robinson-european-elections-mep-north-west-england-ukip-edl-far-right-a8886376.html (accessed 22 May 2019)

23 www.pinknews.co.uk/2017/06/14/lesbian-ally-of-the-edls-tommy-robinson-stand ing-to-be-ukip-leader/ (accessed 1 July 2017)
24 www.forbritain.uk/ (accessed 1 May 2019).
25 www.stern.de/investigativ/projekte/terrorismus/blog--politically-incorrect--die-off ene-gesellschaft-und-ihre-feinde-3061282.html (accessed 1 July 2017)
26 www.bbc.com/news/world-europe-30776182 (accessed 1 April 2016)
27 http://time.com/3668889/pegida-germany-islamization/ (accessed 15 August 2016)
28 www.wp.de/staedte/hagen/neue-pegida-frontfrau-stammt-aus-hagen-id10559375. html (accessed 3 September 2016)
29 www.dailymail.co.uk/news/article-3443786/Forget-decency-fight-sex-jihad-Femme- fatale-extremist-Pegida-group-accuses-Muslims-targeting-Western-women-gay-men- calls-public-grab-pitchforks.html#ixzz4r9OioBiq (accessed 12 July 2016)
30 https://web.archive.org/web/20020306021624/www.katholieknieuwsblad.nl/ actueel19/kn1920a.htm (accessed 9 December 2016).
31 www.hoover.org/profiles/ayaan-hirsi-ali (accessed 10 December 2016); www.nyti mes.com/2017/08/24/opinion/southern-poverty-law-center-liberals-islam.html (accessed 25 August 2017); www.washingtonpost.com/opinions/the-islam-reformers- vs-the-muslim-zealots/2015/03/27/acf6de6c-d3ed-11e4-ab77-9646eea6a4c7_story. html?utm_term=.2ced0e3a2b08 (accessed 10 December 2016).
32 www.washingtonpost.com/opinions/the-islam-reformers-vs-the-muslim-zealots/ 2015/03/27/acf6de6c-d3ed-11e4-ab77-9646eea6a4c7_story.html?utm_term=.2ced0 e3a2b08 (accessed 14 January 2016).
33 www.nrc.nl/nieuws/2016/05/05/ed-aus-holland-het-gezicht-van-pegida-1616 000-a472998 (accessed 7 August 2016)
34 www.b.dk/kultur/web-kriger-ser-roedt (accessed 12 September 2015)
35 www.information.dk/kultur/2008/01/stadig-marxist (accessed 23 September 2015)
36 http://demos.dk/2015/04/17/2488/ (accessed 23 May 2015)
37 www.youtube.com/watch?v=yyb2L7fSNFE (accessed 24 August 2016)
38 http://idag.no/nyheter/en-ikke-representativ-elite-domminerer-nyhetsbildet/19.6547 (accessed 24 August 2016)
39 See for instance his Master's thesis, "The Holocaust: execution and response: an appraisal".
40 www.dagbladet.no/kultur/siv-jensen---landets-ledende-feminist/66259298 (accessed 24 August 2016)
41 Interview with Storhaug from 2010.
42 https://www.minervanett.no/islam-er-en-voldelig-ideologi/ (accessed 10 December 2016).
43 https://www.vg.no/nyheter/innenriks/i/05V0E/vendepunktet-kom-da-egyptiske- naboer-feiret-paa-11-9 (accessed 10 December 2016).

Bibliography

Klandermans, B., & Mayer, N. (2006). *Through the magnifying glass: The world of extreme right activists*. London: Routledge.
Rydgren, J., & Van Holsteyn, J. (2005). Holland and Pim Fortuyn: A deviant case or the beginning of something new? In J. Rydgren (Ed.), *Movements of exclusion: Radical right-wing populism in the Western World* (pp. 41–59). New York: Nova Science Publishers.
Vossen, K. (2011). Classifying wilders: The ideological development of Geert Wilders and his party for freedom. *Politics, 31*(3), 179–189.
Vossen, K. (2016). *The power of populism: Geert Wilders and the party for freedom in the Netherlands*. Abingdon: Taylor & Francis.
Wilders, G. (2005). *Kies voor vrijheid: een eerlijk antwoord*. Amsterdam: Groep Wilders.

APPENDIX II

Network data

TABLE I Anti-Islamic network broken down by community and the groups they contain in March 2015

Community	Groups in community
Stop Islam	766
Defence Leagues	631
PEGIDA	556
US Republicans	509
Pro-Israel	397
Document.no	259
British Patriots	102
Canadian conservatives	96
Feminist and LGBT	73
Iranian groups	69
Mainstream news	34
Stuttgart	34
Indian Lake	31
Hindu nationalists	25
SIAD	10
Animal rights	10
Polish nationalists	7
Nordic neo-Nazis	5

Notes: Number of groups = 3,615, number of communities = 18. Community labels given on the basis of which groups are predominant, as identified by manually trawling the list of groups.

TABLE II Anti-Islamic network broken down by community and the groups they contain in March 2016

Community	Groups in community
PEGIDA and Stop Islam	1,262
Defence Leagues	922
Pro-Israel & Stop Islam	869
Document.no	327
Polish nationalists	248
British Patriots	201
US Republicans and Tea Party	186
Feminist and LGBT	184
Christian Defence Leagues	118
Stuttgart	61
German AfD	57
Lega Nord	53
SIAD	43
Indian lake	31
Sports	11
UK Police	8
Paganists	7
Russian media (Sputnik)	4

Notes: Number of groups = 4,594, number of communities = 18. Community labels given on the basis of which groups are predominant, as identified by manually trawling the list of groups.

TABLE III PEGIDA and feminist community rises in importance for the anti-Islamic movement, US Tea Party declines; brokerage score by community clusters within anti-Islamic Facebook network in March 2015 and March 2016

	Pure brokerage	*Weak brokerage*
2015		
Defence League	0.267	0.067
Pro-Israel	0.286	0.096
Stop Islam	0.578	0.089
Tea Party	0.472	0.167
2016		
Defence Leagues	0.5	0.143
Pro-Israel	0.333	0.19
PEGIDA	0.643	0.179
Tea Party	0	0.167
Feminist and LGBT	0.167	0

Notes: honest brokerage is divided into three scores ranging from 0–1; pure brokerage: no tie between any pair of alters joined by broker; weak brokerage: one directed tie allowed between pairs of alters joined by broker; non-brokerage: alters who have a tie to broker have also have a two-way tie with each other.

TABLE IV Density matrix of the anti-Islamic network in March 2015

	Defence Leagues	Indian Lake	Pro-Israel	Mainstream news	Document.no	British Patriots	Feminist and LGBT	Stop Islam	Nordic neo-Nazis	SIAD	Stuttgart	PEGIDA	Polish nationalists	Iranian groups	US Republicans and Tea Party	Animal rights	Canadian conservatives	Hindu nationalists
Defence Leagues	1.75%	0.16%	0.04%	0.00%	0.00%	0.36%	0.02%	0.31%	0.00%	0.00%	0.00%	0.01%	0.00%	0.00%	0.03%	0.00%	0.00%	0.03%
Indian Lake	0.00%	13.98%	0.00%	0.00%	0.00%	0.00%	0.00%	0.00%	0.00%	0.00%	0.00%	0.00%	0.00%	0.00%	0.01%	0.00%	0.00%	0.00%
Pro-Israel	0.02%	0.00%	2.59%	0.00%	0.01%	0.00%	0.09%	0.12%	0.00%	0.00%	0.00%	0.00%	0.00%	0.00%	0.10%	0.00%	0.00%	0.07%
Mainstream news	0.00%	0.00%	0.00%	11.14%	0.01%	0.00%	0.00%	0.00%	0.00%	0.00%	0.00%	0.00%	0.00%	0.00%	0.00%	0.00%	0.00%	0.00%
Document.no	0.00%	0.00%	0.02%	0.01%	1.22%	0.00%	0.01%	0.00%	0.00%	0.00%	0.00%	0.00%	0.00%	0.00%	0.01%	0.00%	0.00%	0.00%
British Patriots	0.12%	0.00%	0.00%	0.00%	0.00%	8.69%	0.00%	0.01%	0.00%	0.00%	0.00%	0.00%	0.00%	0.00%	0.03%	0.00%	0.00%	0.00%
Feminist and LGBT	0.00%	0.00%	0.06%	0.00%	0.01%	0.00%	7.38%	0.01%	0.00%	0.00%	0.00%	0.00%	0.00%	0.00%	0.00%	0.00%	0.00%	0.00%
Stop Islam	0.42%	0.00%	0.34%	0.00%	0.00%	0.05%	0.04%	1.18%	0.05%	0.00%	0.00%	0.02%	0.00%	0.00%	0.18%	0.16%	0.01%	0.08%
Nordic neo-Nazis	0.00%	0.00%	0.00%	0.00%	0.00%	0.00%	0.00%	0.05%	40.00%	0.00%	0.00%	0.00%	0.00%	0.00%	0.00%	0.00%	0.00%	0.00%
SIAD	0.00%	0.00%	0.00%	0.00%	0.00%	0.00%	0.00%	0.00%	0.00%	27.78%	0.00%	0.00%	0.00%	0.00%	0.00%	0.00%	0.00%	0.00%
Stuttgart	0.00%	0.00%	0.00%	0.00%	0.00%	0.00%	0.00%	0.00%	0.00%	0.00%	10.43%	0.00%	0.00%	0.00%	0.00%	0.00%	0.00%	0.00%
PEGIDA	0.02%	0.00%	0.01%	0.00%	0.00%	0.00%	0.00%	0.04%	0.00%	0.02%	0.01%	1.79%	0.03%	0.00%	0.01%	0.00%	0.00%	0.00%
Polish nationalists	0.00%	0.00%	0.00%	0.00%	0.00%	0.00%	0.00%	0.00%	0.00%	0.00%	0.00%	0.00%	19.05%	0.00%	0.00%	0.00%	0.00%	0.00%
Iranian groups	0.00%	0.00%	0.00%	0.00%	0.00%	0.00%	0.00%	0.02%	0.00%	0.00%	0.00%	0.00%	0.00%	2.37%	0.00%	0.00%	0.00%	0.00%
US Republicans and Tea Party	0.01%	0.00%	0.15%	0.00%	0.00%	0.03%	0.01%	0.09%	0.00%	0.00%	0.00%	0.00%	0.00%	0.00%	1.54%	0.02%	0.00%	0.00%
Animal rights	0.00%	0.00%	0.00%	0.00%	0.00%	0.00%	0.00%	0.00%	0.00%	0.00%	0.00%	0.00%	0.00%	0.00%	0.04%	21.11%	0.00%	0.00%
Canadian conservatives	0.00%	0.00%	0.01%	0.00%	0.00%	0.00%	0.00%	0.00%	0.00%	0.00%	0.00%	0.00%	0.00%	0.00%	0.00%	0.00%	10.78%	0.00%
Hindu nationalists	0.01%	0.00%	0.04%	0.00%	0.00%	0.00%	0.00%	0.05%	0.00%	0.00%	0.00%	0.00%	0.00%	0.00%	0.00%	0.00%	0.00%	8.00%

TABLE V Density matrix of the anti-Islamic network in March 2016

	Sports	British Patriots	Russian media (Sputnik)	News (Document. no)	Pro-Israel	Indian lake	UK Police	US Tea Party and Trump:	Defence Leagues	Paganists	Feminist and LGBT	Christian Defence Leagues	SIAD	Stuttgart	AfD	PEGIDA	Lega Nord	Polish Patriots
Sports	11.82%	0.05%	0.00%	0.00%	0.00%	0.00%	0.00%	0.00%	0.01%	0.00%	0.00%	0.00%	0.00%	0.00%	0.00%	0.00%	0.00%	0.00%
British Patriots	0.00%	6.63%	0.00%	0.00%	0.02%	0.00%	0.00%	0.00%	0.02%	0.00%	0.00%	0.00%	0.00%	0.00%	0.00%	0.00%	0.00%	0.00%
Russian media (Sputnik)	0.00%	0.00%	33.33%	0.00%	0.00%	0.00%	0.00%	0.00%	0.00%	0.00%	0.00%	0.00%	0.00%	0.00%	0.00%	0.00%	0.00%	0.00%
News (Document. no)	0.00%	0.00%	0.00%	0.99%	0.01%	0.00%	0.00%	0.00%	0.01%	0.00%	0.01%	0.01%	0.00%	0.00%	0.00%	0.00%	0.00%	0.00%
Pro-Israel	0.00%	0.02%	0.00%	0.00%	0.84%	0.00%	0.00%	0.06%	0.12%	0.00%	0.03%	0.07%	0.00%	0.00%	0.00%	0.01%	0.00%	0.00%
Indian lake	0.00%	0.00%	0.00%	0.00%	0.01%	14.19%	0.00%	0.00%	0.00%	0.00%	0.00%	0.00%	0.00%	0.00%	0.00%	0.00%	0.00%	0.00%
UK Police	0.00%	0.00%	0.00%	0.00%	0.00%	0.00%	53.57%	0.00%	0.03%	0.00%	0.00%	0.00%	0.00%	0.00%	0.00%	0.01%	0.00%	0.00%
US Tea Party and Trump:	0.00%	0.00%	0.00%	0.00%	0.16%	0.00%	0.00%	3.05%	0.03%	0.00%	0.01%	0.03%	0.00%	0.00%	0.00%	0.01%	0.00%	0.00%
Defence Leagues	0.01%	0.15%	0.03%	0.01%	0.25%	0.11%	0.15%	0.03%	1.29%	0.02%	0.01%	0.24%	0.00%	0.00%	0.01%	0.02%	0.00%	0.00%
Paganists	0.00%	0.00%	0.00%	0.00%	0.00%	0.00%	0.00%	0.00%	0.00%	16.67%	0.00%	0.00%	0.00%	0.00%	0.00%	0.00%	0.00%	0.00%
Feminist and LGBT	0.00%	0.00%	0.00%	0.00%	0.03%	0.00%	0.00%	0.01%	0.00%	0.00%	2.96%	0.00%	0.00%	0.00%	0.00%	0.01%	0.00%	0.00%
Christian Defence Leagues	0.00%	0.00%	0.00%	0.01%	0.06%	0.00%	0.00%	0.00%	0.12%	0.00%	0.00%	3.90%	0.02%	0.00%	0.00%	0.00%	0.00%	0.00%
SIAD	0.00%	0.00%	0.00%	0.00%	0.00%	0.00%	0.00%	0.00%	0.00%	0.00%	0.00%	0.00%	5.43%	0.00%	0.00%	0.00%	0.00%	0.00%
Stuttgart	0.00%	0.00%	0.00%	0.00%	0.00%	0.00%	0.00%	0.00%	0.00%	0.00%	0.00%	0.00%	0.00%	5.08%	0.00%	0.01%	0.00%	0.00%
AfD	0.00%	0.00%	0.00%	0.00%	0.00%	0.00%	0.00%	0.00%	0.00%	0.00%	0.00%	0.00%	0.00%	0.00%	14.97%	0.02%	0.00%	0.00%
PEGIDA	0.00%	0.00%	0.00%	0.00%	0.03%	0.00%	0.00%	0.08%	0.04%	0.00%	0.00%	0.09%	0.02%	0.04%	0.21%	0.56%	0.01%	0.01%
Lega Nord	0.00%	0.00%	0.00%	0.00%	0.00%	0.00%	0.00%	0.00%	0.00%	0.00%	0.00%	0.00%	0.00%	0.00%	0.00%	0.00%	9.83%	0.00%
Polish Patriots	0.00%	0.00%	0.00%	0.00%	0.00%	0.00%	0.00%	0.00%	0.00%	0.00%	0.00%	0.00%	0.00%	0.00%	0.00%	0.00%	0.00%	5.97%

INDEX

Note: Page numbers in *italics* indicate figures; page numbers in **bold** indicate tables.